UNIVERSITY OF NORTH CAROLINA AT CHAPEL HILL
DEPARTMENT OF ROMANCE LANGUAGES

NORTH CAROLINA STUDIES
IN THE ROMANCE LANGUAGES AND LITERATURES

Founder: URBAN TIGNER HOLMES

Editor: CAROL L. SHERMAN

Distributed by:

UNIVERSITY OF NORTH CAROLINA PRESS

CHAPEL HILL
North Carolina 27515-2288
U.S.A.

NORTH CAROLINA STUDIES IN THE
ROMANCE LANGUAGES AND LITERATURES
Number 259

CONVERTING FICTION

CONVERTING FICTION

Counter Reformational Closure
in the Secular Literature
of Golden Age Spain

BY
DAVID H. DARST

CHAPEL HILL

NORTH CAROLINA STUDIES IN THE ROMANCE
LANGUAGES AND LITERATURES
U.N.C. DEPARTMENT OF ROMANCE LANGUAGES

1998

Library of Congress Cataloging-in-Publication Data

Darst, David H.
  Converting fiction: counter reformational closure in the secular literature of Golden Age Spain / by David H. Darst.
  p. – cm. – (North Carolina studies in the Romance languages & literatures; no. 259).
  Includes bibliographical references.
  ISBN 0-8078-9263-7 (pbk.)
  1. Spanish literature – Classical period, 1500-1700 – History and criticism. 2. Religion and literature. 3. Counter-Reformation-Spain. 4. Conversion in literature. 5. Closure (Rhetoric). I. Title. II. Series: North Carolina studies in the Romance languages and literatures; no. 259.

PQ6066.D37   1999   98-41810
860.9'382 – dc21   CIP

Cover: El Greco. *San Francisco meditando ante un crucifijo*. Private Collection

Cover design: Shelley Gruendler

© 1998. Department of Romance Languages. The University of North Carolina at Chapel Hill.

ISBN 0-8078-9263-7

DEPÓSITO LEGAL: V. 817 - 1999

ARTES GRÁFICAS SOLER, S. L. - LA OLIVERETA, 28 - 46018 VALENCIA

TABLE OF CONTENTS

	Page
Preface	9
Chapter One: Converting Source Materials	13
Chapter Two: Converting Ideology	33
Chapter Three: Converting Genres	51
Chapter Four: Converting Others	71
Chapter Five: Converting Oneself	91
Chapter Six: Converting History	115
Chapter Seven: Converting Landscapes	135
Chapter Eight: Converting Affective Expectations	155
Bibliography	175

PREFACE

This book explores some of the ways in which the Counter Reformation initiated by the Roman Catholic Church after 1563 affected Spanish secular literature in the seventeenth century. It will begin by explaining how the writers in the late sixteenth century first assumed the task of converting the extant materials to a Catholic posture by transforming the secular writings *a lo divino*. Courtly poetry, Classical literary forms, pastoral novels, the "romancero," popular songs, and the emblem tradition were all made *contrafacta* into religious literature. The book will then examine how, after 1598, this initial *a lo divino* effort was replaced by more subtle modes of conversion which appropriated a secular form or theme or narrative and, while retaining it as a secular vehicle, manipulated the closing moments to establish a religious closure resulting from some kind of conversion. In other words, seventeenth-century writers retained the secular discourse (rather then transforming it *a lo divino*), but replaced the attendant finale with a religious conversion of the circumstances, of the outcomes, of the motivations, of the people involved, of the characters' peripeteias, and of the very terrain peopled by the characters. Furthermore, the writers programmed the ending moments of their literature to direct the affective expectations of the spectators about motivations, history, prevalent outcomes, national identity, and physical geography.

The specific kinds of conversion at closure examined here are, in Chapter Three, appropriation of earlier genres, in particular the ruined city poem and the *novela cortesana*; in Chapter Four, conversion of non-Christian literary types, especially the "moro sentimental"; in Chapter Five, personal conversion of the native Spaniard through the Catholic ritual of confession, penitence and absolution; in Chapter Six, conversion of the nation's historical material by creating a divinely orchestrated pattern for the peninsula's heroes, whose feats of prowess against the non-Christian interlopers come to depend on direct intervention by heavenly agents in their lives; in Chapter Seven, conversion of the very physical terrain upon which Christians walk in their *peregrinatio vitae* by accommodating the expansive trajectories of the Byzantine novel to a Catholic blueprint of the risk-filled life guided by legitimate desire ending in restful union with one's society.

This book's concluding remarks in Chapter Eight attempt to describe the immediate consequences for Spanish literature that the various techniques of conversion brought to fruition. First and foremost, the lives and events in Spain's Counter Reformation literature become transparently "directed" towards the religious goal of conversion, the social goal of marriage, or the ontological goal of death. In all three closures, the outcome is usually unexpected by the participants (although not by the readers/spectators/listeners), who view their ends as remarkably different from the expectations they as individuals had held. The works thus have a "programmed" quality about them that demonstrate an "agenda" of action leading inexorably to the appropriate closure, which in turn accommodates all those personages who have willingly reached a role of passive compliance with the directing forces in their lives.

Additionally, these many events that lead to conversion intentionally appeal to the affections of both the characters and the readers/spectators/listeners. The narratives move them by means of emotional arousal to applaud freely and joyously the outcomes presented in the literature as the most appropriate and most accommodative program for closure, evoking thereby the devotion of them all to those divine forces which brought about the finale. In the early literature of the first decades of the seventeenth century, which is the major focus of this book, the awe-struck devotion is experienced as a capitulary love, a surrender to the other, in one of the only two possible career goals for the Christian creature, either marriage or conversion.

These closed endings, however, should not lead the reader to suppose that the fictions lack artistic quality or an open aesthetic posture. As Charlotte Stern argued so eloquently in a study of the *comedia* as a propagandistic instrument of the state, a fiction can present a monolithic view of society and still be a great piece of literature.

Closure has been an important topic of literary discussion since the "open-minded" sixties, and especially since Frank Kermode's *The Sense of an Ending*, which argued that fiction by definition manages to convey values of temporal openness. The more recent postmodernist movement has dropped all notions of closure in fiction for an infinite eternal openness, as the introductory remarks in a popular anthology declare: "Postmodernity's assertion of the value of inclusive 'both/and' thinking deliberately contests the exclusive 'either/or' binary oppositions of modernity. Postmodern paradox, ambiguity, irony, indeterminacy, and contingency are seen to replace modern closure, unity, order, the absolute, and the rational" (*Postmodern* ix).

We will see here that the writers of the specific fictions with Counter Reformational closure consciously intended to create works precisely the opposite of the postmodernist view, because they wished to establish a clear-cut ending without paradox, irony, indeterminacy or contingency in regard to the doctrinal message. On the other hand, it goes without saying that the uniform doctrinal message of this literature does not detract in any way from the ingenious and innovative techniques utilized to convey the message to the reader. All the literary works examined here are fine pieces of artistic endeavor, and perhaps more than the standard secular fare of the time, because this literature attempts to subvert in new and often shocking ways the literary secular canons of the day.

We thus have a paradoxical kind of writing that presents a closed message with a prescribed ending, but has a completely open and subversive methodology for conveying its propaganda. Moreover, the presence of this institutional propaganda does not deny nor berate in any way the presence in seventeenth-century secular literature outside the scope of this study, as well as in many of the fictions included here, of "multiple discourses of power and ideology" (Simerka) or "contradictory subjects" (Mariscal), as will be seen in *El remedio en la desdicha*, *El burlador de Sevilla*, and *Guzmán de Alfarache*.

Some of the material in this book has appeared previously in article form, but never with the emphasis given it here nor within the context of closure by conversion. The most pertinent studies which have contributed in some way to this text – however minimally – are "The Unity of *Las paces de los reyes y judía de Toledo*," *Symposium* 25 (1971): 225-35; "The Two Worlds of *La ninfa del cielo*," *Hispanic Review* 42 (1974): 209-20; "The Thematic Design of *El condenado por desconfiado*," *Kentucky Romance Quarterly* 21 (1974): 483-94; *Tirso de Molina's 'The Trickster of Seville': A Critical Commentary* (New York: Simon & Schuster, 1976); "La muerte y el matrimonio en el teatro de Tirso de Molina," *Immagini riflesse* (Napoli: ESI, 1990): 217-24; "The Conceptual Design of Rodrigo Caro's 'A Itálica,'" *Hispanófila* 108 (1993): 11-17; "The Theology of Expectations and Outcomes in *El esclavo del demonio*," *Journal of Interdisciplinary Literature Studies* 4 (1992): 155-67; and "Una comedia, dos argumentos, tres historias: La estructura de *El remedio en la desdicha*," *Hispania* 76 (1994): 46-53.

The present form of this book owes much to the valuable contributions of its anonymous reviewers and to Professor Carol Sherman who guided it to completion. Publication was also facilitated by generous grants from Florida State University's College of Arts & Sciences and Department of Modern Languages as well as from the Program for Cultural Cooperation between Spain's Ministry of Education and Culture and United States' Universities.

CHAPTER ONE

CONVERTING SOURCE MATERIALS

In the little chapel to the back left in the Royal Basilica of El Escorial the pious visitor can purchase for a small donation a prayer card that has an ornate monstrance on the front – and on the cover of this very book – and the following words on the back:

> El Real Monasterio de San Lorenzo de El Escorial es un verdadero relicario de maravillas, de las cuales la más estimada es la Sagrada Forma, todavía incorrupta después de más de cuatro siglos que fue profanada por un hereje, en compañía de otros zvinglianos, en Gorcamia (Holanda). En ella se notan tres roturas que, al parecer, fueron producidas por los clavos que llevaría en el calzado el que la pisó, y de las que brotó sangre en el momento de cometer el sacrilegio. Ante este prodigio, el profanador se convirtió a la religión católica, haciéndose más tarde religioso franciscano.

It is simply astonishing that at the close of the twentieth century the Spanish Church still places so much emphasis on the early modern conflict that divided Protestants and Catholics. The legend on the back of this card mentions a "heretical" group surely unknown to the average Spaniard and probably to modern day Protestants as well. The story, however, is the canonical Catholic conversion brought about by direct divine intervention in an individual's life, causing a recognition of sin, a conversion, and an incorporation of the body and the soul within the Catholic fold, in this case as a Franciscan monk. The barbaric Zwinglian who had accepted faith alone as the road to salvation, had rejected all sacred images in the church, and had destroyed all the convents and monasteries of the religious orders, upon conversion becomes a member of the Catholic group most dedicated to good works, the cult of images, and the monastic life. All of this occurs, furthermore, because the man desecrated what his belief considered to be the mere sign of a commemorative feast, when it actually was the very transubstantiated blood of Christ, which gushed from the three nail holes made by the Zwinglian's boot exactly as the Lord's own blood flowed from the three nail holes made in his very body at his crucifixion.

We traditionally call the aggressive Catholic response to the Protestant Reformation epitomized in this card the Counter Reformation, assuredly one of the most precise terms we have for any cultural movement in Western Europe. It refers to the efforts of the Catholic Church to "Counter" the "Reformation" of the Christian religion undertaken by the Protestants in northern Europe. Its first manifestations were efforts to counter Erasmian criticism of established Church practices, but the Lutheran heresy quickly became the focus of attention, and by the 1520s concerned people like Ignatius Loyola had determined to dedicate their lives to countering the German's protests against Rome.

By 1540, with the establishment of Loyola's Society of Jesus, the movement to counter the Reformation with a reinforcement of Christian doctrine became a sanctioned part of papal policy. Five years later, Church authorities met in Trent to begin to codify what would become "Catholic" dogma; and by 1563, when the Council of Trent closed its twenty-fifth session (and coincidentally when King Philip II began to construct the Royal Monastery of San Lorenzo de El Escorial), the process of creedal codification was complete.

The materials converted directly to Catholic use during the next fifty years are the foundation for the literary constructions of the seventeenth century, which will be the concern of this book's later chapters. The examination of the sixteenth-century accomodation of religious thought in secular modes in this present chapter and the intellectual underpinnings of Counter Reformation doctrine in Chapter Two will facilitate the reader's understanding of the religious tenets that characterize the fictions studied in the later chapters.

The literature produced in the initial period from 1545 to 1563 is virtually untouched by the Church's response to Protestantism. If anything, it is reformist and Erasmian in outlook. After 1563, however, countering techniques appear with persistent rapidity. By 1598, the year of King Philip's death, one can speak with assurance of a Counter Reformational mode in Spanish literature. It is those techniques which were introduced between 1563 and 1598, a period appropriately called by Ludwig Pfandl Spain's Second Renaissance, that are the subject of this first chapter. Although it is a difficult period to discuss in general terms because it includes a variety of modes, the techniques examined here all concern the conversions of previous secular literature or secular ways of thought to a spiritual context. In the seventeenth-century Counter Reformation literature, by contrast, the religious context will become an integral component of the secular literature or secular mode of thought and will serve mainly to close the world-bound text with a spiritual resolution precipitated by some kind of personal conversion.

First, there are a number of important trends in late sixteenth-century Spanish letters that have nothing to do specifically with the Counter Reformation, but do affect tremendously the direction of all Spanish literature in the next century. One trend is the neo-traditional popularizing tendencies of the "romancero" by Lope de Vega, Cervantes, Luis de Góngora and many other minor writers which began in the 1550s with the first printed volumes of ballads and reached its peak around 1600. The same nationalistic movement to create an autochthonous literature creates such masterpieces of Philippine literature as the pastoral novel, which transfers an Italian genre to Spanish soil, the neo-traditional native letrillas, redondillas, glosas, and other popular-appearing poetry that Lope, Góngora, and others began publishing in the 1580s to compete with the Italian meters introduced in the first half of the century, and the collection and publication of native proverbs and adages, such as those of Juan de Mal Lara and Sebastián de Horozco.

Another trend is the flowering in southern Spain of a Classical school of writers, almost all poets, appropriately called the Sevillan school, which creates for the Spanish language a sober Horatian style of elegaic poetry of skillful elegance to compete with the Renaissance Latin tradition (also initiated by the Italians).

A third trend is the ardent defense of the Spanish language for all endeavors, whether scholarly, political or religious, that began with the widely diffused apologies of Fray Luis de León in *Los nombres de Cristo* (1583) and Pedro Malón de Chaide in *La conver-*

sión de la Magdalena (1592) and was still going strong in the late seventeenth century when the *Historia y magia natural* (1692) by the Jesuit Hernando Castrillo (1586-1667) was finally published. As had his predecessors, Castrillo felt he needed to defend his use of Spanish rather than Latin for a philosophical treatise with the standard nationalistic arguments that the language will reach more people, that it is the "mother tongue" and therefore the most natural, and that it is the oldest vernacular idiom, with its roots in pre-Classical Egypt ("Prólogo" n. pag.).

Finally, there is a continual trend of emulative appropriation of various Italian artistic and literary forms such as the commedia dell'arte, the Boccaccian novella, emblem books, the contemporary epic, and the bucolic eclogue.

Virtually all of the above Spanish literature is published in the second part of Philip's reign, traditionally marked from 1568 when the King shifted to a more Catholic political stance with his selection of Cardinal Antonio Perrenot de Granvela (1517-1586) as his private secretary. It is during this period that two distinct Counter Reformational religious endeavors emerge alongside the secular nationalistic trends. The best-known new enterprise is the mystical impetus spearheaded by Teresa de Cepeda (Santa Teresa de Jesús), Juan de Yepes (San Juan de la Cruz) and Fray Luis de León; but it is just the tip of the iceberg. The few publications of these mystical geniuses were bulwarked by hundreds upon hundreds of minor religious writings on lives of the saints, biographies of contemporary defenders of the faith, commentaries of the scriptures, handbooks for meditation, guidebooks for penitents, and every other conceivable kind of religious material, all intended to provide the Spanish reading public with accessible spiritual literature.

The second new enterprise is the virulent *a lo divino* movement by religious writers (and later by secular writers), which involves converting to proper Counter Reformation credence the contents of the Renaissance Spanish literature by Garcilaso de la Vega, Juan Boscán, Jorge de Montemayor, and others, attempting thereby to compete with secular literature by "counter-writing" it, for which Bruce W. Wardropper coined the term *contrafacta*. Interestingly, most of the *contrafacta* publications were directed at the new forms of literature imported from abroad, which were viewed as especially pagan and lascivious by the Spanish conservative thinkers. Eventually, however, even indigenous forms considered especially dangerous because of their blatant non-religious message or association with Spain's Arab past, like the "romancero," the traditional "cantigas de amigo," and the chivalresque novel, were converted to the religous realm by turning them *a lo divino*.

Most of these pre-Baroque late sixteenth-century innovations have one thing in common. They are all attempts at appropriation, at stealing a genre or style, clothing it in a new native garb, and presenting it to the public as something better than its alien predecessor. The initial manifestation of the Counter Reformational mode, in other words, is not a new form of literature but rather the incorporation of religious ideas within preexisting forms, especially those forms brought in from the outside and seen as generically alien, but also popular forms considered particularly pagan or non-Catholic. It was, to speak plainly, a process of religious conversion of the materials and forms used by the secular writers.

The *a lo divino* literature took at least four forms in the sixteenth and early seventeenth centuries. One is the case of authors attempting to reproduce exactly a sacred version of a specific popular secular literary work, such as Sebastián de Córdoba's *Obras de Boscán y Garcilaso trasladadas a materias cristianas y religiosas* (1577), Bartolomé Ponce's *Clara Diana a lo divino*, Jaime de Alcalá's *Libro de la caballería cristiana* (1570) and Juan Francisco de Villava's *Empresas espirituales y morales* (1613).

The second is the more common case in which the author presents a work as a cleansed substitute for a genre or a particular reading public. Alonso de Ledesma wished his book of popular sacred poetry *Conceptos espirituales y morales* (1612) to replace all the secular ballads and songs on the market; Alonso Remón wanted his popular book *Entretenimientos y juegos honestos y recreaciones christianos para que en todo género de estados se recrean los sentidos sin que se estrague el alma* (1623) to replace all the secular games children and adults played; Fray Luis de León hoped his *De los nombres de Cristo* (1583) would displace all the works of fiction read so avidly by the women of his time; and Malón de Chaide wrote his *Conversión de la Magdalena* (1592) to serve the same purpose.

The third is those authors who wrote "counter-fictions," transcribing their own literary work into an *a lo divino* format, as Lope de Vega did when he penned *Pastores de Belén* (1612) to be a counterweight to *La Arcadia* (1598) or *Rimas sacras* (1614) to atone for his earlier *Rimas* (1602); and Tirso de Molina's *Deleitar aprovechando* (1635) offsets his earlier *Cigarrales de Toledo* (1621).

Fourthly, other writers practiced a more sophisticated form of intellectual transference, appropriating outright the secular piece and converting its entire form and substance into a religious work, often without altering the vehicle. The lyric poems of Spain's great mystic pair Santa Teresa de Jesús and San Juan de la Cruz are the best-known examples of this wholesale divinization of a poetic form, and their success spawned hundreds of similar efforts by all the Golden Age poets, especially Lope de Vega and José de Valdivielso. The latter stated specifically, in fact, that the purpose of his *Romancero espiritual* (1612) was the conversion of the reader: "He tomado por instrumento algunos de estos versos para conversión de algunas almas envejecidas en culpas; persuadiéndome que leyéndolos muchos, se podrán reducir algunos" (9); and, effectively, the very first ballad is a spiritual rendition of a famous Cid ballad now titled "Romance a la conversión de un pecador." A close examination of one or two items in each of these four categories hopefully will illustrate sufficiently the techniques utilized by *a lo divino* writers.

(1) Juan Francisco de Villava's *Empresas espirituales y morales* is the first and only Spanish emblem book truly *a lo divino*, which is curious, because of its late publication date – 1613 – and the popularity of the genre both in Spain and abroad. As will be explained later, the reason for only one *a lo divino* emblem book is due to the wholesale appropriation of the genre for religious purposes in the second half of the seventeenth century.

An emblem is a complex of poem, illustration, motto, and prose commentary working together to present a single idea to the reader. The genre appeared *ab ovo* in 1531, when the Augsburg printer Heinrich Steyner published Andrea Alciati's *Emblematum Liber* of 97 woodcuts with accompanying mottoes and epigrams. The book's popularity prompted Alciati to add more emblems, and the final version contained 211. The first Spanish edition was done by Bernardino Daza Pinciano and appeared in 1549 with the title *Los emblemas de Alciato traducidos en rhimas españolas*; and a second rendition with commentary came out in 1615 by Diego López entitled *Declaración magistral sobre los emblemas de Andrés Alciato*.

The popularity of the genre led to a number of excellent imitations in Spain. Juan de Borja, son of the Jesuit general Francisco de Borja, published one hundred original emblems in 1581 in a volume titled *Empresas morales*, which initiated a series of "moral" emblem books whose purpose was to present in a concise way a clear and pithy statement about the ethical life. As Borja's grandson remarked to Charles II in a 1680 prologue to the book, the emblems are "de gran servicio de Dios, y de V. M. su enseñanza, por contener lo más Heroyco, y acendrado de las Virtudes morales, y políticas, y con la concisión de que necessitan los Príncipes, y personas públicas, por su mucha ocupación" (ed. 1680, n. pag.). This political end for emblems experienced an upsurge in popularity in the late Baroque when Diego Saavedra Fajardo published his *Idea de un príncipe político-cristiano representada en cien empresas* (1640), and initiated a slew of imitations.

The immediate successors to Borja's book are all of the highest quality. The first and most popular is *Emblemas morales* by Juan de Horozco y Covarrubias, first published in Segovia (1589), with a second edition quickly appearing in 1591 and a third in 1604. The book contains a long introduction on the nature and function of emblems, followed by two parts with fifty emblems in each. The next effort is Hernando de Soto's *Emblemas moralizados* (1599), which contains sixty emblems in the same style and with the same doctrinal attitude as those of Horozco. In 1610 the last true moral emblem book is published by Horozco's brother Sebastián de Covarrubias y Orozco. Also titled *Emblemas morales*, it is the most ambitious of them all, containing three hundred different emblems, with a royal octave below each device and a prose commentary on the page's back (or left) side. Yet another contribution is *Proverbios morales* by Cristóbal Pérez de Herrera in 1618. While more a collection of enigmas than a full-fledged emblem book – there are only thirteen woodcuts – the volume definitely belongs in the genre.

After 1618 the moral emblem tradition dies out. It is not due to a decline in the popularity of emblems, however, for works in the genre continue to increase in supply and demand. What changes is the subject matter, because the moral, humanistic emblem books are replaced by the sub-genre of religious Counter Reformational ones.

The first volume of the religious type to appear was a kind of proto-emblem book by Francisco de Monçón entitled *Norte de ydiotas* (1563). It was not a true emblem book because there were no mottoes to the devices, nor did the pictures come from the Alciati repertoire. The volume is important to the emblem tradition, nevertheless, because its proloque expressed the new Tridentine attitude towards the use of images for meditative inspiration. Monçón explained that all the church fathers and general councils approved the use of images in prayer, and noted:

> Muchos provechos se siguen generalmente de la vista y adoración de las ymágines, y principalmente a las personas simples y sin letras, que según se dize son sus libros adonde leen y aprenden los hechos de aquellas personas illustres que allí se representan, que éste es el fin que la sancta madre yglesia regida por el Spíritu Sancto tuvo, quando ordenó que en los templos y aun en las casas se pusiessen Retablos de tanta diversidad de figuras, avisando y aun vedando que no se pusiesse ninguna deshonesta, sino de cosas sanctas y verdaderas, de adonde el spíritu se pueda provocar a devoción y se incide a imitación de sus virtudes. Este género de leción en las ymágines es tan conveniente como la de los libros, y en la una también como en la otra se puede fundar la escala espiritual. (4v-5r)

Monçón's views on religious images are strikingly similar to the statements that were coming out of Trent at the same time, such as the following declarations in the section "Concerning the Invocation, Worship, and Relicks of the Saints, and holy Images:"

> The holy Synod commands all Bishops and others that have the Charge and Care of Teaching, that according to the Usage of the Catholick and Apostolick Church, received from the primitive times of Christianity, the Consent of the holy Fathers, and Decrees of Councils, they diligently instruct the People, chiefly concerning the Intercession and Invocation of Saints, Honour of Relicks, and the lawful Use of Images: Teaching them, that the Saints, reigning together with Christ, do offer up their Prayers to God for Men; That it is good and profitable humbly to invocate them, and to have recourse to their Prayers, help and assistance, for the imploring benefits from God by his Son Jesus Christ our Lord, who is our alone Saviour and Redeemer. (*Council* 145-46)

As with every reaffirmation at Trent, the probational declaration is always followed by a penal one: "But that those, who deny that the

Saints, enjoying eternal happiness in Heaven, ought to be invoked; or who assert, that they do not pray for Men; and that it is idolatry to Invoke them to pray for us particularly or singularly; or that it is repugnant to the Word of God, and contrary to the honour of the *one Mediator* between God and Man, *Jesus Christ*; that it is a foolish thing, to pray to those that are Reigning in Heaven, either with Heart or Voice; do entertain wicked and ungodly Thoughts and Opinions" (*Council* 146).

Concerning images and other visual aides, the text declares: "Moreover, That the Images of Christ, of the Virgin, and of other Saints, ought especially to be had and kept in Churches, and to have due Honour and Veneration given them. ... The Bishops also shall diligently Teach and suggest, that by the Histories of the Misteries of our Redemption, expressed in Pictures, and other Similitudes, the people are instructed and confirmed, in remembring and daily calling to mind the Articles of Faith" (*Council* 146).

These texts and all similar ones show the strong influence, directly or indirectly, of Saint Ignatius's *Ejercicios espirituales para vencer a sí mismo y ordenar su vida sin determinarse por afeción alguna que desordenada sea* and his innovative theory of Composition of Place, which influences in one way or another the vast majority of Counter Reformation literature. Succinctly, Loyola defined the meditative procedure as follows:

> El primer preámbulo es composición viendo el lugar. Aquí es de notar que en la contemplación o meditación visible, así como contemplar a Christo nuestro Señor, el cual es visible, la composición será ver con la vista de la imaginación el lugar corpóreo donde se halla la cosa que quiero contemplar. Digo el lugar corpóreo, así como un templo o monte, donde se halla Jesu Christo o Nuestra Señora, según lo que quiero contemplar. En la invisible, como es aquí de los pecados, la composición será ver con la vista imaginativa y considerar mi ánima ser encarcerada en este valle, como desterrado entre brutos animales; digo todo el compósito de ánima y cuerpo. (221-22)

It should come as no surprise that the Jesuits dominated the seventeenth-century emblem tradition, authoring as a group more secular and religious emblem books than anyone else. The Jesuits were more prolific and influential outside of Spain than within, yet just the list of Spaniards includes Sebastián Izquierdo (1605-1681), Andrés Mendo (1608-1684), Juan Eusebio Nieremberg (1595-1658), Francisco Núñez de Cepeda (1616-1690), Lorenzo Ortiz (1632-1698), Juan de Pineda (1557-1637), Jerónimo Nadal (1507-1580), and Pedro de Salas (Campa *passim*).

As noted earlier, the first and only true *a lo divino* emblem book to appear in seventeenth-century Spain was Villava's *Empresas espirituales y morales*. The book contains ninety-nine rather crudely designed woodcuts, most from the Italian emblem tradition (Villava cites Paolo Giovio, Girolamo Ruscelli, Luca Contile, Claude Paradin, Gabriele Simeoni, Camillo Camilli, and Giulio Cesare Capaccio as sources) and totally secular in figure and motto. Each is followed by a one or two page commentary giving the emblem a religious meaning. The first fifty emblems concern spiritual or morally acceptable types of persons. After twelve on God's divine aspects, the remainder attempt to personify personalities such as the just, the faithful, the confident, the charitable, the prudent, the temperate, etc. The second part contains forty-nine emblems that typify sinners, such as those who commit the seven deadly sins, the slanderer, the ingrate, the vainglorious, the profane, the dandy, etc. The third part is an extensive diatribe on heretical sects, culminating with a condemnation of the *alumbrados*.

Of equal importance here is Villava's rationale for converting emblems to the Catholic cause. Echoing in many aspects Monçón's ideas, Villava declares *in nuce* the theory behind *a lo divino* writings:

> Siempre me pareció zelo piadoso, y digno de ingenios virtuosos, el de los que qualesquier invenciones, que se ha usurpado el mundo tyranicamente para su servizio, las procura reduzir a la obediencia de su dueño que es Dios: que éste ha de ser el fin y blanco de nuestras obras. ... En tiempo pues que tan despierto anda este negocio, y tantas invenciones busca Satanás, para enriquezer su Reyno, es bien, que pues los gustos están tan estragados y dolientes, se hagan algunas salsillas y picantes, para que les sepa bien la doctrina del Cielo, y les dé algún gusto la virtud. Tomado an algunos esta empresa, bolviendo los versos humanos en divinos, trocando la materia, y guardando la composición, aunque si el no salir tan agudos y aceptos nazca de no acudir nuestro entendimiento con tan presto y acertado buelo, a las cosas del espíritu, como a las de la carne; o de que al paladar hu-

mano (por estar tan corrompido) no les saben tan bien como en materias profanas, no es negocio que tiene tan fácil resolución. No (empero) dexa de ser grattísimo a Dios, y a los buenos en su nombre, el buen zelo con que estas pieças se arrebatan de las manos del mundo como de injusto posessor, para hazerles venir bolando a servir al Evangelio, pues a todas las artes llama la Theología y les toca caja para que acudan a su alcaçar. ... Yo bien quisiera entrar en este número, como lo he significado en las ocasiones que se an ofrecido, bolviendo algunas cosas profanas, y haziéndoles servir a Christo nuestro bien. (1r-2r)

Villava's insistence that he is not converting at all, but simply "recovering" the literary function that the secular world usurped from the sacred world is a constant theme in these kinds of apologies and had been used earlier by Fray Luis de León and Pedro Malón de Chaide. The former stated categorically that "poesía no es sino una comunicación del aliento celestial y divino" (158-59) which by its very nature has a profound influence on its hearers, and this is why profane poetry, which transmits a message of lascivious secular love, is so pernicious.

Villava's statement that the *a lo divino* methodology is simply "bolviendo los versos humanos en divinos, trocando la materia, y guardando la composición" is also right on the mark, because most *contrafacta* writers insist quite adamantly that their objections to secular literature are exclusively with the *res*, the subject matter, and not with the *verba*, which is the medium or form of the composition. Fray Luis de León also saw this problem, and expressed it succinctly. The original religious poems, he claims, used order and number to imitate the spiritual sense of their desire, "para que el estilo del dezir se assemejasse al sentir, y las palabras [*verba*] y las cosas [*res*] fuessen conformes" (159). Popular songs, using the same techniques of number and harmony to inspire their hearers (here, innocent young women), insert base words into the format, creating thereby "cantarcillos de argumentos livianos, los cuales hablan con ellas a todas horas, y sin recatarse dellos, antes aprendiéndolos y cantándolos, las atraen a sí y las persuaden secretamente, y derramándoles su ponzoña poco a poco por los pechos las inficionan y pierden" (159).

The bitter arguments among the secular writers concerning the legitimacy of forms that masked a lascivious content or that paraded alone without bringing any content at all to the listener, such as the polemic over *cultismo* which I examined in an earlier study ("Palabras"), come later and are related to *a lo divino* literature only in that religious-minded thinkers consistently rejected *cultismo* because they considered it either useless, since it had no message to convey, or – as had Fray Luis de León – the coverup of a lascivious content. Tirso de Molina, for example, specifically equates cultistic language with cosmetics in his saint's play *Santa Juana I* and ironically concludes that poets who praise beautiful women with elegant metaphors are twice decieved about the object they describe because they see only the painted face rather than the real person: "¿Por qué ha de ser luna y sol / lo que es solimán y sebo?" (1: 772a-773a). Other thinkers go so far as to equate *cultismo* directly with heresy. Francisco de Quevedo repeatedly associates Góngora with the Jews because he considers the Cordoban's poetry to be anti-Spanish and anti-Christian (2: 439-46); and Lope de Vega denounces Góngora's cultistic style as inappropriate for religious matters, urging in his sonnet *Contra los que predican en culto*, "dejad, ¡oh padres!, los conceptos vanos, / que Dios no ha menester filaterías / sino celo en la voz, fuego en las manos" (*Obras completas* 2: 278b).

The books by Monçón and Villava are probably the only *a lo divino* emblem books in Spanish because so many were written in Latin or were translations of Latin works. Of the latter, the most famous is unquestionably the *Affectos divinos con emblemas sagradas* (1658) by the Jesuit Pedro de Salas, which is a translation of the immensely popular *Pia Desideria* (1624) by Herman Hugo. Salas's book also contains an introduction defending "poesía divina" against "poesía profana," as he terms it. His volume will "reparar con poesía divina los daños de la poesía profana reduziéndolo a su fin, que es el que escribe Horacio: Et prodesse volunt et delectare poetae" (n. pag.).

Another reason for the dearth of true *a lo divino* emblem books is that so many anomalies appeared. The aforementioned *Entretenimientos* of Alonso Remón is one example. Another is Laurencio de Zamora's enormous *Monarquía mística de la yglesia hecha de hieroglíficos sacados de humanas y divinas letras* (1604), which has an interesting "Apología contra los que reprehenden el uso de las humanas letras en los sermones y comentarios de la santa escritura" (1-89).

(2) Alonso de Ledesma is another *a lo divino* writer who published a number of religious works between 1600 and 1625, employing emblems, hieroglyphs, enigmas, devices, and other visual techniques. The volumes are not strictly speaking within the emblem tradition, but they certainly partake of the same philosophy and function in the same way. Ledesma's overall intention is more aggressive than Villava's, because Ledesma wants to convert the pagan poetry he considers to be corrupting the morals of his countrymen. To accomplish his mission he leaves no poetic stone unturned, writing popular religious sonnets, romances, villancicos, redondillas, glosas, seguidillas, quintillas, décimas, ensaladas, endechas, letras, conceptos, and coloquios. He also includes scores of hieroglyphics, which function precisely as emblems do by presenting the reader with a theme, a visual image (described), a motto, and a poetic commentary. The following, which is part of a series of poems dedicated to the glorious beatification of Ignatius Loyola, is typical:

>   Al extassis que tuuo de ocho dias en Manressa
>
>   Hierogliphico
>
>   Pintose a Hercules abraçado con Anteon, leuantado en el ayre
>   Quae sursum sunt sapite, non quae super terram (ad. colos 3)
>   Con tal de por muerto al mundo,
>   pues el Alma en esta guerra
>   haze el cuerpo perder tierra. (3: 337)

In an introduction to the reader for the first part of the work, the Augustinian prior Juan de Arenas states openly the belligerent substitutive intent of Ledesma's poems. Arenas claims that Spain's customs have been undermined by profane books – especially those containing poetry – which induce people to practice what they read. Yet in the midst of this turmoil, "despierta Dios los coraçones de otros, a quien tambien dio galano talento, para que le empleen en aficionar a lo diuino, ... porque tanto fruto se puede esperar destos libros a lo diuino, quanto mal acarrean los que son a lo humano" (1: 14-15).

Fray Luis de León and Pedro Malón de Chaide both establish the same rationale for their literary compositions. Fray Luis begins *De los nombres de Cristo* with the line "de las calamidades de nuestros tiempos" (47) and complains that the Christian community has degenerated from its pristine state of pure virtue, "que se han entregado sin rienda a la lición de mil libros no solamente vanos sino señaladamente dañosos; ... destos libros perdidos y desconcertados, y de su lición, nasce gran parte de los reveses y perdición que se descubren continuamente en nuestras costumbres. ... A mi juyzio el principio y la rayz y la causa toda son estos libros ... porque muchos destos malos escriptos ordinariamente andan en las manos de mugeres donzellas y mozas" (50-51). The only possible remedy is to take the field in a belligerently aggressive way by creating an alternative literature that will wrest the vicious rivals from people's hands, "algunas cosas que o como nascidas de las sagradas letras, o como allegadas y conformes a ellas, suplan por ellas cuanto es possible con el común menester de los hombres y juntamente les quiten de las manos, succediendo en su lugar dellos, los libros dañosos y de vanidad" (51).

It is not clear precisely what kind of literature fray Luis wished to supplant with *De los nombres de Cristo*. Pedro Malón de Chaide was much more specific about the usurpative purpose of *La conversión de la Magdalena*: "Libros de amores, y las *Dianas* y Boscanes y Garcilasos, y los monstruosos libros y silvas de fabulosos cuentos y mentiras de los *Amadises, Floriseles y Don Belianís*, y una flota de semejantes portentos como hay escritos" (279). All are profane and lascivious books which destroy proper customs and lead their young readers astray. The only remedy is to repair the damage by competing with the secular literature on its own ground, offering exciting material with pretty verses in a clear "ordinary language" (276) that will appeal to the young female reader. Malón de Chaide thus closes his prologue in the book with the hope that his Spanish-language tale of Mary Magdalene will supplant his readers' addiction to secular fiction:

> Dije al principio deste prólogo que hacían gran daño a muchos los libros de poesía profana; y por si pudiese yo reparar alguna parte deste daño, he querido probarme a hacer algunos versos y salir *velut anser inter olores*, que suelen decir. Bien sé que no son los más escogidos ni más bien trabajados del mundo; mas lo que les falta de curiosidad en la compostura les sobra de bondad en la materia y de grandeza en el sugeto. Podría ser que, hecho el gusto a estos salmos y canciones divinas, vengan algunos a desgustar de las profanas. (282)

(3) Some writers who produced counter-fictions of their own previous publications also followed an aggressively belligerent path of literary emulation. Such is apparently the case with Tirso de Molina, whose secular *Cigarrales de Toledo* is "counter-placed" (the term is his) by *Deleytar aprovechando* in a competitive way. While the two works are not mirror images, they both have the typical Boccaccian cycle of days and hosts, they both include interpolated poetry, and they both end each day with a dramatic performance (three *comedias* in the former and three *autos sacramentales* in the latter). *Cigarrales* is wholly courtly, representing perhaps the highest-quality purely secular literature about beautiful young nobles in Spain's Golden Age. *Deleytar* is wholly religious and desires to supplant its secular counterparts, "los Belianises, Febos, Primaleones, Dianas, Guzmanos de Alfarache, Gerardos y Persiles en nuestro castellano" ("A don Luis Fernández de Córdoba," n. pag). His method will be "contraponiendo lo devoto a lo atrevido, al vicio la virtud, a las máscaras los sermones, a los teatros los templos, a las burlas las veras, los jubileos a los disfraces" (2v).

Lope de Vega's counter-fictions are less combative and more apologetic. Whereas Tirso never mentions his previous work as the object of his counter-placing novel, Lope writes explicit detractions expressing regret for his secular production and proffering the new material as an act of contrition as well as a substitute for the profane literature.

In effect, after 1612 Lope de Vega produced a series of counter-fictions to many of his earlier works in an attempt to change his life. In early 1610 he had joined an oratory sponsored by the Congregación de Esclavos de Dios, and in 1611 he entered the congregation of the Orden Tercera de San Francisco. That same year both his wife Juana de Guardo and his beloved son Carlos Félix became ill, prompting him to write the intimate *Cuatro soliloquios* and to begin *Los pastores de Belén*, which he dedicated to the sick child. Carlos Félix died the next year, and Juana the year after that. Devastated, Lope decided to become a priest, and spent almost all of 1614 going through the procedures of minor orders, major orders, subdeacon, deacon, and priest. That same year he allowed a friend to publish his *Rimas sacras*, and 1619 saw another counter-fiction in the form of religious ballads published as the *Romancero espiritual*. Given all these facts, one can safely assume that Lope's religious projects were serious and well-intentioned.

In late 1611, Lope wrote a letter to his benefactor the Duke of Sessa: "Sepa Vuestro Excelentísimo Señor que estos días he escrito un libro que llamo *Pastores de Belén*, prosa y versos divinos a la traza de *La Arcadia*. ... Hartas veces he pensado cuán mal empleé mis servicios y mis años en el dueño de aquellos pensamientos de *La Arcadia*" (*Obras escogidas* 2: 1193). The book is dedicated to his sick son Carlos Félix, to whom he writes: "Será bien que cuando halléis Arcadias de pastores humanos sepáis que estos divinos escribieron mis desengaños, y aquéllos, mis ignorancias" (2: 1194). Indeed, *Pastores de Belén* is a virtual mirror to its predecessor, a "traza" or outline having the same length, the same five sections, and the same closing "Belardo, a la zampoña," in which the author again apologizes for his youthful secular production. "Esta vez," Belardo announces to his panpipe, "habéis empleado vuestro talento en sujeto dignísimo, y satisfecho en parte aquellas fábulas vanas, inútiles, copiosas de mentiras y lisonjas, halagadoras de hermosuras que en tan breve tiempo feas han sido luz de mis engaños" (1342).

The *Rimas sacras*, dedicated to his confessor Martín de San Cirilo, are a substitute for the *Rimas humanas*, which initially appeared in 1602 and were then republished almost every year thereafter with many additions and emendations. The sacred poems were actually collected by Antonio Flórez; but they have an interesting poem by Juan de Piña addressed to Lope that claims "vos mismo os imitáis":

> Si en el arte de amor
> os vio el mundo peregrino,
> hoy, en el arte divino,
> divino os pueden llamar.
> (*Obras poéticas* 308)

Another laudatory poem by Fernando Bermúdez de Carvajal makes the same connection between the "old" Lope who sang of human love like a swan and the "new" Lope who has been reborn as a phoenix, "porque quien se vuelve a Dios / muere cisne y fénix nace" (309).

The one hundred sonnets in *Rimas sacras* (matching the two hundred in the earlier *Rimas*) form a comprehensive palinode for Lope's past secular life. Sonnet I, "Cuando me paro a contemplar mi estado," is a *contrafacta* of Garcilaso's first sonnet. The next fifty are all personal confessions, expressing sorrow for past sins and a desire for forgiveness in which Lope speaks directly to himself or to Christ. In Sonnet XIX Lope denounces the lyre with which he has sung so many profane songs and swears henceforward to sing only with the lyre that is Christ; and in Sonnet XXIX he promises to consecrate pen and voice, mind and hand, to Christ rather than to mortal beauty: "A la hermosura vuestra eternamente / consagro pluma y voz, ingenio y mano" (330). Sonnet L is titled appropriately *A la Resurrección*, and ends the personal cycle of conversion poems, because the remainder (with the exceptions of the repentant sonnets XC, XCI, and XCIV) are devotional poems to saints, biblical figures, and religious occasions.

(4) The fourth kind of *a lo divino* literature practices the "craft of literary transference" (Darst, "Techniques") whereby a genre originally intended for one purpose or audience is manipulated in such a way that it is converted into a vehicle for a different – perhaps dialectical – message with another purpose for a new audience. When San Juan de la Cruz transmits *Noche oscura del alma*, he intentionally omits any clear reference to specific religious items. If the poem were read by a totally innocent reader, in other words, it would relate the tale of a young woman who sneaks out of her house by a secret stairway late one night when everyone is asleep and goes to meet her beloved, guided by her flaming love. They consummate their mutual affection, and he falls asleep on her breast as the soft winds cool his brow and wound her softly, causing her also to fall into a state of unconsciousness.

Llama de amor viva also is devoid of direct religious references. The bare content expresses the orgasmic exclamations of a lover in the ecstasy of intimate union with the beloved. In both poems, San Juan de la Cruz has transferred the secular love poem over to the religious side so completely that – paradoxically – the poem remains secular in all appearances but spiritual in every sense of the word. He must have known that the poems would be difficult to interpret as he wished them to be, because he wrote extensive line-by-line commentaries for both of them detailing the mystical meaning.

San Juan de la Cruz's long poem *Cántico espiritual*, which also has an extensive prose commentary, is in the same category of literary transference. It is a secular canticle that the author wants the reader to interpret in a spiritual way, although the entire poem has only two direct biblical references ("Judea" and "Aminadab"), both of which are corrupted by pagan attachments ("ninfas" of Judea and "caballería" of Aminadab).

The poet's reasons for writing this kind of poetry are many. He admits in the prologue to *Llama de amor viva* that he really does not like to write commentaries about his poems because they describe moments so intimate and inneffable that words cannot explain them, "por ser las cosas tan interiores y espirituales, para las cuales comúnmente falta lenguaje, porque lo espiritual excede al sentido, y háblase mal de las entrañas del espíritu si no es con entrañable espíritu" (216). He elaborates on this notion of communicating the incommunicable in the prologue to *Cántico espiritual*, noting that "sería ignorancia pensar que los dichos de amor e inteligencia mística, cuales son los de las presentes canciones, con alguna manera de palabras se pueden bien explicar" (143). Therefore, he has resorted to tropes, similes, and metaphors – "figuras, comparaciones y semejanzas" – to convey the love and understanding he has experienced, "las cuales semejanzas, no leídas con la sencillez del espíritu de amor e inteligencia que ellas llevan, antes parecen dislates que dichos puestos en razón" (143). It is for this reason that San Juan appends an interpretative commentary, although he warns his reader that his own interpretation of the poetry is merely a partial, rational description and should not be taken as a definitive view, since in matters of faith there is no such thing as a clear understanding: "Porque es a modo de la fe, en la cual amamos a Dios sin entenderle claramente" (143).

For San Juan de la Cruz, then, these poems attempt to express feelings that are inexpressable and describe meaning that is indescribable. Clearly, any attempt to specify either feelings or meaning with references to concrete religious notions would create immediate interpretative associations contrary to the inexplicable sense of mystical union the poems are attempting to convey; so the poet simply writes the simplest poems he can, avoiding all pointed references to anything but retaining a recognizable story line. Furthermore, within the context of San Juan de la Cruz's personal experience, all three poems describe the same intimate union of the soul with God or with Christ, the soul's husband. Within this context, for the mystical poet, the poems are wholly religious without any secular references. The spiritual union of the soul with her beloved is true, real love, of which carnal union is a corporeal parody, a sham imitation which functions on the sensitive level much the same way that the intelligence of lower animals functions in comparison to the intelligence of angels. Sexuality, in other words, can be on a vegetative level, a sensitive level, or a rational level the same way as understanding or acts of good will can. In the true sense of literary transference, these poems express a valid state of love far beyond even reason, one that is universal for angelic beings but very rare for humans because it requires separation of the soul from the body.

These poems are therefore "real" love songs, now appropriately transferred to the spiritual realm, while all the other canticles are "false" love songs, or at least a hazy simulacrum of true love. San Juan's poems look like carnal verses to the secular-minded reader only because that earth-bound person is incapable of conceiving that love can be anything other than physical union. If read "con la sencillez del espíritu de amor e inteligencia que ellas llevan," however, they will be seen as the spiritual songs they truly are.

Ample studies are available on the popular *a lo divino* poetry from the Spanish Second Renaissance, in particular Wardropper's ground-breaking *Historia de la poesía lírica a lo divino en la cristiandad occidental*, Damaso Alonso's perceptive discussion of the material in *Poesía española* (219-68), and John Crosbie's strange *A lo divino Lyric Poetry: An Alternative View*. As regards the Spanish mystics, San Juan de la Cruz wrote about 20 of the typical kind of *a lo divino* poems which emulate popular ballads and villancicos, wherein he sketches the traditional content but converts its meaning with specific references to God or Christ or Mary or some other specific religious item. Sta. Teresa de Jesús also composed many religious songs based on popular themes. Although she was constantly exchanging her songs with other "trazadoras de versos," as she called those who wrote popular villancicos *a lo divino* (*Obras* 502), only about 30 of her compositions have been preserved.

By 1598, all the experimental efforts at the appropriation of secular literature for Counter Reformational purposes have been completed, and the truly creative writers will be able to compose outstanding works of uniquely Spanish literature in which an apparently secular argument is generated, but which leads by way of a conversion to a Catholic denouement. The plot will invariably involve Spanish persons and will take place on Spanish soil. The setting will be contemporaneous or at least will be couched in contemporary garb. The action will appear to be a secular one, but will shift, sometimes quite imperceptibly, into the religious camp so that the only proper appreciation of the closure intended by the author will include willy-nilly a Catholic response to the converted material.

But first things first. The process began back in the early 1520s, a century earlier, and it is that time period to which this study will go in the next chapter to show how the Counter Reformation developed precisely as a movement "counter" to the "Reformation." This will clarify the motivations which led in the seventeenth century to the ingenious manipulation of secular materials so they would acknowledge at closure a Catholic view of Spanish existence.

CHAPTER TWO

CONVERTING IDEOLOGY

An understanding of the Counter Reformational mode and its use of closure in seventeenth-century Spanish literature requires first at least some knowledge of what it was that generated such a profound response. The father of the Protestant Reformation is of course Martin Luther, but behind him stands Erasmus of Rotterdam, the man who laid the egg that Luther hatched. Behind Erasmus lies a long tradition of reform movements and protests, which include the Hussites in Bohemia, the Lollards in England, the Waldensians in Switzerland and France, and other suspicious groups throughout northern Europe, all of which accounted for the impetus in the sixteenth century to break with Rome.

Erasmus belonged to a less radical reformed group called the Brothers of the Common Life, initiated during the Papal Schism (1378-1429) by Gerard Groote. Known also as the *devotio moderna*, the Brothers made their living first by copying books, then after the invention of printing by teaching. They stressed the teachings of the Gospels, the primacy of the Bible over church doctrine through reading the Testaments, reform of the monastic orders, imitation of the primitive Christians, and economic self-sufficiency. All these factors made them leaders in the anti-Scholastic movement, which rejected the use of Aristotelian logic as the sole way to analyze religious matters.

Also behind Erasmus was a full century of Renaissance Humanist thought culled from close philological readings of the classics, many only recently recovered. From the Greek and Roman thinkers, Humanist scholars like Erasmus and his friend Thomas More learned that their intellectual colleagues in ancient times directed their lives by reason, without recourse to miraculous intermediaries or good luck. Those earlier Europeans believed that a life based on reasoned conduct would create a career of virtuous actions, which alone bring a sense of happiness, and that the beatitude one experienced here on earth, based on virtue and employed to assist the community, would carry over into the afterlife. Thomas More envisioned much the same world view for his Utopians, and described it in the following way:

> They define virtue as living according to nature. We have been ordained, they say, by God to this end. To follow nature is to conform to the dictates of reason in what we seek and avoid. The first dictate of reason is ardently to love and revere the Divine Majesty, to whom we owe what we are and to whatever happiness we can reach. Secondly, reason warns us and summons us to lead our lives as calmly and cheerfully as we can, and to help all others in nature's fellowship to attain this good. (48)

This felicitous marriage of Classical ethics and a provident God capable of being known by reason alone is the hallmark of Christian Humanism. Unfortunately, as even the Protestants realized, it had little to do with the Christian tenets of sin, Christ's sacrifice, grace, salvation and entrance into a Kingdom of God at Judgment Day. Martin Luther would declare in one of his letters: "Bear in mind that to be a pious man and accomplish many great works and lead an honorable and virtuous life is one thing; to be a Christian is something quite different." His appreciation for Christian Humanism was not very high, to say the least. Another famous comment by Luther is explicated by Delio Cantimori:

> *Res sine verbis Lutheris*
> *verba sine rebus Erasmus,*
>
> se mofaba Lutero en las *Tischreden*: palabras sin sustancia. Idólatras, "estoicos," es decir, fatalistas, indiferentes a las cuestiones teológicas, no movidos por el deseo de salvación y por el sentido apocalíptico de la gracia y la vocación: tales eran los humanistas para Lutero, que tantos dardos suyos había aprovechado. (163)

At the time, however, the Humanists were more concerned with reconciling Classical thought with Christianity to establish a new anthropocentric soteriology without the centuries of intervening accretions. When Erasmus published the first complete statements of his Christian Humanism in the *Enchiridion Militis Christiani* (1503), virtually all the reform ideas of the *devotio moderna* were included, but now with the emphasis on a philosophy based on Christ's own words which could lead the pious Christian to a good life here on earth: imitate the *man* Christ and his teachings, following the lead of St. Paul the Apostle rather than Church doctrine; read the word of Christ directly from the Bible rather than through the abstruse commentaries of the Scholastics; use prayer and knowledge (not faith) to reach God, including knowledge of the classical writers who described the blessed secular life one can experience while still here on earth; do away with the exterior trappings of religion and return to a *prisca theologia* as practiced by those who walked and talked with Christ; and write in a clear, direct, Ciceronian style which uses rhetorical eloquence to convince the hearer rather than convoluted syllogisms that only bewilder the mind.

By the eve of the Reformation, Erasmus had fine-tuned his Christian Humanist message into a true *philosophia Christi*, a simple Biblical doctrine meant by its divine speaker to be accessible to all and easily understood by the simplest of believers. In his *Paraclesis*, written as a preface to the famous Latin translation of the New Testament published by Frobenius in February 1516, Erasmus offered the Bible as the only way to Christ himself through his own words, to which "the journey is simple, and is ready for anyone. Only bring a pious and open mind, possessed above all with a pure and simple faith" (101). The Word of God itself is all that is needed to sway a pious person, for God would never have spoken such simple truths in a language so obscure that the gentlest heart would not understand it and by it be transformed into a new person of Adamic purity:

> Only a very few can be learned, but all can be Christian, all can be devout, and – I shall boldly add – all can be theologians. Indeed, this philosophy easily penetrates into the minds of all, an action in especial accord with human nature. Moreover, what else is the philosophy of Christ, which He Himself calls a rebirth, than the restoration of human nature originally well formed? (104)

About the same time Erasmus was proposing the Humanist view of Jesus as a Socratic teacher of gentle wisdom rather than a divinely incarnate theologian of Church doctrine, the Augustinian friar Martin Luther was undergoing a spiritual transformation in his cold Wittemberg cell. He had read Erasmus's works many times, but he realized that the problem of reform was not a Humanist endeavor concerning how one should live one's life on earth; rather it was how one should address the question of salvation. Specifically, how is it possible for any human to be judged as worthy to enter heaven if every human is too steeped in sin to ever merit by one's own merits a place in Heaven? If salvation depends on our own sinful efforts, Luther concluded, as Erasmus's rationalistic arguments and the Church's humanitarian policies indicated, then no one would ever receive salvation. In the Winter of 1512-1513, Luther finally came upon an answer to his quandary. He had been troubled for some time with a bad conscience, feeling that he was a sinner unworthy of salvation. He began reading Paul over and over to see if there wasn't something in the Apostle's words to soothe his mind.

> Night and day I pondered until I saw the connection between the justice of God and the statement that "the just shall live by his faith." Then I grasped that the justice of God is that righteousness by which through grace and sheer mercy God justifies us through faith. Thereupon I felt myself to be reborn and to have gone through an open door into paradise. The whole of scripture took on a new meaning, and whereas before the "justice of God" had filled me with hate, now it became to me inexpressively sweet in greater love. This passage of Paul became to me a gate to heaven. (Bainton 49-50)

This fundamental idea that "the just shall life by his faith" (the notion of *sola fide*) is the core of Lutheran – and Protestant – theology. By 1520, when Luther wrote a conciliatory open letter to Pope Leo X titled *Christian Liberty* concerning the reformed beliefs that were sweeping northern Europe, faith was the dominant theme. Luther separated for Leo the individual into a "spiritual, inner, or new man" and "a carnal, outward, or old man" and averred that "no external thing has any influence in producing Christian righteousness or freedom or in producing unrighteousness or servitude" (7-8). Religious vows, fasts, prayers, and practices do not help one to be a Christian, nor do secular callings, eating habits and duties deter one from being a Christian. The only thing necessary for the Christian Life is the Word of God, the Gospel of Christ (the notion of *Scriptura Sola*):

> The Word of God cannot be received and cherished by any works whatever but only by faith. Therefore it is clear that, as the soul needs only the Word of God for this life and righteousness, so it is justified by faith alone and not any works; for if it could be justified by anything else, it would not need the Word, and consequently it would not need faith. (9)

This simple idea obviates the need for all the western Church's hierarchy of cardinals, bishops, priests, monks and nuns; it eliminates all images and icons; it throws out of the Christian spiritual community all the saints and other intermediaries that accumulated over the past fifteen centuries. It ingeniously boils the Christian doctrine down to one easy lesson: "Faith alone, without works, justifies, frees, and saves" (11).

Yet, continues Luther, Christians who have faith constantly perform remarkable deeds of charity in every area of their lives; in fact, faithful Christians become true priests and dedicate their lives to serving God and neighbor. Hating idleness, these people are driven and compelled to do many good works for God. "Nevertheless, the works themselves do not justify him before God, but he does the works out of spontaneous love in obedience to God" (22). In sum,

> Good works do not make a good man, but a good man does good works; evil works do not make a wicked man, but a wicked man does evil works. ... As works do not make a man a believer, so also they do not make him righteous. But as faith makes a man a believer, and righteous, so faith does good works. (24)

This was Luther's "conciliatory" message in his letter on Christian liberty. Earlier, on 31 October 1517, he had more specific doctrinal complaints against the Church, which he posted on the Wittemberg cathedral door in the form of 95 theses he was ready to defend in open debate. There, the denunciations were directed at the Church's elaborate process of repentance, confession, and satisfaction, both in this life and in the afterlife of Purgatory. The very first thesis, in fact, broached the conflictive interpretation of Matthew 3:27 (*et passim*), which was translated in the Vulgate as *Paenitentiam agite*, "Do penance," but was interpreted by Erasmus and all the Protestants as a simple "Repent Ye." Luther's first thesis thus broke with a twelve-century tradition of being able to "do" penance to wash one's soul of sin to propose in its place the idea of a process of "changing one's mind" (*metanoia*) and becoming another kind of person through a mental decision to live another way: "When our Lord and Master Jesus Christ said 'Repent,' he willed the entire life of believers to be one of repentance" (Thesis 1).

Sacraments and confession now mean nothing for this wholly spiritual act of "true inner repentance" (Thesis 4). Hence, all the Church rituals and obligations become just fanciful stage events, including the hocus-pocus (the phrase comes from a corruption of *hoc est corpus meum*) of the Mass. The Pope, in fact, has no power to forgive sins in this life nor in Purgatory; so the myriad of indulgences and papal bulls and monks' prayers serves no purpose at all and should be eliminated. Luther could thus conclude his critical remarks with the statement that "Christians should be exhorted to be diligent in following Christ, their head, through penalties, death, and hell; and thus be confident of entering into heaven through many tribulations rather than through the false security of peace" (Theses 94 and 95).

The Catholic reaction to the Protestant rebellion is what scholars now call the Counter Reformation. Its history has been well-documented in scores of books. Here it suffices to note that the movement was indeed viewed from the beginning by the Spanish prelates as an action "counter" to Martin Luther's reforms, as one famous case will demonstrate. Pedro de Ribadeneyra (1527-1611) became an early disciple of Ignatius, served the Society in Flanders, and eventually held the post of lieutenant general in charge of Spain and Portugal. In 1572 he published the official biography of his leader, *Vita Ignatii Loiolae*, which he later translated into Spanish with the same title (1583). After describing Loyola's saintly death on 31 July 1556, Ribadeneyra wrote the following:

> Varón por cierto valeroso y soldado esforzado de Dios, el cual con particular providencia y merced envió su Majestad a su Iglesia, en estos tiempos tan peligrosos, para ir a la mano a la osadía

de los herejes, que se rebelaban y hacían guerra a su madre. Vese ser esto así claramente, porque, si bien lo consideramos, hallaremos que Ignacio se convirtió de la vanidad del mundo a servir a Dios y a su Iglesia al mismo tiempo que el desventurado Martín Lutero públicamente se desvergonzó contra la religión católica. Y cuando Lutero quitaba la obediencia a la Iglesia romana y hacía gente para combatilla con todas sus fuerzas, entonces levantaba Dios a este santo capitán para que allegase soldados por todo el mundo, los cuales con nuevo voto se obligasen de obedecer al sumo Pontífice y resistiesen con obras y con palabras a la perversa y herética doctrina de sus secuaces; porque ellos deshacen la penitencia, quitan la oración e invocación de los santos, echan por el suelo los sacramentos, persiguen las imágenes, hacen burla de las reliquias, derriban los templos, mofan de las indulgencias, privan a las ánimas del purgatorio, de los píos sufragios de los fieles, y como furias infernales turban el mundo, revolviendo cielo y tierra y sepultando, cuanto es de su parte, la justicia y la paz y la religión cristiana. Todo lo contrario de lo cual enseñó Ignacio y predican sus hijos, exhortando a todos a la penitencia, a la oración y consideración de las cosas divinas, a confesarse a menudo y comulgarse con devoción, a reverenciar y acatar las imágenes y reliquias de los santos, y aprovecharse a sí y a los fieles difuntos con las indulgencias y perdones sacados del riquísimo tesoro de los merecimientos de la pasión de Jesucristo y de sus santos, que está depositado en su Iglesia, en manos de su vicario. Finalmente, todos los consejos, pensamientos y cuidados de Ignacio tiraban a este blanco, de conservar en la parte sana o restaurar en la caída por sí y por los suyos, la sinceridad y limpieza de la fe católica, así como sus enemigos la procuran destruir. (234-35)

If the Protestants renounced penitence, eliminated prayers and invocation to the saints, rejected the sacraments, destroyed images, mocked relics, razed churches, scoffed at indulgences, deprived souls in Purgatory of the pious offerings by the faithful, and turned heaven and earth upside down with their infernal madness, then Ignatius and his followers asserted the opposite. They exhorted everyone to do penance, to pray and contemplate things divine, to confess often, to take communion devoutly, to revere and respect images and relics of the saints, and to take advantage for themselves and for the dead of the indulgences and other pardons which the Pope has garnered from the rich treasure of merits won by Jesus and the saints. Ribadeneyra thus describes the Jesuits' actions as a one-to-one opposition that enumerates all the major issues in religious practice rejected by Protestants and resolves them for the believer by simply stating that they are the true and efficacious way to salvation.

The official Church organization that had been charged with establishing these religious aspects which Ribadeneyra found so obviously Catholic and anti-Protestant in 1572 was the Council of Trent. Pope Paul III had begun the process of convening a general council in 1532, shortly after the Protestants' Augsburg Confession had definitively separated their beliefs and Rome's. The Council finally gathered in 1545 at Trent in north Italy. It met in twenty-five general sessions during three periods of work in 1545-47 (sessions I-VIII), 1551-52 (sessions IX-XIV), and 1562-63 (sessions XV-XXV). The Spaniards were aggressively present at all three convocations and managed to push through most of their conservative legislation. In 1547, the Dominican Domingo Soto successfully defended Scholasticism and imposed wording that rejected the Humanistic reforms of Erasmus. In the second period, the Jesuits gained control, and in the final years Pedro Guerrero, the archbishop of Granada, organized the Spanish attendees so well that he caused a revolt by the Italian members which led to fighting in the streets of Trent. In this period the two Jesuit leaders Diego Laínez and Alfonso Salmerón pushed through important doctrinal statements about the Mass.

At its close, the Council of Trent had passed a body of legislation larger in bulk than the total left by all the previous eighteen general councils of the Church and had created thereby one of the greatest monuments of committee-thinking in the whole history of religion (Dickens 108, 133). Specifically, the twenty-five sessions of the Council of Trent reaffirmed, in order of sessions, the creed, canonical scripture, the edition and use of sacred texts, original sin, justification (the fifth session of the council and the most theological), the sacraments, the eucharist (the most anti-Protestant session), penance, education, communion of both kinds, the mass, holy orders, marriage, and the physical apparatus of the Church (*Council* "Index"). In practice, the decrees of the Council led in the seventeenth century to the following reaffirmations of Christian belief.

1) Sancta Romana Ecclesia. The Church is a Roman Catholic organization whose head is the Pope. He has absolute authority

over spiritual matters and indirect authority (*potestas indirecta*) over secular matters.

2) The Scriptures *and* unwritten traditions about the Holy Family and the Community of Saints are valid sources of reverence. The latter include the sophisticated writings of the Greek and Latin fathers and as well all the legends, tales, and stories about the heavenly host of Virgin Mary, Christ, angels and saints who have actively participated in people's lives since Biblical times. Of special value is the *Flos Sanctorum* approved for the Church calendar.

3) The Latin Vulgate is the only authorized form of the Bible. The competing Latin translations, whether by Erasmus or others, and all the vernacular versions are prohibited because they are the works of uninspired individual minds, whereas the Vulgate is the product of twelve-hundred years of research.

4) The Church is the only recognized interpreter of the Bible. The Bible is a complicated collection of inspired writings, many of which have mystical meanings beyond the reach of the ordinary secular reader. The text should therefore be protected and dispensed through the Church by qualified interpreters trained in Biblical matters.

5) The original sin of Adam is washed away by Baptism, and one's own sins (whether incurred at birth or by actions against God and neighbor) are alleviated by acts of penance. It is therefore not enough to live a good secular life, nor even to live a saintly life; the devout Catholic must also participate fully in all the propitiatory functions made available within the Church structure by recognizing, confessing, and paying for past sins.

6) Justification is by faith *and* by good works. Faith in God's mercy is absolutely necessary, but it must be accompanied by conscious acts of service, which demonstrate the understanding's recognition of a higher wisdom and the will's submission to the divine will.

7) There are seven sacraments: Baptism, Confirmation, Eucharist, Penance, Holy Orders, Matrimony, Extreme Unction.

8) Purgatory exists, and the purgation of sins there can be facilitated by the pious offerings of the living here. Further, Purgatory is close enough to the terrestrial state that the souls dwelling there can appear to the living here to convey their thoughts and desires, but especially to serve as a warning to those who live in a state of sin.

9) Indulgences and pardons can be granted by the Pope, who

distributes the unused gifts won by Christ and the Saints for their blessed lives and acts of sacrifice. The indulgences can be used to free the souls of loved ones from Purgatory or to accumulate blessings to facilitate an individual's own passage to Heaven.

10) Parochial education is necessary for the young to assure their proper indoctrination in Church matters. Priests, nuns, friars, and all other members of the Church must be trained properly as teachers of the young, and must be willing to perform teaching duties at home and abroad in missions.

11) Those who participate in religious orders are more sanctified than those who lead a secular life, provided they adhere to the triple vow of poverty, chastity, and obedience. These vows are also recommended for all Catholics, but are not necessary for salvation.

12) Humans have Free Will which they must exercise properly in their lives to choose those things advantageous to their salvation and to reject those which would damn them. They must therefore examine carefully their conscience at every opportunity to assure that the decisions they make are not clouded by the passions or by errors in reasoning.

13) The Creator is a good and just lord who has distributed to each being precisely what is sufficient and appropriate for that particular person to reach salvation in this life. Believers therefore should not worry about what their role or "calling" may be, since any particular role in life, if one feels accomodated and comfortable in it, is as good and efficacious for salvation as any other; nor is salvation imputed by success in one's role, but rather is assured by good works of charity. The important thing is therefore not what one does, nor how successful one may be in a particular career, but whether one practices a devout Catholic life and complies with the tenets of the Catholic faith, which have been shown to be the most efficacious way to save one's soul.

14) The Creator is a loving God who ardently desires everyone's salvation, which everyone can win by cooperating with Him actively and passionately through love of God, of neighbor, and of self. The ardent believers must therefore be always ready to express their love through acts of personal devotion, acts of outward charity to others, and acts of obedience to the Lord. These can be fulfilled by participation in the sacraments, adoration of images, wearing insignia of allegiance, and by active manifestations of love in religious functions such as Mass, feast day festivals, homages on saint's days, and pilgrimages to sanctuaries.

These principal reaffirmations appear in every possible form and medium throughout the Counter Reformation. Some are of course more prevalent in secular literature than others, because they appealed to a certain author or were relevant to a person's role in society or held a special message about proper comportment. Others appear almost exclusively in strictly religious writings. A few, like the doctrine of Free Will (as opposed to Predestination), the importance of Good Works (as opposed to *sola fide*), and the idea of a divine love freely and patiently extended to all people so each individual receives every possible opportunity for salvation (as opposed to Election), infiltrate every nook and cranny of Spanish letters because they are the cornerstones of the reformed Catholic creed.

Eventually, the goals of the original Counter Reformation thinkers and writers will be met, and a different notion of Catholicism's place in Spanish society will become so firmly established as a part of Spanish life that, as Sánchez Lora has tried to explain, the interrelationships between religion and Spanish culture become so entwined that it is equally valid to say that Spanish culture becomes part of religion in the Counter Reformation:

> Cuando *todos* los aspectos de una vida permiten ser estudiados desde la óptica de su vinculación eclesiástico-religiosa, no parece difícil percibir que, en realidad, no se trata de una conducta vital influida de religiosidad, sino de una religiosidad construida con los actos vitales. ... La vida cotidiana es entonces el vehículo y la herramienta y la religión el objetivo y la esencia. Tamaña distorsión facilita el entendimiento de ese clima peculiar que suele denominarse la religiosidad barroca. (9)

It is difficult to establish a precise time when this fulfillment of the Church's purpose is achieved for Spanish literature, since some authors go in directions different from the others. Nevertheless, there is general agreement among most scholars that during the 1620s Spain began to soften its harsh tone about practicing Catholicism in an orthodox way, quite simply because by those years the Church had accomplished its project of conformity and no longer needed to pursue its ends so adamantly.

One way to see the change in direction in the seventeenth century is to examine the shift in painting from a "Barroco" (1610-1630) style as practiced by Jusepe de Ribera, Juan Ribalta, Francisco de Zurbarán, the young Diego Velázquez, Alonso Cano, and Fray Juan Rizi, to a "Barroquismo" (1630-1670) style as practiced by Murillo, Valdés Leal, Lucas Jordán, Antolínez, and Claudio Coello (Gállego 3-6).

Another more precise date would be 1621, when Philip IV ascends the throne and Gaspar de Guzmán, the Conde-Duque de Olivares, begins a new strategy of international accomodation. This innovative period of political rather than religious hegemony has been called by José Luis Abellán the "segunda Contrarreforma" because the Church takes a less visible part in the manipulation of power but still exercises its will as a *potestas indirecta* (2: 60-61).

Yet another justification for the use of an end date somewhere in the early 1620s as a good time to note the general change in Counter Reformation attitudes is the simultaneous canonization on 28 June 1622 of the three great Spanish Counter Reformation figures Saint Francis Xavier, Saint Ignatius Loyola, and Saint Theresa of Avila, along with San Isidro "Labrador," the long-standing patron saint of Madrid, and the Italian reformer Philip Neri (1515-95). The official recognition of these near-contemporary Spaniards as examples of popular piety, valiant missionaries, promulgators of the Faith, and mystical communicators with God put to rest any doubts the Spanish people may have had about the direction of the Church and permitted a softening of the belligerent tone that characterized the Catholicism of the previous half century.

An interesting chart in Sánchez Lora's *Mujeres, conventos y formas de la religiosidad barroca* substantiates the apex of religious fervor in the first three decades of the seventeenth century. The following statistics are the number of hagiographic books reported published in Spain during the century and a half between 1530 and 1680, as listed in Nicolás Antonio's *Bibliotheca Hispana Nova*:

1530-39: 5	1580-89: 36	1630-39: 50
1540-49: 1	1590-99: 46	1640-49: 35
1550-59: 7	1600-09: 79	1650-59: 58
1560-69: 10	1610-19: 97	1660-69: 43
1570-79: 11	1620-29: 124	1670-79: 41. (375)

The Counter Reformation obviously did not stop in the early 1630s; but, as the above figures suggest, it took a turn away from saints and martyrdoms into other fields. Indeed, the new direction was a more positive and comprehensive one away from emphasis on an individual's conversion to a life of piety and toward attention to the area of political matters. It was made precisely because its promulgator, the Spanish Church, had been successful in its efforts to infiltrate and gain influence over practically every aspect of Spanish society, especially printed materials. It is in effect this positive dynamism to which the Council of Trent's major apologists point when they attempt to justify the totalitarian indoctrination of the State by the Church. H. Outram Evennett's influential *The Spirit of the Counter Reformation*, for example, presents the active posture of the Church as an enlightening endeavor: "The effect of the Tridentine decrees was to make doubly sure in practice that the spirituality of the Counter Reformation would be one in which activity of all kinds was to play a very large part; in which active striving after self-control and the acquisition of virtues would be vital; in which zeal for good works of mercy and charity, and labour for the salvation of souls, were to predominate; a spirituality which was to reflect the bustle and energy and determination of sixteenth-century man, feeling at last that he had a power over himself and over things, to be applied, in the Counter Reformation, for the greater glory of God and the revival of his Church" (31-32).

Specifically, as will be seen repeatedly in the works studied in the following chapters, in the 1630s even this aggressive strategy of ideological domination fades and gives way to a friendlier social program of open-armed inclusion. The ideas of love shift from mystical ecstasy to divine friendship, and the convent emerges as a warm-hearted place of refuge for lost souls rather than a locale for acts of contrition and penitence.

There is a similar shift in literary themes from closures with conversions of the pagans, heretics, and mockers of the faith to ones with doctrinal messages about the eucharist or religious orders or free will that stress conformity and obedience to the Church rather than harrowing experiences of personal salvation. The English scholar John Crosbie has even gone so far as to claim that the very techniques of *a lo divino* writing, whose initiation he puts at 1580, become no longer appropriate for poetry: "By 1620, in fact, *a lo divino* poetry in the strict sense had to all intents and purposes ceased to exist" (13-14).

Much of the literature examined in the following chapters will present closures that illustrate this shift from a religious militantism beginning in the 1570s (the second half of Philip II's reign) and lasting through the early decades of the seventeenth century to a conformist obedience facilitated by an amiable and inviting Mother Church beginning in the 1620s (the initiation of Philip IV's reign) and lasting well into the eighteenth century. Two non-literary comparisons here will help to establish the trend.

The first is the evolution in the emblem tradition where, beginning in 1640, there was the simultaneous disappearance of religious-moral books and the creation of a third genre of political tractates. The sixteenth century had seen a flowering of political writings because of the many problems arising concerning the governace of the newly discovered territories in America, the intricacies of defining the messianic nationalism of Philip II, and the anti-Machiavellian polemic that fomented political writings in every European country. Then, as Maravall has affirmed in *Teoría española del estado*, when the Counter Reformation mentality began to infiltrate political thought in Spain in the last two decades of the century, the treatises and histories there became more oriented towards establishing the religious orthodoxy of the prince rather than his political astuteness.

Paradigmatic of the new trend is the Jesuit Pedro de Ribadeneyra's popular 1595 treatise whose full title intentionally covers all the topics of interest at the time: *Tratado de la religión y virtudes que debe tener el príncipe cristiano para gobernar y conservar sus estados, contra lo que Nicolás Maquiavelo y los políticos deste tiempo enseñan*. Ribadeneyra's book dedicates fully one-half of its space to the prince's training in religious matters, and only after exhausting this topic does the Jesuit turn to matters of political governance. A good prince, in other words, must first be a good Catholic, because a good Catholic will be the most appropriate prince for his people.

By 1640, the Church has instilled its thought so effectively that the theorists can dedicate their minds to the consideration of governance in and of itself as undertaken by a christian prince. Diego de Saavedra Fajardo can thus title his treatise *Idea de un príncipe político-cristiano* and leave doctrinal Catholicism out of his discussion; Saavedra's prince is already a devout Catholic who recognizes the *potestas indirecta* of the Church, wherein, as José Luis Abellán explains in his history of Spanish thought, the prince recognizes that "el poder espiritual es superior al temporal, y sin implicar imperio ni dominio, esto quiere decir que puede actuar sobre lo temporal pura y exclusivamente en aquello que afecta a cuestiones espirituales, llegando a poder deponer al Príncipe y privarle de sus bienes cuando realiza algo contrario a la religión" (3: 61). The prince is free to act as he wishes in purely temporal circumstances, yet always with the proviso that his actions conform with the moral and ethical teachings of the Church and the practical dictates of prudence.

These two sources form the "político-cristiano" ruler who always does the right thing because his actions are framed by objective decisions made apart from any personal desires based on the lower faculties of the imagination, the fantasy, the senses, or the passions. It is in fact this marriage of "Religion of the Church" and "Reason of the State" that most characterizes later anti-Machiavellian statecraft (Bireley 239) and that likewise most distinguishes it from the separation of Church and State advocated by Protestant thinkers.

The second illustrative comparison concerns the general notion of one's possible relationship with God. The works of the great mystics Saint Theresa of Avila and Saint John of the Cross are paradigms of the arduous but emotionally charged journey of the soul to God in the seminal decades prior to the Counter Reformation. They were read voraciously by thousands of Spaniards, along with the scores of other religious books that appeared at the time, as Caro Baroja has noted (31). The emotional impact of Mystical Love on the literature and art of the period was immense, and it is generally considered to be the catalyst for the new Baroque style in art. Werner Weisbach referred specifically to the mystical aspects of Catholicism – including martyrdoms, sacrifices, heroic deeds, and penitential sainthood – in his influential book on Counter Reformation art, and the eminent scholar Frederick Hartt has only Mystical Love in mind when he describes the Baroque experience in his brief study *Love in Baroque Art*:

> One widely prevalent pattern of Baroque experience can, in these typical examples, be tentatively anatomized. It seems to comprise the following aspects: a. The uniting of the individual with an infinite realm outside the confines of his previous experience, by means of b. A sudden climax beyond the individual's expectations or control, and even contrary to his natural reason.

> For it is certainly contrary to natural reason that people should ascend into the air, that ceilings should dissolve, that clouds should appear through solid vaults, that architecture should burst asunder. For want of a better title, and with understandable misgivings, I have called this experience the Baroque breakthrough. (5)

Hartt's description fits precisely the many miraculous events that occur to close Counter Reformation literature during the first decades of the seventeenth century. The fact is, however, that after the 1620s the dramatically sudden and erotically-charged confrontation with a divine being ceases to be the accepted mode of communication with God, for it is replaced by a more familial relationship based on an idea of religious friendship quite different from the capitulatory love of the mystics and early energetic believers in the first two decades of the century. The new form of friendly and familial love, which can best be termed a Cooperative Love, has few adherents in the writers presented here, but becomes the core of established Catholic belief in the centuries to come. Its first great spokesman and proponent was Saint Francis of Sales (1567-1622), who almost single-handedly introduced this new kind of Catholic love to European sensibilities.

Here is the perfect representative of the later Counter Reformation in action. Born in Savoy of aristocratic parents, Francis entered the priesthood in 1593 against his father's wishes and initiated campaigns to convert Protestants to Catholicism. He moved to Geneva in 1599 and became its bishop in 1602. He was especially concerned about the education of the masses, and set up many schools in his diocese. He also founded (with St. Jane Frances de Chantal) the Visitation for Women as a non-austere order of nuns for those who wished a normal religious life without the harsh penitential rules of the great established orders. In 1608 he published his *Introduction to the Devout Life*, which Francisco de Quevedo translated into Spanish in 1634. Its contents, influenced by Jesuit ideas which St. Francis acknowledges in his prologue, start with a description of the ways to purify oneself of sin through meditation followed by a general confession and a resolution to serve the Lord. Then comes a section on the value of submission of the individual will by humility, obedience, and chastity when exercising the virtues, which leads to a discussion of true love and false love.

Those chapters (17-22) in Part Three are literally the center of the text. This love isn't the mystical ascent of the soul to God, however, nor is it the universal egalitarian charity of the medieval friars. It is a new kind of Christian love modelled on Ciceronian friendship, an *amistad espiritual*, a *santa y sacra amistad*, a *casta amistad* proffered only to those who are worthy of one's friendship. As in Aristotle's *Ethics* (Book VIII), Sales separates friendship from the passion of love by noting that, unlike love, 1) the friendship must be reciprocal, 2) there must be an acknowledgement of the friendship by the parties involved, and 3) there must be communication between the parties for the friendship to continue (Quevedo, 1: 1646).

This is the fundamental relationship that the Church will suggest that the soul have with the Lord. It is a reciprocal, cooperative, sexless love unrelated to the sacred marriage model in The Song of Songs and to the Platonic ascent of the soul to the divine essence by rejection of this world; rather it is a conscious selection of the best possible friend one can have by rejection of one's false, mundane friends. The notion of a "spiritual friendship" with a cooperative, accomodating divinity with whom one can communicate freely about all of one's most heartfelt matters is certainly a lot easier to embrace for the majority of Catholics than a tortuous route of self-annihilation to an unknowable, although anxiously passionate, bridegroom.

One of the first Spanish literary examples to express this shift from the capitulatory mysticism expressed by the religious reformers of the late sixteenth century to the new accomodative attitudes expressed by the gentler religious figures in the next century is the description of the nunnery in which Alonso, "mozo de muchos amos" and protagonist of *El donado hablador* (1624), is serving as a lay-brother when he narrates the first part of his life. After a lengthy approbation of the nun's conventual life, Alonso justifies the need for entertainments and diversions, since "en carne viven, y no en espíritu; de sujeto flaco son, y no de ángel. ... Tiempo ha de haber para la oración, para el coro, para el refitorio, y tiempo también para una honesta y virtuosa recreación y alivio" (1267b). Times have changed, explains Alonso, and God's attitude about our service has changed also: "Ya, padre, con nosotros Dios no quiere usar de aguel rigor que antes acostumbraba ni es el Dios de las venganzas, sino el de las misericordias" (1268b).

In pictorial terms, the shift is the same as the one from the harsh tenebristic estatic visions of Jusepe de Ribera's martyrs and Francisco de Zurbarán's monks done in the early 1600s to the amiable difused-light domestic scenes of the Holy Family that Bartolomé Esteban Murillo did in the later 1600s.

The next six chapters will present a number of ways in which Spanish writers inserted Counter Reformational notions directly or indirectly into their ostensibly secular texts. The scope of the study is thereby limited to those texts which contain in their closing narratives some kind of religious reference, as minimal as it may appear at first glance. In other words, strictly secular literature such as Gongora's "Polifemo y Galatea," the *comedia de enredo*, Cervantes' *Don Quijote de la Mancha* or Quevedo's *Vida del Buscón* will not be examined. Further, the sacred reference will invariably be lodged in a socially popular, direct context usually not associated with purely religious matters, which eliminates the sixteenth-century religious thinkers like Fray Luis de Granada and Beato Juan de Avila as well as the prose commentaries of Santa Teresa, San Juan de la Cruz, and Fray Luis de León. The sacred reference, in other words, will be embedded blatantly or surrepticiously in a popular secular mode of fiction which it has appropriated to convey its message in a process that involves what has been called "dialectical imitation" (Greene 45). Furthermore, the study will concentrate on the insertion of this material at the very end of the literary discouse as a closing mechanism of conversion for the fiction's action. It is thus the appropriation of the same secular fiction, used in apparently the same secular way, but with a Counter Reformation purpose that – as will be see in the cases examined in the next chapter – is proffered only as closure of the discourse or in such a way within the context of the discourse that the reader remains convinced that the religious conversion was what generated the successful closure experienced by those who opted for it and the unsuccessful end by those who did not.

CHAPTER THREE

CONVERTING GENRES

A pristine example of the use of Counter Reformation closure in Spanish literature is Rodrigo Caro's transformation of the ruined city theme in his poem "Canción a la ruinas de Itálica." Poems about ruined cities (which have been conveniently anthologized by Vranich) entered Spanish literature about 1530 with several imitations of Baltassare Castiglione's Latin sonnet *"Superbi colli,"* basically a courtly love poem utilizing an apostrophe to the ruins of ancient Rome to concretize the aspiration that perhaps the lover's torment also might cease with time. The Renaissance poets Garcilaso de la Vega and Gutierre Cetina wrote sonnets that tracked Castiglione's courtly love motif, and then in the "Second Renaissance" the Sevillan classical school appropriated the ruined city theme to express the Stoic notions of the passing of material things and the fortuitous nature of the glory associated with transitory matters. The impersonal poems of *consolatio*, as López Bueno calls them, like Juan de Arguijo's "A las ruinas de Cartago" and "Remedio engañoso," Fernando de Herrera's "Del peligro del mar," Francisco de Rioja's "A las ruinas de Atlántida," Villamediana's "Las pompas con que Roma vio superba" and "Estas de admiración reliquias dignas," and even Quevedo's "A Roma sepultada en sus ruinas," all express a philosophy of disillusionment contrary to the earlier one of Renaissance optimism. Moreover, most of them can be considered pessimistic, if one means by this term the absence of any suggestions for remedying the destruction of human glories by time and fortune. Villamediana is the only poet who retains a positive secular vision in his ruins poems by stressing individual achievement:

> La virtud es el medio peregrino,
> el valor y el talento prestan vuelo,
> sin que el tiempo contrario lo limite. (37)

Later in the seventeenth century the ruined city theme will be appropriated and manipulated in a variety of ways. Lope and Quevedo will personalize it to speak about their own lives, while other poets will deflate the classical theme by treating the ruined city as precisely a complex of broken-down buildings. The unique exception is Rodrigo Caro's famous poem "Canción a las ruinas de Itálica."

1. Estos, Fabio, ¡ay dolor!, que ves ahora
   campos de soledad, mustio collado,
   fueron un tiempo Itálica famosa.
   Aquí de Cipión la vencedora
   colonia fue. Por tierra derribado
   yace el temido honor de la espantosa
   muralla, y lastimosa
   reliquia es solamente.
   De su invencible gente
   sólo quedan memorias funerales,
   donde erraron, ya sombras, de alto ejemplo.
   Este llano fue plaza, allí fue templo;
   de todo apenas quedan las señales.
   Del gimnasio y las termas regaladas
   leves vuelan cenizas desdichadas.
   Las torres que desprecio al aire fueron
   a su gran pesadumbre se rindieron.
2. Este despedazado anfiteatro,
   impio honor de los dioses, cuya afrenta
   publica el amarillo jaramago,
   ya reducido a trágico teatro,
   ¡oh fábula del tiempo!, representa
   cuánta fue su grandeza y es su estrago.
   ¿Cómo en el cerco vago
   de su desierta arena
   el gran pueblo no suena?
   ¿Dónde, pues fieras hay, está el desnudo
   luchador, dónde está el atleta fuerte?
   Todo desapareció. Cambió la suerte
   voces alegres en silencio mudo;

       mas aun el tiempo da en estos despojos
       espectáculos fieros a los ojos;
       y miran tan confusos lo presente
       que voces de dolor el alma siente.
3.   Aquí nació aquel rayo de la guerra,
       gran padre de la patria, honor de España,
       pío, felice, triunfador Trajano,
       ante quien muda se postró la tierra
       que ve del sol la cuna, y la que baña
       el mar también vencido gaditano.
       Aquí de Elio Adriano,
       de Teodosio divino,
       de Silio peregrino
       rodaron de marfil y oro las cunas.
       Aquí ya de laurel, ya de jazmines,
       coronados los vieron los jardines;
       que ahora son zarzales y lagunas.
       La casa para el César fabricada,
       ¡ay!, yace de lagartos vil morada.
       Casas, jardines, Césares murieron,
       y aun las piedras que de ellos se escribieron.
4.   Fabio, si tú no lloras, pon atenta
       la vista en largas calles destrüidas,
       mira mármoles y arcos destrozados,
       mira estatuas soberbias, que violenta
       Némesis derribó, yacer tendidas,
       y ya en alto silencio sepultados
       sus dueños celebrados.
       Así a Troya figuro,
       así a su antiguo muro;
       y a ti, Roma, a quien queda el nombre apenas,
       ¡oh patria de los dioses y los reyes!;
       y a ti, a quien no valieron justas leyes,
       fábrica de Minerva, sabia Atenas:
       emulación ayer de las edades,
       hoy cenizas, hoy vastas soledades,
       que no os respetó el hado, no la muerte
       ¡ay! ni por sabia a ti, ni a ti por fuerte.
5.   Mas, ¿para qué la mente se derrama
       en buscar al dolor nuevo argumento?
       Basta ejemplo menos, basta el presente.
       Que aun se ve el humo aquí, aun se ve la llama,
       aun se oyen llantos hoy, hoy ronco acento.

Tal genio o religión fuerza la mente
de la vecina gente
que refiere admirada
que en la noche callada
una voz triste se oye que llorando
"Cayó Itálica" dice; y lastimosa
eco reclama "Itálica" en la hojosa
selva, que se le opone resonando
"Itálica"; y el caro nombre oído
de Itálica, renuevan el gemido
mil sombras nobles en su gran rüina.
¡Tanto, aun la plebe a sentimiento inclina!
6. Esta corta piedad, que agradecido
huésped a tus sagrados manes debo,
les do y consagro, Itálica famosa.
Tú (si lloroso don han admitido
las ingratas cenizas de que llevo
dulce noticia asaz, si lastimosa)
permíteme piadosa
usura a tierno llanto
que vea el cuerpo santo
de Geroncio, tu mártir y prelado.
Muestra de su sepulcro algunas señas,
y cavaré con lágrimas las peñas
que ocultan su sarcófago sagrado.
Pero mal pido el único consuelo
de todo el bien que airado quitó el cielo.
Goza en las tuyas sus reliquias bellas
para invidia del mundo y las estrellas.

This magnificent poem, first published only in 1774 by Juan José López de Sedano, now occupies a place in almost every anthology of Spanish poetry. It actually exists in three major rewritings dating from an *in situ* attempt in 1595 when Caro was twenty-two to the final version examined here, which could date to 1647, when Caro passed away (Blanco Suárez 284).

Caro's presentation of the theme of the ruined city in the first five strophes of his poem is typical of most of the other presentations in the genre. Strophe One presents a dense use of temporal and spatial imagery. Its seventeen lines interweave thirteen verbs, six in the present and seven in the preterite, with subjects and objects that juxtapose a constructed past of tall edifices and ordered space to a deconstructed present of deserted ruins and disorderly landscapes, complemented with epithetic adjectives and prepositional phrases to reinforce the counterbalance. The images of the past are all vertical, erect, frightening, proud, invencible: "Itálica *famosa*," "la *vencedora* colonia de Escipión," "el *temido* honor de la *espantosa* muralla," "*invencible* gente," "sombras *de alto ejemplo*," "plaza," "templo," "gimnasio," "termas," "torres." The images of the present, on the other hand, are all horizontal, flat, pitiful, broken-down, crushed to dust: "campos *de soledad*," "*mustio* collado," "por tierra *derribado*," "*lastimosa* reliquia," "memorias *funerales*," "señales," "cenizas *desdichadas*." The former have turned into the latter, "fueron," "se rindieron." This vertical-horizontal, temporal-spatial conceit runs throughout the entire poem as a constant mark of past erections in all their proud grandeur that become present prostrations of deserted countryside; that become even less, since they are now no more than pitiful relics, funeral memories, traces, blown ashes.

The next four strophes continue the themes and motifs established in the first verses. Strophe Two is an elaborate conceit on the idea of tragic performance, as E. M. Wilson explained in an early study of the poem. Exercising the same vertical-horizontal temporal imagery, Caro makes the great ampitheater a tragic playhouse; and the arena with its strong, naked athletes is now a redundant "silencio mudo" where remain only wild beasts. Strophe Three turns the palace gardens of Trajan's, Hadrian's, Theodosius's, and Silius's birth places into briar patches and swamps. Strophe Four converts the tall walls of Troy, Rome, and Athens into the same "cenizas" and "soledades" evoked in the first lines of the poem to describe the state of present-day Itálica. Strophe Five returns to the present case of the Iberian city to dwell on the ashes that still harbor some smoke and an occasional flame, on the loneliness that still emits a random wail or hoarse voice, echoes of echoes of echoes.

As Strophes One and Two elaborate the specific conceits of ancient monuments destroyed, so Strophes Three and Four establish a progression from birth in the cradle to death in the grave, utilizing thereby the poem's up-down language specifically for movements from an initial high noble posture to a final low humble burial in the earth. Strophe Three thus has allied words such as "nació," "padre," "cunas," "casas," which counterpoint opposite terms such as "se postró," "yace," "vil morada," "murieron." Furthermore, the images are now of hard, permanent, immortal things – "sol," "mar," "marfil," "oro," "laurel," "jazmines," "piedras" – all turned into the most base, putrid elements of the lowly earth, where live the commonest forms of existence in the plant and animal kingdoms: "tierra," "zarzales," "lagunas," "vil morada de lagartos."

Strophe Four takes this destruction, death, and burial of the royal houses in which those famous men were born and raised to its logical conclusion in the destruction of all signs of their historical immortality. The famous marbles, the triumphal arches, and the proud statues, all these have been knocked down by Némesis and lie stretched out on the ground, dead: "yacen tendidas," "en alto silencio sepultados." This destruction, death, and burial of the statues and monuments to heroes is followed logically with the death of the ancient cities they peopled. Troy, Rome, Athens are all ashes, vast deserts.

In Strophe Five, Caro continues the imagery begun in Strophe Three with "nació" by including Itálica, which today has become only the eco of an eco in the forest of a thousand shadows' laments. What was once real substance now deteriorates line by line from loud complaints ("llantos") to hoarse sounds ("ronco acento") to sad voices ("voz triste") to pitiful echoes ("lastimosa eco") to resonances ("resonando") to shadowy moans ("gemido").

In sum, Strophes One and Two presented a temporal contrast between then and now by describing the physical state of the present-day ruins in spatial terms of horizontal presence and vertical past; and the next three strophes continued the imagery with references to the rich palaces of Itálica's famous offspring and the streets with their arches and monuments, then extended the vision to ancient cities, and finally returned to Itálica itself. Within the elaborate imagery of past glory juxtaposed to present ruin, Caro threaded the standard trope of the birth, splendor, and decay of Itálica, a progression that began in the very first lines of the poem with the founding of Itálica by the conquering armies of Scipio and grew through the birth and great deeds of the city's famous sons, enumerated in Strophe Three, to the solid, enduring monuments of marble and stone cited in Strophe Four. All then ended in the vocal nothingness of Strophe Five's regressive moans of resonances of echoes of voices of sounds of complaints.

Now comes the Counter Reformational Strophe Six, which intentionally breaks the downward march of the poem that culminated in the aural regression of Strophe Five. In this last strophe, the reader is faced with a series of religious terms couched in an apostrophe to the lost city. "Piedad," "sagrados manes," "consagro" all move the poem to a higher plane of meaning. "Agradecido huésped" and "debo," furthermore, introduce the poet himself for the first time and replace his previous ironic and mocking tone with a humble and ingratiating one. So there is indeed a sharp and clearly intentioned turn upward and inward by the poet in Strophe Six.

Nevertheless, there are also a number of conceptual threads that penetrate the first three lines of this last strophe and bind it to the rest of the poem. The linking sign from Strophe Five to this one is the very word *Itálica*, to whom Caro now responds after hearing "mil sombras nobles" call out the city's name. Further, those audible "sombras" in the earlier strophe are the same "sagrados manes" to whom Caro now dedicates his poem. Yet as brilliantly as these lines lead the mind from one strophe to the next, they as well set the new tone of Counter Reformational closure by utilizing a series of religious terms ("piedad," "sagrado," "consagro") which will occur later in the strophe in reference to the true but as yet unmentioned purposeful object of the poem ("piadosa," "santo," "sagrado").

The uplifting words contrast, however, with a battery of equally depressing terms that dominate the middle section of seven lines to maintain thereby the sober, leveled equilibrium of this last strophe. The gift is "lloroso," the news is "lastimosa," Caro presents a pious payment of "llanto" to see the body of a martyred Christian prelate. This particular section is, in fact, the most sophisticated series of imagery in the poem. It plays with the idea of a noble lord giving some kind of gift to the poet as payment for dedicating the song to him. In this case, the benefactor is the ruined city and Rodrigo Caro is requesting the body of a Christian martyr as his boon. "Itálica famosa" is thus the apostrophied recipient of the poem. Rodrigo Caro is the "agradecido huésped" who has – like the early bards – been staying with his host. "Corta piedad," "dulce noticia asaz, si lastimosa" and "tierno llanto" all refer to the proffered poem. "Lloroso don," "piadosa usura" and "cuerpo santo" all refer to "Geroncio, tu mártir y prelado." The poet offers his tearful elegy to the city and asks as his equally tearful payment to see the body of Geroncio, the first bishop of Itálica, who died for Christ in jail but whose tomb holding the incorrupt body became a pilgrimage site for later Christians until the destruction of the city by the Moors. The "cenizas ingratas" thus refer to the ruined city of Itálica, about whom he brings sweet yet sad news (Caro's song), and from whom he wants the gift (Geroncio's body), although it too will be tearful. The privilege of seeing Geroncio's incorrupt body becomes the pious payment for his tender weeping.

Finally, the last seven lines of the poem close the entire argument by ingeniously recapitulating a number of ideas and words first used in Strophe One to describe a city that had fallen into terrible decay and which are now repeated to refer to an incorruptible sainted body. "Algunas señas" of Geroncio's remains evoke the barely visible "señales" of the pagan temple in Strophe One; the "sarcófago sagrado" brings to mind the "memorias funerales" that remain of those invencible Romans; and the "reliquias bellas" poignantly obviate the "lastimosa reliquia" of the fearful city wall. Ironically, all the man-made, material things of pagan Itálica have turned to ashes and dust, have become no more than echoes of ghostly voices; but the body of a simple Christian has remained whole, incorrupt and permanent. Geroncio's corpse is, in truth, the only thing that the ruined city has to give to Rodrigo Caro in payment for his song, the only relic among its relics that is worth coveting, because angry heaven took all the other goods away: "pido el único consuelo / de todo el bien que airado quitó el cielo."

The poem thus ends at the opposite pole from where it began, among the stars rather than on the lonely fields and gloomy hill of Itálica. Interestingly, it does not make any reference to contemporary Spain, to the country's inhabitants, or to any overarching personal philosophy; and the absence is even more surprising when one reads in the prose sections of Caro's *Memorial de la villa de Utrera* the following strongly moralistic words: "Parece que aquellos derribados edificios están llorando la larga ausencia de sus dueños, y amonestando a los que los miran, con un mudo sentimiento, cuán breve es la gloria de este mundo y cuán flaca la mayor firmeza. Leen aquí los ojos la destrucción de aquella fuerte ciudad, y recelan los ojos del alma la de su propio cuerpo, flaco y miserable" (Caro 203-04).

"Canción a las ruinas de Itálica" is a sad poem, but it is not a poem of disillusionment like Quevedo's "Miré los muros de la patria mía" or Lope de Vega's "Vivas memorias, máquinas difuntas"; nor does Caro intrude in any personal way into his own work, as

Quevedo and Lope do, where, as Begoña López Bueno has noted, there is a two-fold purpose: "Oposición entre un pasado glorioso y la destrucción presente; y la extrapolación del motivo para aplicación personal de consuelo" (133). Caro's poem virtually stands alone in its supreme objectivity, what Stanko Vranich has called "una percepción aguda del objeto observado, enfoque que le hace participar de la poderosa constante de la literatura castellana desde *El Cid* a Cela, y explica, según mi criterio, su mayor autenticidad" (21).

The major reason for this poem's difference is its Christian context, which is unique to the genre. It gives the elegy a self-confident tone missing in all other examples of poems about ruined cities. Caro thereby creates the temporal opposition so typical of all ruins poetry; but rather than couch it in the Baroque *desengaño* of glorious past and present destruction, he frames a unique Counter Reformational dichotomy between the pagan classical world and the Christians who came to inhabit it. For Caro, the glorious past now fallen to ruins and turned to ashes is not a reflection on present destruction, and therefore is not a motive for pessimism or disillusionment, quite simply because that past was not Christian. On the contrary, only the Christian component of Itálica – Geroncio's body – is what has endured whole and immutable.

What is most surprising is that it occurred only to Rodrigo Caro to insert a Christian message into a poem about a ruined city, for which he had no imitators. Caro had legitimate doctrinal reasons for targeting the incorrupt body of a Christian martyr as the boon for his poetic enterprise. The Council of Trent had specifically recognized sacred cadavers as rightful objects of veneration: "That the sacred bodies of Holy Martyrs, and others Reigning with Christ, who were the living Members of Christ, and the Temple of the Holy-Ghost, and by him to be raised up unto eternal Life and Glorification, are to be worshipped by the Faithful, for whose sakes God shews many kindnesses and benefits to Men" (*Council* 146).

By 1595 Caro also had tremendous historical motivations to do what he did, for the poem extols the appreciation of precisely the kinds of relics which were most in vogue in Spain in the last quarter of the sixteenth century. In 1578 a series of intact catacombs were discovered on the Roman estate of Bartolomé Sánchez de Alda, an Aragonese nobleman (Bouza Álvarez 47-56). Many of the corpses were exhumed and sent to Spain as relics of Christian martyrs from the early days of persecution. They fueled an already established cult of relics that Philip II had initiated only six years earlier when he dispatched Ambrosio de Morales to catalog Spanish religious treasures and to determine which ones were appropriate for transference to El Escorial. Such efforts must have paid off, because José de Sigüenza, the contemporary Jeronimite chronicler of the construction of El Escorial, claimed that Philip's collection contained 507 reliquaries with a total of 7,422 relics (Bouza Álvarez 35). To further stimulate the relics craze, in 1588 some Granadan priests claimed that they had discovered a cache of early Christian artefacts and relics on the Sacromonte, and new finds were made periodically up to 1595, with increasingly more strident religious enthusiasm. It should come as no surprise, then, that in the same year of 1595 Rodrigo Caro visits the Hispanic ruins of Itálica, a parallel city to Italy's Rome in the emergence of Christianity, and desires to uncover by any means possible the remains of an early martyr, for it would not have been possible for him to remain oblivious to a nationwide cult which, in the words of José Luis Bouza Álvarez, "favorecía la adhesión afectiva e irracional a la ortodoxia y fortalecía la unidad y cohesión político-religiosa del beligerante catolicismo reformado, contribuyendo a preservar ideas e intereses de la clase dominante durante la crisis general del siglo XVII" (476).

Of equal interest is the existence of an enormous amount of art and literature about martyrs, relics, and artefacts, but only one religious ruined-city poem. Caro's song – and to some degree all Counter Reformation literature – elaborates a *mimesis* quite different from that of its thematic relatives but quite typical of Counter Reformation thought because it attempts to transform the very purpose of the genre by installing a finale that closes the poem on a religious note alien to the mold. All the other ruins poems participated in some way in the typical forms of imitation practiced by Renaissance and post-Renaissance writers. According to a model developed by G. W. Pigman III, imitation of a classical model (in this case of the "modern" classical poem written in Latin by Baltassare Castiglione) can take three progressive stages:

> [1] *Following*, or nontransformative imitation, is the gathering or borrowing of phrases, sentences, passages which amounts to a transcription of the model(s) into the text. ... A certain amount of transforming occurs by virtue of inclusion in a new context,

and complete transcription without changing a word is very rare indeed. Consequently one occasionally has difficulty distinguishing following from [2] *imitation*, in which the note of transformation is strong. In an imitation the differences between text and model are at least as pronounced as the resemblances. ... Critical reflection on or correction of the model distinguishes [3] *emulation* or eristic imitation from (transformative) imitation, and this criticism is often grounded in an awareness of the historical distance between present and past. (32)

While eristic poems like Góngora's "Castillo de San Cervantes" and Quevedo's "Funeral a los huesos de una fortaleza que gritan mudos desengaños" and "A los huesos de un rey que hallaron en un sepulcro, ignorándose, y se conoció por los pedazos de una corona" are patent examples of [3] *emulation*, Caro's poem practices what can only be called "dialectical imitation," characterized, according to Thomas M. Greene, as a process that looks like something from the past but which functions in a way totally different from the Classical model (45). In this case, what looks like a typical "Fabio" poem of moral import elaborating the ruined city theme is in truth a Counter Reformational religious poem extolling the permanence of a fellow Christian amid the transitory glories of the pre-Christian Roman past. Caro thereby contradicts the very model he imitates, on the one hand creating a dialectic between the pagan classical world and its early Christian inhabitants that demonstrates the supersession of the former by the latter, and on the other penning a Christian Baroque poem that voids by way of its religious message the very Stoic philosophy so inherent to the genre. In other words, as the relics of Geroncio's tender body supplanted and replaced the seemingly eternal pagan marbles, so Caro's Spanish poem supplants and replaces the imperishable classical tradition in literature.

It is assuredly this daring enterprise of subversive "dialectical imitation" of Counter Reformational closure that Caro undertook in his poem, wherein the Christian message contradicts by opposition the rightful Stoic function of traditional literature about ruined cities, what has made "Canción a las ruinas de Itálica" so popular and enduring. It is also what separates the poem – and all explicitly Counter Reformation literature – from the Humanist tradition based on continuity from Classical times to a present-day rational existence. The following schema of six stages of national self-awareness in Spain during the course of the sixteenth century which José Antonio Maravall delineated in his monumental *Antiguos y modernos* means little to the Counter Reformation mind intent on establishing an agenda of religious conformity based on the subversive manipulation of the Humanist literary tradition:

> [1] El sentido de continuidad, sobre cuya base puede eficazmente desenvolverse con toda su fuerza el mito de los clásicos; [2] la corriente de emulación, suscitada por la reconocida ejemplaridad de aquéllos; [3] el despertar de la conciencia histórica que permite distinguir y comparar épocas y grupos humanos; [4] el sentimiento de comunidad política que, renovado bajo la influencia de los antiguos en forma de patriotismo, compromete a la defensa e ilustración del propio grupo; [5] la preferencia por los modernos que, a través de tan larga polémica, se afirma como fruto del Renacimiento; [6] la confianza en la crítica del principio de autoridad: tales son los factores que en la crisis del siglo XVI, sobre la base de las nuevas condiciones socio-económicas que trae consigo el crecimiento de la burguesía, se desarrollan y articulan para dar origen a la teoría del progreso como visión general del curso de la historia. (477-78)

The closure practiced by Counter Reformation writers simply does not fit into this generally accepted survey of European letters because the Counter Reformation mind subverts the last stage of criticism of authority (which will itself be replaced in the nineteenth century by personal testimony based on experience) for reaffirmation of authority based on the doctrines and tenets of the Holy Roman Catholic church.

Another tipical example of Counter Reformational closure will clarify further the techniques involved. Tirso de Molina's novelette "El bandolero," one of the many tales published in *Deleitar aprovechando* (1635), is essentially a *novela cortesana* of amorous intrique, and it also has elements of the *novela pastoril* and the *novela bizantina*, but the events in the last chapters of the novel convert the material into the dialectically antagonistic *vida de santos*.

Alberto Armengol and his wife have a son, Pedro, whose career is foreseen by a hermit and an astrologer to lead to a disgraceful death: "A este niño un patíbulo ha de hacerle santo. ... Sus fuerzas han de ser bizarras, pero su empleo tan desbaratado que, caudillo de salteadores, atajará sus travesuras un dogal infame que de un árbol le suspenda" (10-11). Alberto therefore announces the son was still-born and places him with a family of shepherds. A few years later, his wife bears a daughter, to whom the name Saurina is given.

Years pass, and the two young people, naturally drawn to each other by their affinities despite the apparent disparities in their social status, spend so much time together that Saurina comes to adore Pedro. They go to Barcelona one day for the Candelaria festival (February 2), where Pedro meets Laurisana, the sister of Count Berenguel. They immediately fall in love with each other, while Saurina becomes the object of desire of both Berenguel and the wicked Count Manfredo of Sicily.

The courtly intrigues that this circle of affections precipitates come to a climax when Pedro and Laurisana decide to elope and the evil Manfredo determines to abduct Saurina, whom King Jaime II has promised in marriage to Berenguel. Confused identities abound, and Pedro mistakenly flees with his sister while Manfredo unwittingly takes Laurisana to Sicily.

The King declares Pedro a traitor, so the young man becomes a bandit with a group of other disaffected nobles. They are quickly caught and taken to a hanging-tree to die; but Berenguel, who has discovered that Manfredo is the real culprit in all the deceits, arrives in the nick of time to save their lives. Pedro is reconciled with his father, Saurina marries Berenguel, Manfredo commits suicide, and Laurisana, who had taken refuge in a Sicilian religious house, becomes a nun.

The tale could very well have ended here, as do scores of other *novelas cortesanas* by Zayas y Sotomayor, Castillo Solorzano, Salas de Barbadillo, and others. Tirso decides to close his story quite differently, however. In Chapter thirty-four (of thirty-seven), the Mercedarian creates a remarkable "examen de conciencia" for his protagonist based on the young man's personal experiences in life:

> Enmudecido hasta este tiempo le habían tenido a Pedro Armengol sus bien encaminados pensamientos, discurriendo por los sucesos presentes la inestabilidad de la fortuna, lo quebradizo de sus prosperidades, la incertidumbre de su duración y la fallida seguridad de las humanas confianzas.

> – ¡Cuán poco permanecen floridas primaveras de juventud y gallardía! ¿Qué aprovechan – se decía a sí mismo – favores príncipes que, pisando vidrios, tan fáciles se quiebran, y cuando durables se resistan, aún no tiene la majestad monarca poder, para un instante siquiera, de limitar jurisdicciones a la muerte? ¿Qué la destreza, el valor, las posesiones, la sangre ilustre, los estudios, los amigos, si vinculado todo en la caduca consistencia de la flor, del heno, del humo, de la sombra, el hielo las desmaya, el sol las seca y el aire las desvanece? A la nave compara Job la vida más robusta, que cargada de manzanas, sale del puerto de la cuna, naufraga piélagos de miserias y desembarca en el sepulcro la fruta corrompida. ¡Discreta y venturosa mil veces Laurisana, que de tanto escollo, tantos huracanes combatida, sobre la tabla de su conocimiento burló bajíos, y ya en el faro religioso, a la fortuna, triunfó de sí misma! (198)

Such is Baroque *desengaño*. It is expressed no differently by Tirso here as the catalyst for Pedro's conversion to a religious life than by Arguijo, Medrano, Quevedo, Villamediana, Gracián, and countless others as the neo-Stoic rationale for leaving the Court life to cultivate one's spiritual side in tranquillity. One comes to one's senses, sees the topsy-turvy world as a physical sphere dominated by fortune, elects to refrain from being subject to it, and thereby reaches a state of self-knowledge.

In Tirso's Counter Reformational trajectory, however, the Humanist safe harbor is converted into the haven of Religion. Pedro Armengol joins the Order of Mercy, dedicated to redeeming captive Christians from Moorish lands, and thereby becomes a "bandolero santo":

> Banderizó pasiones y afectos contra el mundo, contra el demonio y contra el más que estos dos ejecutivo, por más doméstico, enemigo avecindado en nuestra carne. Bandolero, pues, nuestro Armengol, salteaba estrategemas de estos tres corsarios, saliendo tan airoso de sus ardides como en el siglo de las empresas a que se expuso. (209)

Armengol makes many trips to Granada, Algiers, Tunis, and Bizerte to ransom prisoners. On a trip to Bejaïa, however, the ransom money he has promised for the released Christians does not arrive on time, and the vile and malicious Moors decide to hang him:

> Padeció en el ínterin el mártir catalán las vejaciones que la descortesía infiel y atrevimiento idólatra ejercitan con sus cristianos huéspedes, pues entre aquella bárbara república hay quien, a persuasiones de sus morabitos, tiene por cierto que quien mata a un católico se va derecho al paraíso, ... pues el más vil moro, el rapaz entre ellos menos atrevido, se juzga para poco si con bofetadas, con palos, no escarnecen y maltratan a los que por mofa llaman pápaces. (212)

Pedro is suspended from a gallows for three days, but when they return to cut him down he is still alive. He preaches to them about the redemptive power of the Virgin and their own eventual destruction by Christian forces, and many are converted. They allow him and all their Christian prisoners to return to Barcelona, where Pedro decides to retire to La Guardia de Montblanch, dying ten years later of natural causes. His tomb quickly becomes a pilgrimage site accredited with many miracles, "porque Armengol divino, Redentor segundo, retrato del primer Hijo de su Virgen Madre, si en la Tierra redimió afligidos, en el Cielo, a imitación del primero, le tenemos abogado, todo lo socorre y para todos es maná celeste que sabe a todo" (219).

These are the words that end the otherwise secular tale of love, intrigue, adventure, and banditry. With them Tirso has exercised the same strategy of dialectical imitation as did Rodrigo Caro, transferring meaning of a traditional, secular literary mode into the sacred realm by generating an unexpected religious closure for the text. As in Caro's poem, the reader of Tirso's novel is entertained and *then* indoctrinated, rather than simultaneously entertained and indoctrinated, as in *a lo divino* literature. In Tirso's novel, as in Caro's poem, the disillusionment is a result of seeing the material world as a worthless physicality which for the poet became a moan of a resonance of an eco of a voice of a sound of a complaint and for the novelist became the faded, dried up, and dispersed flower, hay, smoke, shadow, ice. In the first, the response was a desire to see the enduring miraculous body of a saint, while in the second the response was to become the very enduring miraculous body of a saint.

Both fictions thus prompt the reader to concur with a number of Tridentine affirmations. Some of the most obvious are the veneration of relics, the mediation of saints, the real possibility of ongoing miracles, the value of the religious calling, and the superiority of the Roman Catholic faith over paganism and Islam. One less obvious affirmation is the efficacious role of the body of Christ in the transubstantiation of the Mass. It is Geroncio's "body" that has lain incorrupt for fourteen centuries, and it is Pedro's "body" that is hung Christ-like for three days and then later buried to become a provider of miracles; and it is not happenstance that caused Tirso to end his novel with the reference to celestial manna, a Biblical antitype for the host. Another less obvious Tridentine message is the assurance that God's efficacious work can take place anywhere at any time to any person, regardless of the secular circumstances. Even in Itálica, the Catholic presence remains. Even a noble-born man who grew up among shepherds, disobeyed his father, became a bandit, and defied his king can become a Catholic saint. Everyone, regardless of birth, position, race, or nationality, can become a martyr to the Catholic faith, because God's plans for Catholics are egalitarian and comprehensive. Moreover, those who reject the freely offered Catholic life, such as Manfredo or the Moors, are vile, wicked people who will never see heaven's glow.

Finally, the two pieces have in common the way in which disillusionment converted the minds of their protagonists – the poet Rodrigo Caro and the fictional character Pedro Armengol – to a religious closure. Many others visited Itálica, and some wrote melancholy poetry about it; but Caro was moved to perceive the sacred significance of the ruined city in a uniquely organic way. When he first observed the ruins he saw a "lastimosa reliquia," "memorias funerales," and a "templo," all religious items. In Strophes Three and Four he contemplated the passing of all the great pagan sons of Itálica, and observed that they lie stretched out in their sepulchres. So the idea of a religious presence and of bodies lying in tombs is on his mind when he evokes the sacred spirits whose moans of "Itálica" have inspired him to write the poem. Now, remembering that Geroncio, another favorite son of Itálica, is also buried among the ruins, Caro decides to dedicate his poem to the sacred spirits in hopes that they will lead him to the sight of the bishop's sepulchre.

Tirso's transition is much more mechanical. In his presentation of the denouement for all his novelesque personages, he creates a contemplative moment for his hero in which the bandit exercises the three powers of the soul – memory, understanding, and will – to recollect the events in his past life and to bring his understanding in conformity with his will: "Haciendo discursos dignos de tan acertado espíritu, enmudeció los labios, careó con la voluntad su entendimiento, y terciando la memoria de sus trágicos sucesos, salió de esta consulta un propósito tan ilustre que, cuando llegó a efecto, le perpetuó blasones inmortales para entrambas vidas" (196).

Perhaps of most importance for the topic of conversion at closure, both Caro (as the protagonist of the poem rather than as the author) and Armengol reach the religious stance they adopt through a disillusionment that is totally rational and elective. "Careó con la voluntad su entendimiento" is not just an idle phrase. The two men demonstrate by their actions that election of the religious life can be a natural outcome of deep thought about one's past and present circumstances. Moreover, neither of the processes was intentionally motivated from outside by hearing a sermon, reading a sacred book, contact with a religious person, visitation by a divine being, miraculous occurrences, or self-imposed periods of religious meditation, as will be the case in most other literary closures.

A well-known case similar to Armengol's but with a different outcome that will serve to close the topic of self-directed conversions is Segismundo's famous decision at the end of *La vida es sueño* to seek "lo eterno" (1: 530b). In the first Act of the play, the youth has been led to believe that he is beast-man, "un hombre de las fieras, / y una fiera de los hombres" (1: 503a), subject only to the same laws of Nature as the animals. In Act Two he is dressed in princely garb and expected to comport himself in accordance with the laws of Man. He fails and is again placed in his cage dressed as a beast; but his tutor Clotaldo, who concurs with the young prince's conclusion that his day at the palace was a dream, advises that "aun en sueños / no se pierde el hacer bien" (1: 522a).

Segismundo takes the advice seriously and decides to repress his fierce nature so that the pain next time will be less: "Pues reprimamos / esta fiera condición, / esta furia, esta ambición, / por si alguna vez soñamos" (1: 522a-b). In the first scenes of Act Three, the youth indeed represses his passionate desires in five distinct moments, and in every case announces that his good actions are due to his desire to lessen his deception when he awakes, "que llevándolo sabido, / será el desengaño menos" (1: 524b). His efforts at self-control are thrown into question, however, when he discovers from Rosaura that his day in the palace was real and that he really is a prince who has been manipulated by his father.

Segismundo's immediate reaction is to conclude, as did Armengol, that all of this life's glories and pleasures are dreams, because all are transitory. One day they will be gone, and we will think that even our memory of them is a dream. What, then, does not perish with time as if it were a dream?

> Si es sueño, si es vanagloria,
> ¿quién por vanagloria humana
> pierde una divina gloria?
> ....
> .... Pues si esto toca
> mi desengaño, si sé
> que es el gusto llama hermosa,
> que le convierte en cenizas
> cualquier viento que sopla,
> acudamos a lo eterno;
> que es la fama vividora
> donde ni duermen las dichas,
> ni las grandezas reposan.
> (1: 530 a-b)

Despite allegations that there are no references to the otherworldly in this play (Heiple 123), it is patent that this "acudir a lo eterno" is the same Counter Reformation Catholic conclusion reached by Pedro Armengol. Neither of the young men necessarily had to see the divine realm as the only place of refuge, because many other thinkers before and after Tirso and Calderón viewed "desengaño" as an end in itself which fulfilled the Stoic dictum *nosce teipsum*, know thyself. Segismundo's later actions as the perfect prince who magnanimously resolves all the issues by pardoning his father, marrying Rosaura to Astolfo, condemning the rebel soldier, and marrying Estrella show him to be the "discreto y ... prudente" (1: 533b) so finely described in Baltasar Gracián's books *El discreto* and *El héroe*. Essentially, there is no need for a religious reference in this political denouement, just as Gracián felt no need to insert religious references in his books on the subject. However, Calderón, like Tirso, is a Counter Reformation thinker. By having Segismundo recognize the heavenly realm as the only fixed eternal entity, Calderón shows his personage operating at the very highest level of human existence through the use of will and wisdom to choose the ultimate good of divine glory. Calderón thus adjusts the long-lived psychological programs associated with memory, will, and understanding to a Catholic framework in which the powers of the soul will by their very nature lead a person to select religious options over secular ones, even over the highest Humanist goals of virtue and wisdom.

The great Humanist Juan Luis Vives (1492-1540), certainly no spokesman for Counter Reformation doctrine, was merely transmitting common knowledge about the will when he wrote in his *Tratado del alma* that "creado el hombre para la felicidad eterna, se le ha concedido la facultad de aspirar al bien, para que desee unirse a él. Esta facultad se llama voluntad" (55). What the Counter Reformation does in the next century is take this statement literally; the good that brings eternal felicity is voluntary recognition of the divine in one's life and the refuge it offers from life's turmoils.

Segismundo, like Pedro Armengol, exercises his will to make decisions about his future. Armengol chose the religious life of a monk; Segismundo chooses to take his proper role as a Prince by exercising his will to make completely objective decisions void of personal desires. These objective actions demonstrate that the young prince is utilizing the highest form of understanding, where one's physical, emotional, and personal desires no longer have any effect on one's rational faculties. Juan Luis Vives had also described this kind of ultimate understanding in *Tratado del alma* in a passage that encapsulates the complete itinerary of human consciousness:

> Conocen las cosas presentes los sentidos; las que no lo están la imaginación; luego viene la reflexión que investiga el interior de la mente y refleja a ésta como en sí propia para que reconozca su contenido, apreciando su cualidad y cuantidad. Por último, la razón saca de los objetos concretos y obvios los recónditos y carentes de cuerpo, de lo particular a lo general; todo ello lo comunica a su entendimiento, y después a la contemplación, si está libre. Y así como los ojos corpóreos necesitan una luz exterior para ver, el ojo mental también necesita una interior para conocer y entender. Las cosas son, o de índole mudable y temporal, o inmutables y perpetuas. Para ver estas últimas es menester una luz sobrenatural cuyo conocimiento se llama sabiduría. (93)

Essentially, the philosophical Calderón attached a Counter Reformational meaning to the Classical-Christian idea of a "luz sobrenatural" and made it "lo eterno," the religious touchstone with which Segismundo had to come into contact in order to forthwith make the discrete and prudent decisions concomitant to his legitimate role as Prince. Calderón could have made Segismundo into a monk, as Tirso did with Pedro Armengol; but *La vida es sueño* is a play about the appropriate roles in one's secular existence, and Segismundo's God-given role is that of a Prince, not a monk. The play presents Segismundo as reading that role on his own by learning through personal experience to use his memory to control his passions, so that his will can communicate freely with his understanding to make indifferent decisions, as described so succinctly by Tirso for Pedro Armengol and demonstrated so poetically by Rodrigo Caro. In every case, the reader surmises that diligent people who reflect on their lives can undergo a spiritual transformation that will lead them through conversion to a religious conception of existence.

Moreover, if they can not or will not reflect on their own circumstances, there is a good possibility that God or some other divine intermediary will intervene in their lives to prompt a proper religious closure for them, as will occur to the marginalized characters discussed in the next chapter.

CHAPTER FOUR

CONVERTING OTHERS

The ultimate Spanish Counter Reformation event is not the Inquisition's *auto de fe*, nor the forced conversion of native populations in America, nor Alba's Court of Blood in Holland, nor Philip's Invencible Armada against England, nor even the Thirty Years War that ravaged northeastern Europe. These actions have received attention mainly because they were manipulated by the Protestant nations to create the *leyenda negra* still present in the literature today about the religious fanaticism and ruthless absolutism of Spanish culture. The ultimate event is the expulsion of the Moriscos from Spain in 1609.

The number of Arab peoples who were forced to leave the country in which their forefathers had lived for almost nine hundred years could have been as high as 300,000 (Domínguez Ortiz 200), making the forcible expulsion by far one of the largest in European history and a textbook case of ethnic cleansing. Not surprisingly, it was considered as such by all the major writers, who supported the action whole-heartedly. In 1653, almost fifty years after the event, Baltasar Gracián can still look back on the ethnic cleansing as the one great action undertaken by Philip III, comparable in importance to the earlier forced conversions and expulsions of the Moors and Jews by the Catholic Monarchs: "Aquel nuestro inmortal heroe, el rey católico don Fernando, ¿no purificó a España de moros y de judíos, siendo hoy el reino más católico que reconoce la iglesia? El rey don Felipe el Dichoso, porque bueno, ¿no purgó otra vez a España del veneno de los moriscos en nuestros días?" (181).

The hatred runs deep. Nevertheless, there existed in the early sixteenth century a literary view of Moors that was humanistic and egalitarian. It is usually referred to as the motif of the Sentimental Moor because the central element in most of the literature is a romantic love affair between a gentle Moor and his beautiful lady that is frustrated by time, place, social status, money, or some other standard hurdle to the union of two spiritually compatible but circumstantially separated young people. The most famous of the genre is "El Abencerraje," which first appeared in Jorge de Montemayor's *Los siete libros de la Diana* (1561) but was published in a more complete form by Antonio de Villegas in his *Inventario* (1565).

The delightful tale of love and friendship could not be more direct. A group of bored Christian soldiers on the Málaga frontier led by Rodrigo de Narváez, military governor of Alora, come upon and capture a Moorish gentleman on his way to marry secretly his beloved Jarifa. On hearing his story, Rodrigo frees him for three days. The Moor continues his journey, marries Jarifa, and returns as promised to Rodrigo's castle. There the Abencerraje and Jarifa are sumptuously feted while Rodrigo writes to the king of Granada to seek approval of the secret marriage, which is granted. All then return to their homes and exchange gifts of peace and friendship.

What enriches these simple events is the way in which the author weaves an elaborate net of relationships among the characters. The valiant, noble Moor is captured and imprisoned by the equally valiant Rodrigo de Narváez. When the military governor learns that Abindarráez is in love – a kind of spiritual capture and imprisonment – he frees him to continue on his way. This act of pardon, however, morally recaptures and reimprisons Abindarráez by obligating him to respond with the same virtue and honor as his captor. Later, Jarifa will become symbolically captured and imprisoned by Abindarráez in their wedding ceremony; so when he returns to Rodrigo's castle she, as his "captive" spouse, accompanies him to the physical prison in Alora. Her arrival paradoxically "captures" Rodrigo by obliging him to act gallantly towards her and to intercede with the king of Granada on behalf of the young lovers. The latter task is simplified by the fact that the king is also "imprisoned" by Rodrigo through the deep regard and obligations that he owes the Christian. The exchange of letters and gifts finally obligates each again to the other in a lifelong alliance of spiritual captive//captor relationships in which these people of opposite cultures and religious beliefs equal one another in moral qualities. There is thus in this novelette a remarkable absence of social conscience, for Christian and Moor – as dichotomous as they may appear in dress, language, and religious practices – are shown to be equals in the Humanist ability to make decisions based on reason alone and to perform virtuous deeds of friendship.

Within the larger tale of "El Abencerraje" is a smaller one – almost an anecdote – about the Christian knight and a married woman whom he once loved. The interpolated tale appears towards the end of the novelette, when Abindarráez and Jarifa are journeying from Coín, where they have consummated their love in her home during her father's absence, to Alora, where Rodrigo de Narváez awaits the arrival of the Moor as stipulated in their agreement when the Christian captured him two days earlier. The tale (which appears only in the version of "El Abencerraje" published by Antonio de Villegas and not in the more popular rendition from Jorge de Montemayor's *Siete libros de la Diana*) is narrated to the Moorish couple by an old man who is asked to relate something honorable and virtuous about Rodrigo de Narváez.

The knight was once passionately taken with the wife of another gentleman, but she always refused his advances. One day, however, she and her husband were hawking, and their hawk trapped a bird in a bush and skillfully grabbed the victim in its talons, causing the gentleman to comment to his wife that it reminded him of the way the governor of Alora pursued and killed his Moorish enemies. This in turn caused the woman to regret having denied her affections to such a valiant and famous man, so the next time her husband was out of the house she promptly invited Narváez to visit her. On the knight's arrival, she openly told him that she wanted him to have her love because of the wonderful things her husband had said to her. On hearing this, Rodrigo got up, put on his cloak, and said that although he loved her dearly and truly, he could never dishonor a man who had honored him as she said. On the contrary, from henceforward he would try to protect her husband's honor as if it were his own, because that is the only way to repay kind words.

The embedded tale, like the novelette, thus has to do with mutual respect and obligations that outweigh any possible personal desires or projects. Faced with the option of indulging his appetites or acting virtuously by respecting the honor of another, Rodrigo chooses the latter. Equally, throughout "El Abencerraje" the principal characters one by one forego satisfaction of their immediate desires in favor of an outcome honorable to another.

The inspiration for this tale is the well-known "Questions of Love" in Book Four of Boccaccio's *Il Filocolo*, a section of the chivalric-courtly novel so popular that it was published repeatedly in Spain as a separate book (Arce). The fourth question, which is addressed by the Spaniard Menedón, is by far the longest and most sophisticated of the thirteen tales, including the most famous first one about the exchange of garlands, also incorporated into "El Abencerraje."

The fourth tale relates that one Tarolfo is deeply in love with a noble woman, who unfortunately is already married to a wealthy and noble knight. Nevertheless, Tarolfo courts the lady so incessantly that she decides to devise a shrewd trick to force him to cease his pursuit. She calls him to her one day and says that she will do anything he wishes of her on one condition. He must create an abundant garden for her in the month of January; otherwise, he must cease to court her. Tarolfo sets off for warmer climes to see if he can devise a way to bring her the garden. He reaches Thessaly, where he comes upon a wretched little old man, whose name is Tebano, digging for herbs. They strike up a conversation, and Tarolfo tells the old man about his impossible mission. Tebano in turn asks what Tarolfo would give for such a garden, and the young knight offers half of all he owns. Tebano and Tarolfo then return to Spain, and when January arrives Tebano magically creates the wonderful garden, which Tarolfo then presents to his lady and demands his reward.

Greatly troubled, the lady promises to come to him when her husband is out of town. She returns home in such sorrow, however, that her husband becomes worried about her and insists that she tell him of her woes, which she does. The husband's uncharacteristic response is the following:

> Lady, truly I do not want you to kill yourself on this account, or even make yourself melancholy about it; it is no displeasure to me, go and do what you promised, for I shall hold you no less dear to me for it; but once you have done it, next time beware of making such promises, even when it seems to you that the thing you have asked for is impossible to have. (260-61)

The lady then dressed in all her finery and went, accompanied by her handmaids and friends, to Tarolfo's house, where she told him of her husband's consent. Tarolfo was flabbergasted. Considering the loyalty of the lady and the honorable generosity of the husband, he replied:

> Gentle lady, you have done your duty loyally and as a worthy lady, and so I hold you discharged of what I desired of you; and so whenever you please you may return to your husband, and thank him on my behalf for such a favor, and give him my apologies for the folly I have shown in the past, assuring him that in the future such matters will never come up on my part again. (261)

Boccaccio's tale includes yet another act of denial, because when Tebano learns of Tarolfo's generous courtesy he too refuses to accept his reward:

> May it never please the gods, since the knight was generous to you with his lady, and you were not churlish to him, that I should be less than courteous myself. More than anything else in the world, it pleases me to have been of service to you; and I desire that what I was to receive as payment for my services should remain yours as much as it ever was. (261)

The question raised by the tale is clear: which of the three men showed the greatest generosity, the husband who forfeited his honor, Tarolfo who forfeited his pleasure, or Tebano who forfeited his utility? After considerable argument, Fiammetta determines that the husband was the most generous, since honor is of more value that pleasure or utility, a decision affirmed later in the seventh question, which includes a long discussion of the three types of honest love, pleasurable love, and utilitarian love (275-80).

Rodrigo de Narváez's honorable rejection of his lady's proffered love is clearly inspired by this dilemma of generous denials in Boccaccio's hauntingly beautiful tale. Like Tarolfo, the Spanish hero turns down pleasure for virtue: "Usó de gran virtud y valentía, pues venció a su misma voluntad. ... Y pudo más con él la honra del marido que la hermosura de la mujer" (61). His reward is the respect of all those who come into contact with him, as Tarolfo's reward was the reciprocal denial of utilitarian goods by Tebano. Of most importance here, neither of these tales has anything to do with creed, race, nationality, or any other social, religious, or political agenda. Both tales have the sole purpose of offering the reader a Humanist exemplum of virtue and the role it can play in even the most improbable situations of apparently unresolvable contradictions.

In the seventeenth century, this little episode is again utilized as evidence of a person's unwaivable virtue, for Lope de Vega amplifies the characters and events into fully one-half of the entire Abencerraje legend in *El remedio en la desdicha*. The central character in Lope's rendition is still Rodrigo de Narváez, and, as in the original tale, the Christian knight's valor is demonstrated in his choosing to suppress his passionate desires.

At the beginning of the play, Rodrigo enters and expresses his amorous subjugation to a Moorish lady, whose beauty has overpowered him. He decides to send her a love letter, and employs one of his Moorish prisoners to write it for him in Arabic. The prisoner tells Narváez that he is married and that he suffers from bitter jealousy when he thinks about his lovely wife alone and unprotected at home. Rodrigo decides to free the Moor, since "con celos y casado / no quieras mayor prisión" (3: 1178a). Meanwhile, Rodrigo's servant takes the letter to the lady, who turns out to be Alara, the jealous Moor's wife. When she is brought to Rodrigo, ready to fulfill his every desire, he sends her back to her husband, stating the same thing as his prose counterpart did in the original tale: "Sabed que soy caballero, / y que quitalle el honor / contradice a mi valor" (3: 1184a). When she leaves, he delivers the famous sonnet on continence "Si fue mayor la gloria y noble el pago," which ends: "No son los capitanes Cipiones, / ni Alejandros los reyes, si no saben / vencer sus apetitos y pasiones" (3: 1184b).

Lope's initial characterization of Rodrigo de Narváez is thus identical to those of the earlier Rodrigo and of the Boccaccian Tarolfo; but Lope's story continues where the others left off. The Moor Arráez discovers the letter that Rodrigo sent to Alara and returns to the Christian's castle to challenge him to a duel. The Christian explains how he has protected the Moor's honor, and the two part as apparent friends. In Act Three, however, Rodrigo receives a package of bloodied shirts from Alara with a letter complaining that her husband contantly mistreats her. Infuriated, Rodrigo dons a Moorish disguise and leaves immediately for Arráez's home in Coín, where he finds the despicable man whipping his lovely wife.

Rodrigo subjugates him and decides to take both of them back to Alora. There, he forces the Moor to divorce Alara and to give her half of all his possessions.

These events are new to the tale, as are Lope's characterization of the Moor and his wife. Alara, rather than being a happily married woman of the same rank, religion, and status as her admirer, is portrayed here as an unhappily married, lascivious, Moorish housewife. Her husband, rather than being the most magnanimous of the three men because he risks his honor while his rivals only risk their pleasure and utility, is here a wretched little Arab consumed with hatred for Christians and an insane jealousy for his wife. In Act One he has the role of an obsequious prisoner who is slavishly grateful for Rodrigo's generosities. In Act Two he appears as a dirty-minded jealous husband whom Rodrigo forces to swear that he will not harm his wife. In Act Three he appears as a vicious wife-beater whom Rodrigo has to seek out and punish; and, rather than receiving the boon of a restituted noble lady, as do the husbands in Boccaccio's tale and the anecdote in "El Abencerraje," Arráez loses his companion and half his possessions. He has thereby degenerated in moral character from an honorable soldier and husband to a dishonorable coward and misogynist, while Alara, for her part, has evolved to the supreme level of Counter Reformation felicity. In the last scene of the play, Rodrigo presides over the couple's destiny, threatening to enslave Arráez. Alara declares "me he de volver cristiana," and Rodrigo replies: "Si vos cristiana habéis de ser, señora, / daréle libertad, y a Coín se vuelva. / Y vos podréis quedaros en Alora, / donde no se faltará lo que perdiste" (3: 1201b).

Thus ends Lope's version of the brief "question of love." The Moorish soldier is demeaned and humiliated, but the beautiful object of the Christian's passion is rehabilitated from the role of infidel spouse to that of gentle Christian, and thus is saved simultaneously from the clutches of her jealous husband and from the thrall of Islam that had assured her certain damnation.

Such is the difference between a Humanist closure penned by a Boccaccio in 1350 or an anonymous Spaniard in 1550 and a Counter Reformational closure written in 1600. Gone are the symmetry, balance, and harmony of equal parties vying with each other to practice the best good deed imaginable. Gone are the themes of mutual respect, friendship and conjugal reconciliation among peoples of different backgrounds. Now the Christian remains honest and generous and virtuous, but the Moor created by the Catholic mind becomes a stingy, petulant weakling who deserves the disrespect and persecution he has received over the centuries.

Furthermore, the beautiful lady of desire is saved, but only because she converts to Catholicism and chooses to live among the good people. In fact, it is especially significant that Lope presents this Counter Reformation view of Muslims in a play ostensibly about the noble Abindarráez and his lovely wife Jarifa. They escape being codified as aliens quite simply because Lope respects the story too much to change it; but, since he can't bring himself to alter the famous narrative of the Abencerraje, he exercises his Counter Reformation spirit on a slight interpolated tale which he is able to alter, and which he amplifies to one-half of the play, paralleling the career of the gentle Moors and offering a personal intolerant vision of the non-Christian other side, a stance which unfortunately is characteristic of his treatment of Moors and Moriscos in all his other plays (Case 213).

Rodrigo de Narváez thus becomes a character with two roles. As the friend of Abindarráez, he exercises his virtue in a mediating posture among equals: himself, Abindarráez, Jarifa, and Jarifa's father Zoraide. This is the Humanist vision that has come down to Lope from Boccaccio and the Spanish Renaissance. As arbiter in the Alara-Arráez conflict, Rodrigo is the *Aucthoritas*, the supreme commander who imposes his unwelcome decision on others by force. In fact, Alara will be typical of the outsider as viewed by the Counter Reformation mind in that she can do nothing to save herself. While she is not totally passive (she does write a letter to Rodrigo about her husband's abuse), she cannot protect herself from challenges to her personal and social well-being nor can she do anything to change her condition. She is, in short, a "dependent" in the strictest sense of the word; and her dependence is psychological, because she knows that only the Christian military governor can save her from her misfortune. The very title of Lope's play *El remedio en la desdicha* thus takes on a Counter Reformational meaning, for the true remedy to true misfortune is to join the Christian cause.

This part of the play, in sum, presents the Counter Reformation vision of a single authoritative figure who decides the fates of others and expects strict obedience from them. Furthermore, the only remedy within this structure is conversion to Catholicism, a complete break with the pagan world by accepting a new role in life as "cristiana."

Things could have been worse. Lope presents a character whose freedom comes at the price of only a new religion. Mateo Alemán, on the other hand, fabricates the Christian//Moor tale "Ozmín y Daraja" to envision a complete transformation of the neophytes from their religion, their language, their personal comportment, their diet, their dress, and their manners.

Alemán's novelette offers a number of unique problems for the modern reader because it is embedded within the picaresque novel *Guzmán de Alfarache* (1599), whose entire contents will be examined in Chapter Five. Out of its picaresque frame, "Ozmín y Daraja" is a story simple enough to speak for itself. It certainly is not an especially unique tale within the Counter Reformation context. Its immediate predecessor and source of inspiration, for example, is not the Humanist "El Abencerraje" but the equally Counter Reformational *Guerras civiles de Granada* (1595) by Ginés Pérez de Hita. In that novel, the Zegrí tribe jointly accuses Queen Sultana of having an affair with the Abencerraje Abinhamad, and the entire Abencerraje family of plotting to overthrow King Boabdil. The king therefore carries out a massacre of the Abencerrajes; those who escape flee Granada and seek protection under the Castilian flag, becoming Christians and joining the Castilian army or entering into service at Ferdinand and Isabella's court.

Meanwhile, the Granadan queen decides to take her own life rather than face the expected punishment for her alleged crime, but her Christian slave Esperanza de Hita convinces her that if she prays to the Virgin and seeks aid from the Castilian side she will overcome her misfortunes. Sultana agrees, and writes secretly to Juan de Chacón for help. He responds by coming secretly to Granada and defeating the Zegrí who lodged the false accusations. In response, Queen Sultana twice urges Chacón to hasten the taking of Granada so its people can be Christianized: "Y más os quiero hacer saber que la mayor parte de los cavalleros de Granada están de mi opinión y no aguardan más de que el Rey Fernando comience la guerra contra Granada y su Reyno. ... Y por Dios que no me olvidéys, y dad priessa a vuestro Rey que comience la guerra contra

Granada, para que todos los que tienen propósito de ser Christianos, se les cumplan sus deseos" (246, 248).

The novel ends with the anticipated closure. After Fernando and Isabel take the city, the Christianized Abencerrajes recuperate all their lands and possessions (as will Ozmín and Daraja's parents); the young couple Muza and Zelima (who represent the romantic lovers equivalent to Ozmín and Daraja throughout this long episode) become Christians; and Queen Sultana (exactly as will occur to Daraja) asks to become a Christian, is baptized by the Archbishop, takes the new name of doña Isabel de Granada, marries a Christian knight, and receives in dowry two villages for as long as she lives. The Zegrí tribe, however, is rounded up and shipped off to Africa (289-90).

Pérez de Hita thus establishes a clear juxtaposition of Christianized winners to Muslim losers. The former close their lives with a recuperation of their honor, their families, their lands, and their possessions, plus the added benefit of incorporation into the secular Castilian society and the sacred community of faithful Christians. The latter forfeit all of the above.

The "Ozmín y Daraja" version is not remarkedly different from this prototype. It is told by a "buen sacerdote" (50a) to Guzmán in an effort to lift the boy's spirits after he has been beaten by some policemen. Guzmán, however, who as narrator of his own life is telling it to the reader from his prison on a galley, confesses that he has adjusted considerably the priest's tale, since "más dilatada y con alma diferente nos lo dijo de lo que yo la he contado" (75a).

Some recent scholars have seized this statement to interpret the text as a subversion of the priest's stated intention, which was to mollify Guzmán's pain with a tale demonstrating the security that awaits those who submit humbly to the Christian cause (as also transpired in *Guerras civiles de Granada*). Judith Whitenack, for example, argues that the tale, when read closely, attempts to denigrate all the people in it, without exception. The narrator intentionally diminishes the moral character of all the Christians by making them appear to be concerned solely with the conversion of Daraja and her family, and even among the upper classes all the nobler impulses – love, charity, friendship, loyalty, and gratitude – are tainted by self-interest and mercenary impulses ("Alma" 67). The narrator undercuts the vision of Daraja as an idealized heroine by subtly diminishing her presence in the tale and by leaving the door open to speculation about her fidelity to Ozmín because of certain promises she makes to Rodrigo ("Alma" 69). Finally, Whitenack continues, the narrator negates the power of Christian conversion by making it an expedient tactic used by the Moors to retain their presence in Granada, ostensibly because Alemán wants the tale to anticipate Guzmán's own false conversion in order to escape service in the galleys; so Guzmán's "attraction to this tale and his transformation of it support the rhetorical strategies of his entire pseudo-confession while powerfully affirming his own 'alma differente'" ("Alma" 71).

There is no doubt about Alemán perverting the Sentimental Moor theme by diminishing the role and scope of everyone's actions other than Ozmín's, and it is certainly true that the conversion at the end will be manipulative; but the reasons for these perversions may have more to do with a desire for a proper Counter Reformational closure than for a lesson about impenitence. Furthermore, the reader knows nothing about the elderly Guzmán narrating his life except that he is back in the galleys, and the conversion at the end of Part Two (mid-way through Guzmán's life), whether sincere or not, was not related to his liberation. That was a result of his squealing on the shipmates who were planning to mutiny and the fortuitous discovery (although Guzmán also implies that God had a hand in the matter) of the missing hat band and other items he had been accused of stealing.

Interestingly, if Whitenack's new reading of the text as a narrative mechanism to subvert Guzmán's veracity were correct, it would support better the pervasive domination of Counter Reformational closure for secular literature because it would show that Mateo Alemán assumes that the closure he uses is so conventional that it will be recognized by his readers as a hypocritical manipulation (first by the good priest and then by Guzmán de Alfarache) for utilitarian purposes. Anyway, regardless of the appreciation one establishes for the cast of the tale, Ozmín remains a key character whose actions always conform to those expected of the persistent lover who concentrates the entirety of his person on being with the beloved. As will be seen, he achieves his goal only after losing his identity as a Sentimental Moor and becoming the anonymous passive recipient of Christian charity.

The tale is indeed quite simple and direct, with only one rectilinear plot concerning Ozmín's efforts to be with his betrothed (the narrator uses the terms *esposa* and *esposo* throughout for the two young lovers). It begins with Ferdinand and Isabella's seige and conquest of Baza, during which they capture Daraja, daughter of the city's military governor, and take her to Sevilla, where, because of her perfect beauty, discretion, seriousness, grace, and impeccable Spanish, she is befriended by the Queen, who dresses her in Christian clothes "a la castellana" (51b). Desiring likewise that Daraja become a Christian, the Queen lodges her in the home of don Luis Padilla, "para irla saboreando en las cosas de nuestra fe" (51b). There she remains, the passive and helpless object of everyone's desire, for the rest of the tale.

Ozmín's personal journey is quite different. From the moment the brave young man decides to pursue independently the recuperation of his beloved, he becomes subject to fortune and is forced to initiate a linear series of some fifteen transformations, the first totally of his own initiative but the last completely out of his control. They are the following: 1. He adopts a "traje andaluz" to cross into Christian territory. 2. He claims that he is don Rodrigo de Padilla, the son of the family with whom Daraja is lodged (no one accepts this façade). 3. He becomes a "peón de albañilería," dressed in "un vestidillo vil," in order to enter the grounds where Daraja is staying. 4. He becomes a "jardinero" to be even closer to her. 5. He claims he is Ambrosio, a Christian of humble origins who was captured and taken to Baza to serve Ozmín, the young Moor betrothed to Daraja. 6. He is dismissed from the Padilla household because he spoke too often with Daraja in *algarabía* and assumes a "hábito de trabajador." 7. He then becomes friends with Alonso de Zúñiga and serves as his page; 8. but when his worth is esteemed, he dresses as a "caballero" and claims to be Jaime Vives, "natural de Zaragoza" and an intimate friend of Ozmín, the young Moor betrothed to Daraja. Ozmín is immensely successful in his role as Jaime Vives, killing bulls, jousting with the Christian nobility, and teaching Alonso the intricacies of chivalresque combat. 9. He and his friend then decide to dress "de labradores" to serenade Daraja, who has been taken by her new family to the village of El Ajarafe. 10. There, Ozmín gets into a brawl with the yokels, kills four of them, and becomes a "preso." 11. He is immediately put on trial by the townsfolk and ends up a "condenado" sentenced to public hanging, and since he can't reveal his true identity no one can do anything for him.

These eleven transformations portray a fascinating pattern of roles for the young Moor. He fails in his first role as an Andalusian gentleman and in his second impersonation as Rodrigo de Padilla. Clearly, these sudden shifts to the Christian side aren't the appropriate ones at that time in his career. His beloved, on the other hand, has found a niche in Christian society as a *castellana*. Rodrigo de Padilla, his second choice, is a bad one because the reader later learns that Padilla is a vain, arrogant person of little worth: "Por su arrogancia era secretamente malquisto" (67b).

When he arrives in Sevilla, Ozmín decides to begin at the bottom by becoming a hod carrier, assuredly the lowest, most menial profession in Christendom. From there, however, he rises to gardener, and then to day-laborer, page, and Castilian gentleman from Zaragoza. It is no surprise that this is the most successful role for him, since it is the exact Christian equivalent to his Moorish status of "caballero moro de Granada, ... mancebo, rico, galán, discreto y, sobre todo, valiente y animoso en cada una destas partes dispuesta a recibir un 'muy,' y le era muy debido" (51b-52b). The narrator highlights this equality of roles by having "Jaime Vives" tell Alonso that Ozmín was "retrato mío, así en edad como en talle, rostro, condición y suerte" (66a).

When Ozmín then dons the disguise of a farmer, fortune turns against him, and he ends up spiralling down to prisoner and finally to condemned murderer, completely alone, isolated, and passive. In effect, he has become the male equivalent of Alara at the end of *El remedio en la desdicha*, subject bodily to the good will of the Christian overlord to remedy the misfortune each passively and helplessly suffers. As Alara is saved by Rodrigo de Narváez, so, 12. Ozmín's identity is revealed to the Padilla family by Daraja, and don Luis secretly petitions Queen Isabella for a pardon. The unknown condemned murderer thus suddenly becomes a royal protégé, exactly equivalent to the status of his lovely fiancée. Ozmín and Daraja are next taken to their benefactor's court, which is none other than the very Granadan Alhambra that was Ozmín's home only months before.

Back at home with his beloved by his side, Ozmín has undertaken a journey that has brought him to precisely the exactly same physical spot from which he began his quest. Everything is the same, and yet everything is different. The royal authority is Queen Isabella, not Boabdelín. The couple's fathers Alboacén and the military governor of Baza are also present at court serving their king, but now the monarch is Fernando and both men have converted to Christianity. Of most importance, 13. Ozmín and Daraja look at each other and see "castellanos," not "moros," because both are dressed as Castilians surrounded by other Castilians, speak Castilian, and participate fully in Castilian customs such as the "galana máscara" given for their benefit. Only two more transformations are necessary for both to cease being aliens to thus become totally integrated citizens of the new society that has physically replaced the one which has now disappeared forever from the south of Spain:

> La reina se adelantó, diciéndoles cómo sus padres eran cristianos, aunque ya Daraja lo sabía. Pidióles que, si ellos lo querían ser, les haría mucha merced; mas que el amor ni temor los obligase, sino solamente el de Dios y de salvarse, porque de qualquier manera, desde aquel punto se les daba libertad para que de sus personas y hacienda dispusiesen a su voluntad. (74b-75a)

They accept the offer to save their souls by this queen who earlier did so much to save their bodies and to accomodate them in a social milieu parallel to the one they left; and, 14. they are baptized into the Christian faith. Finally, the two lovers initiate the ultimate transformations of their beings, 15. changing their names from Ozmín and Daraja to Fernando and Isabel, becoming thereby spiritual mirror images of the benefactors who saved their bodies and souls.

What, then, is this tale about? First and foremost, it presents the Castilianization of Ozmín the Moor. The youth passes from being a young Arab gentleman through a complex series of roles and disguises which one by one bring him closer and closer to his final destination as a young Castilian gentleman. Daraja experiences the same transformation, but in a wholly passive way, since she is taken to the Castilian camp by force and is dressed in Castilian garb against her wishes.

Second and of equal significance, the tale presents the Christianization of Ozmín the Moor. This, along with the simultaneous change of name, is the last event in his pilgrimage, and it establishes him as a fully-invested member of the new society that has been implanted within the old one to which he belonged, but which no longer exists. The pilgrimage through fourteen transformations has been a series of different moments of *estar*, one could say, which have led to the only destiny appropriate for his *ser*, his underlying nature as a young, rich, gallant, discrete, valiant and brave *persona*. In Counter Reformation Spain, that final appropriate role in life must include incorporation into the Church.

Third, the tale is a true *peregrinatio*. Ozmín thinks that he is participating in a series of adventures that will lead him to a secular physical union with his beloved Daraja, yet ironically his numerous physical changes only lead him farther from both personal security for his body (his imprisonment and condemnation) and national security for his culture (his home in Granada). On the spiritual plane, however, Ozmín undertakes unwittingly a pilgrimage that leads directly and inexorably to his and Daraja's salvation from both their material problems and their lost condition as Muslims.

Fourth and finally, the tale is an object lesson about dependence. Ozmín and Daraja indeed have positive, optimistic attitudes about life and a prosperous outcome to their travails, but their aspirations serve no purpose in the story. Both become totally passive and dependent on the goodwill of another, who for both is Queen Isabella of Castile, the representative of God on earth. So, despite all their efforts and active role-shifting to reach independently their goals, the two lovers fail. Salvation comes only from above; but it comes for all who seek it, whether a wretched abused wife like Alara or two brave young people like Ozmín and Daraja.

The similarities between Lope's treatment of Alara and Narváez and Alemán's treatment of Ozmín and Daraja are now apparent. As well, it is not possible to overemphasize the striking disparities that exist between the original Abencerraje tale embedded in an idealistic pastoral novel and this one embedded in a pessimistic picaresque novel. In "El Abencerraje," the opposing Christian and Moorish forces meet, interchange magnanimous actions of mutual regard, reach a spiritual equality of selves in a climatic reunion, and part physically and socially unchanged, although spiritually transformed into conveyors of Friendship. Essentially, nothing changes in "El Abencerraje," because each group goes its separate way back from whence it came to continue the same life as before; only now each is a friend of the other. "Ozmín y Daraja," on the other hand, narrates the obliteration of the Moorish presence in Spain. The great cities of Baza and Granada are taken, their commanders are either Christianized or exiled, their palaces are Castilianized or razed, and their brave young citizens are transformed into mirror images of the Catholic Monarchs. There is no amiable recognition of the true Humanist worth of the alien presence; rather, it is the total destruction of all evidence of the alien on Spanish soil, and yet at the same time it is the magnanimous accomodation and integration of those outside the pale who choose freely to lose their differentness by joining the Castilian Christian community.

Mateo Alemán makes the cultural and religious transference look easy by presenting it as an evolution through fourteen temporary states of *estar*. Lope presents it as the only possible remedy for a desperate woman; a remedy, moreover, not available to the meanspirited and treacherous members of her tribe. The anonymous author of "El Abencerraje," however, never even considered transference as a possibility; but much had changed in Spain between the 1550s and the 1590s.

One more utilization of the Christian//Moor theme in seventeenth-century Spanish literature deserves mention because it elaborates in a brilliantly sensitive way a person's transformation through various roles within the religious context of the Reconquest. It is difficult to categorize Calderón's *El príncipe constante*. On one level it is a political play about war and conquest in which the characters exercise varying degrees of prudence or imprudence (Fox 51-58). On another level, it is a philosophical play of Stoic disillusionment that dramatizes the failure of all human endeavors to resolve issues (Parker 310). It is also clearly a religious play, a Counter Reformation *comedia de santos* about the suffering and martyrdom of a Christian prince (Lumsden-Kouvel). The one thing that stands out in all these interpretations is the interplay of person and role that propels the character Fernando through the three Acts of the play; for, as Susan L. Fischer, Robert Sloane and many others have observed, Fernando undergoes a number of changes in role throughout the play, some voluntary and some involuntary, but all self-defining. As with Ozmín, the litany of roles is linear and regressive. In Act One Fernando defines his role in political-military terms as Infante de Portugal and Maestre de Avís. As such, he is participating in the conquest of Tangier, which he sees as a Christian enterprise. On capturing Muley, he finds himself in the same role as Rodrigo de Narváez when he captured Abindarráez; he is "un portugués caballero" (1: 257b), "un hombre noble, y no más" (1: 257b) whose sole function is to act virtuously. He therefore allows Muley to go his way, as Rodrigo de Narváez did also with his captive. But Fernando embodies a sense of place and ideology absent in the Renaissance Man. When he sees that his capture is eminent, his only wish is to die a soldier's death – "Por la fe muramos, / pues a morir venimos" (1: 258a) – and to self-define his role exclusively as a warrior knight: "Un caballero soy; saber no esperes / más de mí. Dame muerte" (1: 258b).

Act Two dramatizes Fernando's physical transition from a captive who is treated as a prince to a prince who is treated as a captive. In the first scenes he thus appears in the noble clothing of a courtier and is treated nobly by all, and he defines his present role as a hybrid one of *infante/esclavo* (1: 261a). When he refuses to let himself be traded for Ceuta, however, he makes the decision to self-annihilate himself as príncipe-infante-caballero-cortesano to reduce his *ser*, as he calls it (1: 263b), to that of a mere man: "¿Soy más que un hombre?" (1: 263b). With the assumption of this role he ceases to exist as the person Fernando and becomes the lump of flesh that in Act Three will suffer, rot, die, and be encased in a humble box of wood. Fernando is so aware of his own self-annihilation, in fact, that he verbalizes it in a typically Calderonian regressive accumulation of Fernando, slave, fellow-prisoner, man, sufferer, wretch, woeful one, cadaver:

> Cristianos, Fernando es muerto;
> moros, un esclavo os queda;
> cautivos, un compañero
> hoy se añade a vuestras penas;
> cielos, un hombre restaura
> vuestras divinas iglesias;
> mar, un mísero, con llanto,
> vuestras ondas acrecienta;
> montes, un triste os habita,
> igual ya de vuestras fieras.
> Viento, un pobre con sus voces
> os duplica las esferas;
> tierra, un cadáver hoy labra
> en tus entrañas su huesa.
> (1: 263b-264a)

The remainder of Act Two and the first half of Act Three dramatize the downward movement of Fernando's physicality to that of a corpse carted around the stage in a cheap coffin, a "caja humilde y breve" (1: 277b). Yet, as the buffoon Brito comically declared at the end of Act One, "que, ainda mortos, somos portugueses" (1: 259b). Fernando's physical death frees his spirit to reassume his original role as defender of the faith: *Aparécese el Infante Don Fernando con manto capitular y un hacha encendida* (1: 276B). The dramatic character Fernando is by all appearances the same political-military Infante de Portugal and Maestre de Avís who began the play leading his troops into battle against the Moor; but now the dramatic character is a spiritual entity rather than a physical one. Stripped of all the original human roles he assumed throughout the play, he now emerges in the angelic role of Counter Reformational "divino Príncipe mártir" (1: 278a).

El príncipe constante is thus a uniquely self-defining play, because the prince Fernando undergoes multiple changes in garb and status, but remains constantly the same in the one thing that counts to a Counter Reformation thinker: fidelity to the Church. Because of his fidelity, Fernando ends with his garb and status restored, and on the true permanent plane of immortality rather than the false transitory plane of physical existence.

All the other characters in the play remain outside the gates of immortality, and in this sense they are all failures. Calderón, writing after the crucial decade of the 1620s, lacks the sense of inclusive closure felt by Alemán's narrating priest, whereby all the characters must be inducted into the Castilian corporation. In "Ozmín y Daraja," all the participants without exception are present at the peroration, and all are happy and content with their final lot. The young people are married to their appropriate spouses, and live happily ever after. Neither Calderón nor Lope are so magnanimous with their Moorish characters, for in *El remedio en la desdicha* Arráez is physically and spiritually excluded from the happy finale and in *El príncipe perfecto* all the characters, while included in the final scene's adjustments, are excluded both from the glorious incorporation of Fernando into the heavenly choir and from the achievement of their individual earthly goals.

The reader can easily extrapolate from this the conclusion that all the other characters fail precisely because their goals are earth-centered, as A. A. Parker does when he declares that "spiritual values, as here presented, necessitate the inversion of all human values and the denial that they can be efficacious in constructing a satisfying and reasonable framework for living" (310). This conclusion is substantiated by the constant presence of Death in *El príncipe constante*, which forces Fénix to become aware of the transitoriness of Beauty in its various forms: her own features, nature, and Ceuta.

Lope and Alemán's priest, on the other hand, do not inject the philosophy of disillusionment into their tales, so their creations – especially the women – can begin their new lives optimistically. Ideologically, these lives cannot be lived as aliens, but rather as Catholics in Castilian dress. Incorporative closure, in other words, requires conversion, and conversion brings willy-nilly incorporative closure.

Not all seventeenth-century Spanish literature was to express this closed system of conversion. Miguel de Cervantes presents Humanist options in *Don Quijote de la Mancha*, a novel that belongs to the Counter Reformation culture of ardent Catholicism and strong free-will philosophy, but which avoids the sense of a directed culture prominent in Tirso, Lope, Alemán, and Calderón. In the tale of the "cautivo" Ruy Pérez de Viedma, for example, the Moorish damsel Zoraida is converted by heavenly visitations from a deceased Christian slave girl (1.40) and a vision of the Virgin Mary (1.41). Zoraida, who insists that all the Christians call her María, initiates her own pilgrimage to conversion by contacting secretly the Christian slaves in her father's garden; and she supplies the money, the plan, and the opportunity for her journey to Christendom. At closure, she is bodily incorporated into Spanish society, just as Daraja and Alara were. The more tolerant Cervantes, however, makes it a complete assimilation, because the Moorish lady marries an old Christian and goes to live on his hereditary estates in the mountains of León, erasing thereby, as Michael Gerli lucidly explains, the destructive history of Spanish-Arab relations and replacing it with one of reparation and closure (40-60).

The same Humanist tolerance is shown to the Morisco Ricote and his daughter Ana Félix. She also marries into an old Christian family and is thus fully assimilated, while Ricote appeals his alien status with the proper judicial authorities. Although Cervantes – perhaps deliberately – leaves Ricote's case unresolved, the reader can assume that the Morisco will win his appeal to remain in Spain because he has the support of the Viceroy of Aragón (2.56).

In a way, even the outsiders like Alara, Ozmín, and Daraja have an exceptionally easy transition into Castilian society. It would not be a very good policy to make the conversions appear too difficult or to require overwhelmingly strenuous acts of endurance or discipline from those the Church wishes to coax into its fold. Spanish Christians who undergo a conversion from sinfulness to saintliness, on the other hand, do not enjoy such an accomodative transition. They are already within the fold and therefore should know better, so they must undergo severely harsh and disciplinary transitions before reaching the incorporative closure that conversion assures for them, as the literary figures examined in the next chapter will demonstrate.

CHAPTER FIVE

CONVERTING ONESELF

When Ignatius Loyola settled in Paris in 1529 to study at the College of Saint Barbara, one of the first persons he converted to his new method of spirituality was Pedro Fabro. Ribadeneyra describes the events as follows:

> Lo primero le enseñó a examinar cada día su conciencia. Luego le hizo hacer una confesión general de toda su vida, y después le puso en el uso de recibir cada ocho días el Santísimo Sacramento del altar, y al cabo de cuatro años que pasó viviendo de esta manera, viéndole ya bien maduro y dispuesto para lo demás, y con muy encendidos deseos de servir perfectamente a Dios, le dio, para acabarle de perficionar, los *Ejercicios espirituales*, de los cuales salió Fabro tan aprovechado que desde entonces le pareció haber salido de un golfo tempestuoso de olas y vientos de inquietud y entrado en el puerto de la paz y descanso. (77)

Fortunately for later lay people, the *Spiritual Exercises* themselves would include Fabro's initial stages of examination of conscience, general confession, communion, and service, but would last only four weeks rather than four years.

The key to the process is the *Examen Conscientiae*, which contains the five parts later designated in the handbooks as 1) *gratias age*, 2) *pete lumen*, 3) *examina*, 4) *dole*, 5) *propone* (Dickens 79). Loyola's original statement is amazingly brief:

> *Modo de hacer el examen general, y contiene en sí cinco punctos.* El primer puncto es dar gracias a Dios nuestro Señor por los beneficios rescibidos. El segundo: pedir gracia para conocer los

> pecados y lanzazallos. El tercero: demandar cuenta al ánima desde la hora que se levantó hasta el examen presente de hora en hora, o de tiempo en tiempo; y primero del pensamiento, y después de la palabra, y después de la obra, por la misma orden que se dixo en el examen particular. El cuarto: pedir perdón a Dios nuestro Señor de las faltas. El quinto: proponer enmienda con su gracia. Pater Noster. (220)

These points became the core of the conversion process for Counter Reformation Catholics. It is the procedure, for example, to which Guzmán de Alfarache refers when he calls his autobiography "aquesta confesión general que hago, este alarde público," and advises his reader: "Da vuelta por ti, recorre a espacio y con cuidado la casa de tu alma, mira si tienes hechos muledares asquerosos en lo mejor della y no espulgues ni murmures" (188b).

It is likewise the effectuation of the Council of Trent's declaration on penance in its fourteenth session, where three stages were identified: Contrition, Confession, Satisfaction. These lead to Reconciliation with God, which in turn leads to Peace and Quietness of Conscience with a great Consolation of Spirit (*Council* 61-62). Contrition has three stages, which match Loyola's examination of conscience: Grief of Mind and Detestation of Sin Committed, a Resolution to Sin no more, Confidence in Divine Mercy (*Council* 62). The chapter on confession specifically refers to the necessity of a previous examination of themselves by penitents: "For it is plain, there is nothing more required by the Church of Penitents, than, that every one, after he hath diligently examin'd himself, and tried and search'd every creek and corner of his Conscience, he may confess those sins, wherewith he remembers he has mortally offended the Lord his God; and the rest of his sins, which after diligent examination he does not remember, are understood to be included in the Gross of his Confession" (*Council* 63-64). The final stage of satisfaction is the ministry of absolution, which can only be extended by bishops and priests (*Council* 64).

It is hard for us today to imagine how ubiquitous these three stages were in the Spanish seventeenth century, for the fact is that they permeated every citizen's life on a weekly basis from first communion to extreme unction. They are so instilled in the culture, in fact, that by 1619 Carlos García can use them satirically to close his novel *La desordenada codicia de los bienes ajenos*, where the thief

Andrés declares: "De la penitencia recibimos las dos partes, que son la confesión (porque algunas veces nos confesamos) y la contrición; pero de la tercera, que es la satisfación, no hay que hablar" (1195b).

For the orthodox believer, confession, contrition, and satisfaction are the mental actions that lead to conversion from sinner to saint. The conversion itself of course requires first a decision by the will to reform one's life, followed by voluntary subjection to physical acts of penitence, which cleanse one's soul of sin and prepare it to receive the divine absolution necessary for personal salvation. For this process also Guzmán de Alfarache has a plan:

> El mozo, que tratare de querer ser viejo, deje mis pasos y trate de vencer pasiones. Dispóngase al trabajo y a fuerza de su voluntad ríndala en el suelo, venciendo viejos deseos. Átese una soga de sufrimiento y humildad, que arrastre por algunos días los malos apetitos, gastando el tiempo en virtuosos ejercicios. Que a pocos lances llegará santamente al yugo de la penitencia y con las buenas compañías hará costumbre al arado, con que romperá la tierra de malas inclinaciones. (248a-b)

Guzmán knows the way. He ends the first Part of his life story insisting that all his troubles were due exclusively to "mi mala inclinación" (165a) rather than bad luck or birth or natural causes, and he ends the second Part with an enactment of the stages diagramed in his plan for salvation. The peroration occupies the last two chapters of the book. Guzmán remarks that people like him go to the galleys because God realizes it is the only way they will ever come to recognize their sins. Such was his case, because his present circumstances have caused him to begin to exercise his memory – "vínome a la memoria" (391b) – to consider his past evil life and the eternal punishment awaiting him. On board the ship, he is treated well by the galley sargeant, but at the cost of alienating all the other prisoners. He begins to consider his precarious situation, and decides that the only true friend and master is God. He falls asleep with this idea on his mind, "y cuando recordé, halléme otro no yo ni con aquel corazón viejo, que antes. Di gracias al Señor y supliquéle que me tuviese de su mano. Luego traté de confesarme a menudo, reformando mi vida, limpiando mi conciencia" (399a).

Having thus to all appearances unwittingly fulfilled every stage of Loyola's spiritual exercises, Guzmán is subjected to a series of Christological inflictions by his captors. Falsely accused of stealing a hat band, he is strung up, lashed, beaten, tortured, and hung by his wrists. Close to death, he learns of a mutiny planned for June 25, St. John the Baptist day. As Cayillac (199-200) has observed, the narrator Guzmán sees his own vital situation as analogous to that of John the Baptist preaching in the desert and hoping that those who hear him will be converted by his words.

Rather than join his companions' well-orchestrated mutiny, the youth decides to "convert" to the proper political stance and confesses all he knows to the royal authorities on the galley. His enemies are mutilated and dismembered while his goodness, innocence, and fidelity are recognized and he is promised a royal pardon for his crimes.

Until the 1970s, this denouement was viewed universally as the paradigm of a Counter Reformation confession text; but several recent Hispanists, led by Joan Arias and Judith Whitenack, have written tightly-argued monographs denouncing earlier "critical misinterpretations," as Whitenack calls them (*Impenitent* 42), and proposing Guzmán as an "unrepentant narrator" (Arias) who is shown by his author to be an obstinate degenerate incapable of changing his life but willing to live the lie of a confessed penitent.

The most extreme detractor is Whitenack, who sees no Christian message at all in the novel because it is permeated with hopeless human evil (*Impenitent* 45). Despite Guzmán's ingratiating sermons about the moral Catholic life, his and the other characters' careers present life as an inevitable repetition of evil actions based on deceit as the only expedient form of comportment in a world populated by human beings in existential isolation from one another (*Impenitent* 158). The confessionary structure of the novel is thus a parody of true confession literature, such as the paradigmatic Augustinian *Confessions*, because all the characters in *Guzmán de Alfarache* who make religious confessions do so either under the coercion of exterior circumstances, such as the threat of excommunication or the inability for one reason or another to continue sinning – as with Ozmín and Daraja – or under a serious misconception regarding the nature and purpose of true confession – as with the protagonist Guzmán (*Impenitent* 55). Alemán's vision, according to this view, is "a world in which concealment in the guise of sincerity and self-revelation is the norm. ... Not only can no one be trusted, but human beings are finally unknowable – each one concealed behind an elaborate false self, even at the very moment that one is supposedly baring one's soul" (*Impenitent* 158).

Most traditional critics would assuredly agree with this view of *Guzmán de Alfarache*, and they may also accept Guzmán as an obsequious unrepentant narrator; but they would certainly balk at the notion that Mateo Alemán has written a novel with no Christian message to offer his reader. This present chapter, which concerns self-directed conversions, will hopefully show that an integral part of the novel's internal and external structure is the intention of soliciting from the reader an examination of conscience, an awakening of the memory of past deeds (Alemán's novel thus becomes ostensibly no more than a lectured self-recollection of those things in Guzmán's life that the rogue believed had led him to his present situation in the galleys), a realization of the commitment of sins, a desire to repent, a vocal confession, communion, absolution, and acts of penitence. These steps are all part of the traditional moral conversion, which in *Guzmán de Alfarache* is coupled with the "political conversion" when Guzmán decides to turn against his fellow prisoners in the planned mutiny and to support the State's cause; and both provoke the enactment of the "poetic conversion" represented by the novel itself as a product of Guzmán's transformed social and spiritual being (Cayillac).

Whether the novel is serious or parodic evidently depends on the reader's perception of the material; but the conversions are nevertheless there in the novel and represent the power of Counter Reformation thought on the author. In fact, if the confessionary motif in *Guzmán de Alfarache* were indeed parodic, it would support better the thesis that the Church had successfully appropriated art forms by 1598, since Alemán would be manipulating a religious literary technique created to manipulate secular literature. By the same token, whether one considers the conversions of Ozmín and Daraja to Christianity as sincere or expedient does not affect the real presence of the conversions at the end of the tale as the mode of closure chosen by the fictional priest who tells the tale.

Regardless of the reliability of Guzmán's autobiography or the sincerity of his conversions, the events that close the story of the picaro's life follow the roadway to absolution and freedom from punishment through acts of penitence made by a person converted from sin by a consciously willed decision to refrain from evil thoughts and deeds by guiding his life according to the appropriate dictates of Church and State. Regardless of the possibility of irony or satire, Guzmán satisfies the role that Mateo Alemán announced for him in the second Part's prologue, "que sólo es descubrir como atalaya toda suerte de vicios y hacer atriaca de venenos varios un hombre perfecto, castigado de trabajos y miserias, después de haber bajado a la más ínfima de todas puesto en galera por curullero della" (185).

The epitome of this whole process is the *a lo divino* novel *La conversión de la Magdalena, en que se ponen los tres estados que tuvo, de pecadora, de penitente y de gracia*, the biblical type for all future sinners who repent, confess, make atonement, and receive absolution. As Malón de Chaide tells it, Mary Magdalene was a married woman who, either because she divorced or her husband died, let herself become addicted to fun and parties, slipping thereby into prostitution (303). Sunk in the well of sin, but sensing that something was amiss in her life, she began to examine her conscience: "En cayendo en la cuenta, en comenzando la luz divina a deshacer aquellas tinieblas de su entendimiento, comienza a pensar en su mal estado, en la mala vida pasada, y avergonzarse y afrentarse de sí misma" (335a). She forthwith undertakes acts of penitence by becoming a slave to God (336), publicly confesses her sins (340), and asks for the Lord's pardon (341).

After many tears of remorse, she is able to "volver a desandar lo andado" (381b), like a Catholic Theseus, retracing her way back to her origin by remembering her creation from the dust of the earth: "El acordaros que sois lodo y que en lodo vais a parar, que en eso para todo cuanto acá buscáis, y en lodo pararán vuestros placeres, y en polvo acabaréis vos" (382a). This disillusionment leads to negation of the body's worth and rejection of all the world's comforts for a life of harsh penitential sacrifice in which are scorned fine foods, clothing, beds, gifts, friends, and conversation, but which ends in a union with the divine bridegroom explicitly equal to the one described so eloquently in the Song of Songs (406-07).

There is assuredly no Golden Age author who manipulated the Magdalena motif more than the Mercedarian friar Tirso de Molina (1581-1648), and the remainder of this chapter will present in detail the various manifestations of the motif in Tirso's theater. His drama

La ninfa del cielo illustrates perhaps the most detailed process of Magdalenian penitence in Spanish literature. The first two Acts of the play are to all appearances a typical *bandolera* drama. Ninfa, Countess of Valdeflor, goes hunting one day and meets a noble gentleman who has lost his way while pursuing his hawk. She takes him into her home and, overcome by an ardent passion, invites him into her bedchamber. The hunter seduces her and then flees on a passing ship, leaving Ninfa alone on the beach swearing to avenge the insult by becoming a public bandit.

In Act Two her seducer, whom the spectator learns is Carlos, Duke of Calabria and husband of the beautiful Diana, can't get Ninfa out of his mind and decides to go search for her. Ninfa, meanwhile, full of rage, exacts her cruel vengeance against the men whom she encounters in the forest. She meets Carlos, however, and the two again declare their passion for each other. They are then separated by the arrival of royal soldiers, and Ninfa finds herself alone at nightfall deep within the forest. The stages of her conversion begin.

She lies down to sleep and witnesses a Dance of Death in which she sees – acted out on stage – three dancers dressed as peasants whirl around a well, falling in one by one. She approaches the well and is shocked by the appearance of Death, who questions: "¿Qué buscas en el pozo de la muerte?" (1: 955b). The acute shock of this vision forces upon Ninfa a painful *examen de conciencia* concerning her past sins. She is suddenly aware that she has committed grave crimes against heaven and erroneously thinks she has been condemned: "No me puedo salvar, ya está cerrado / de mi sentencia el último proceso" (1: 955b). She rushes to throw herself from a cliff into the sea, but her guardian angel, who has been by her side since birth, appears to detain her, declaring that she isn't going to be a sea nymph, but a heavenly one.

In the third Act, Ninfa passes through the tortuous "dark night of the soul" (the entire Act transpires in darkness) in which she finds absolution for her sins and eventually achieves the ultimate state of grace and betrothal to Christ. The action is, therefore, more allegorical than literal, with the former increasingly dominant over the latter. This bi-partite representation is also seen in the contrapuntal disposition of scenes between Ninfa's penitence and search for Christ and the pursuit of Carlos for Ninfa. In effect, the two characters enter and leave the stage no less than five times before the final scene. Tirso thus skillfully dramatizes the spiritual world of Ninfa and her divine marriage with Christ in opposition to the terrestrial sphere of Carlos and his carnal love for the Countess.

The dramatization of Ninfa's conversion from sin to grace can be schematized as six distinct moments of action: 1) her repentence and desire for grace, 2) a divine embrace, assuring her of God's love, 3) the penitential washing of sins – as the Council of Trent noted, "Penance by the Holy Father hath been deservedly called a *Laborious kind of Baptism*" (*Council* 61) – and resultant confession and absolution, 4) the victory over death, 5) a momentary sense of abandonment, followed by the vision of Christ and assurance of betrothal, and 6) the climatic *hieros gamos*, taken from The Song of Songs.

Act Three opens on Ninfa, alone in the dark with her conscience. She heartily repents of her past sins, and begins to "desandar lo andado," as Malón de Chaide says, by stripping away the garments representative of her past life that have for so long hidden her from herself. "Como culebra quiero / para nueva vida renovarme" (1: 956a), she comments, utilizing the popular *topos* of the serpent sloughing the old skin to describe the transformation she will undergo. Interestingly, Malón de Chaide employs this very same imagery to describe the movement from nature to grace: "Dejando la vieja piel de la serpiente antigua, que es el hombre viejo, sale del pecado con otra nueva vestidura de *gracia*, y renovada, se goza con su amado" (386a).

Ninfa next comes on stage after crossing a river, and uses mystical language from Psalm 42 (41 in the Vulgate) to describe a *toque* she has experienced:

> Y como de amor me habéis
> herido, Señor, el alma,
> herida y llena de fuego
> vengo, como cierva al agua.
> (1: 959a)

As with the serpent, the wounded deer became a popular emblem in the mystical and aesthetic writings of the time, a typical example of which is the following exegesis by San Juan de la Cruz:

> Compárase el Esposo al ciervo, porque aquí por el ciervo entiende a sí mismo; y es de saber que la propiedad del ciervo es

subirse a los lugares altos, y cuando está herido vase con gran
priesa a buscar refrigerio a las aguas frías, y si oye quejar a la
consorte y siente que está herida, luego se va con ella y la regala y
acaricia; y así hace ahora el Esposo, porque, viendo a la Esposa
herida de su amor, él también al gemido de ella viene herido de
amor de ella. (*Cántico espiritual*, 166a)

Thus the image of the wounded deer not only illuminates the spiritual state of Ninfa's soul at the moment, but also foretells the coming of the Bridegroom to heal her wounds.

Ninfa calls at the entrance of the cave of a hermit, Anselmo, to ask for confession and absolution of sins. She explains to him that she has been guided there by the hand of God and has passed over the river to reach him. "Dame, Anselmo, la más fiera, / la más dura, la más rara / penitencia que mujer / haya hecho en carne humana," she asks him, "que me he ofendido mucho al cielo" (1: 960b). The saintly man is moved by her piety, and takes her into his cave.

Following a brief interruption of the forward progression of events by an encounter with Carlos, Ninfa enters dressed as a penitent with a heavy chain, a garment of animal skins, a hair shirt, a stone, and a skull to announce that she has received the holy eucharist from Anselmo and is now ready to live the life of a penitent hermit. A boatman enters and offers to help her cross the river, but then seizes her, swearing that she is still his slave and belongs to him; but her guardian angel again comes to her rescue, saving her from the clutches of the infernal boatman, who leaves swearing vengeance.

Ninfa next enters pleading in language from The Song of Songs that her beloved Husband not abandon her. It is a situation strongly reminiscent of her sense of abandonment when Carlos left her in the last moments of Act One, for Tirso artfully contrasts the human with the divine to prepare the spectator for the physical juxtaposition of Carlos to the Saviour that follows. As Ninfa calls to her celestial husband, Christ appears in a fountain and reassures her that they will soon be united. When she rushes to the water, however, she sees reflected there the features of Carlos, who has come out on a rock above the fountain. The modulative rhythm of scenes and events thus reaches its zenith in the absolute polarization of lovers earthly and divine. Although Carlos remains adamant in his passionate desire for Ninfa, she now belongs to another, and advises the Duke to look after his soul and to remedy his errant ways.

The climax of the drama begins when Carlos's wife Diana enters in search of her husband. She sees a movement in the brush and, thinking it is a deer, throws her javelin, mortally wounding Ninfa. In death, however, Ninfa encounters the grace of everlasting life, for Christ descends and literally grafts the regenerate Ninfa into his body, lifting her heavenward as his bride.

The drama of the Countess of Valdeflor thus ends at the opposite pole from which it began. Ninfa has progressed from the very human state of innocent nature to a celestial marriage with Christ parallel to the sacred marriage described in The Song of Songs (2: 10-13), for Cristo declares:

> Nuestras bodas se han llegado;
> vestido de boda espero;
> venid, hermosa paloma,
> que ya ha pasado el invierno,
> y en el inmortal Abril
> las flores aparecieron.
>
> (1: 970b)

She has also traced out the penitential way of Mary Magdalene as described by Malón de Chaide, especially the last moment of confession of sins, seeking and receiving Christ's pardon, abandonment of this world for a life of penitence, and a final marriage with the celestial bridegroom; for Malón de Chaide – who could very well have been a source for Tirso – also ended his book with Christ appearing to declare, "Ea levantaos, amiga mía, y dejad ya ese cuerpo mortal; ya es pasado el invierno, ya son acabados los trabajos de la vida, ya es llegada la primavera de la gloria, ya comienzan a florecer las viñas y a dar olor, ya se oye la voz de la tortolilla, que gime sobre el olmo" (407a).

Variations of this dramatic pattern of closure that Tirso utilized in *La ninfa del cielo* appear in a number of his other plays, with interesting results. The same structured universe displayed in Ninfa's fall, desire for revenge, conversion, and penitence is the sub-plot in *La dama del olivar*, a historical-religious drama about the miraculous events that led to the founding of a Mercedarian house in Estercuel, Aragón. The village girl Laurencia is supposed to marry Maroto, but decides to give her love to the noble Guillén, the village's comendador. Why Laurencia succumbs to Guillén is not clear, other than the fact that he is noble and she finds him attractive. After the seduction, however, Guillén gruffly abandons her, and – as did Ninfa – she vows to become a bandit. Shortly thereafter she captures Guillén and ties him to a tree, intending to return later to execute him. Fortunately for Guillén, he is freed by the brother of a noble woman he was supposed to marry (and eventually does), and the plot shifts to the so far unrelated theme of the miraculous appearance of the Virgin in an olive tree.

Laurencia does not appear in Act Three at all until the last scene, where, in an appropriate Counter Reformational closure, she enters to declare that a bright light and an angelic voice emanating from the miraculous olive tree opened her eyes to her sins, so that

> mis vicios dan hoy la vuelta.
> Yo os consagro, insigne imagen,
> mi vida, y desde hoy ordena,
> si en pecados la imité,
> en virtud ser Magdalena.
> (1: 1218b)

How many closures with an mimetic reference to Mary Magdalene can there be? In *Los lagos de san Vicente*, even the converted Moorish princess Casilda becomes a "Magdalena segunda penitente" (2: 49b), despite the fact that she committed no sins nor deviated from the pathway appropriate for her role in life. In *La madrina del cielo*, Dionisio brutally rapes the pious Marcela and then abandons her. She swears to punish him, but his devotion to the rosary causes the Virgin to protect him and to send his guardian angel to fight for his salvation. Dionisio, in the interim, has dressed *con un saco de penitente* in which he wishes to emulate "la desnudez de una Santa Magdalena" (1: 501b). He accomplishes his purpose, for in the following scene *Córrese otra cortina y aparece Dionisio desnudo, salpicado de sangre y una deceplina en la mano con sangre, y alrededor del cuello una soga* (1: 564a). Under these circumstances, Marcela forgives Dionisio and the two become man and wife, with the Virgin serving as godmother.

Tirso's trilogy *Santa Juana*, detailing the life of Juana de la Cruz, a sixteenth-century Madrid nun famous for her prophecies and miracles, has a number of secular sub-plots that close on a religious note. The relationship between Jorge and Mari Pascuala in the second play repeats the Magdalena pattern. Jorge seduces the young village girl and then abandons her. In desperation, she starts to hang herself, but a divine being appears – Santa Juana herself – to tell her that God is merciful and will not punish her if she repents: "Quien perdonó a Magdalena / te perdonará, María, / pues es su misericordia / como entonces, infinita" (854a). Mari Pascuala then delivers in an eloquent soliloquy a general confession of her sins and determines to become a nun in Santa Juana's convent, trusting that God will forgive her: "Confieso y tengo por fe / que a un 'pequé' del alma, olvida / Dios infinitas ofensas" (1: 854b).

It is interesting that Tirso de Molina makes no real distinction between men and women when it comes to falling into sin, recognizing one's error, and seeking divine forgiveness through penitence. Both sexes can participate in the pattern indiscriminately, as Dionisio's case shows. Likewise, the conversions of the men can be just as sudden and eye-opening as those of the women, for which examples abound. Dionisio is awakened to his sinful state by divine music that reminds him of this world's deceits (1: 557b). Bruno in *El mayor desengaño* is awakened by witnessing the momentary resurrection of the supposedly holy Dión, who announces his residence in Hell. Jorge in *Santa Juana II*, Lelio in *Quien no cae no se levanta*, and Guillén in *La dama del olivar* are also pursuaded to change their lives by witnessing the miraculous events that cleanse the women they seduced.

There are three other men in Tirso's theater, however, who participate in a biblical structure which is generally unavailable to the women. In *Los lagos de san Vicente*, the Moor Ali Petrán sets off to avenge an insult by devastating Christian villages, but is stopped when a fig tree opens and the Virgin Mary appears, informing him that he has been chosen to be "un Saulo segundo" (2: 45b) to serve her as a Christian. In *Santa Juana III*, Juana de la Cruz prays to the baby Jesus to help her convert the picaresque Luis, who has seduced Inés by pretending to be her fiancé Diego. Baby Jesus doesn't want to pardon the young man because Luis was disobedient to his father, but Juana promises that "si Vos le reducís / tendréis un Saulo segundo" (1: 895b); so Jesus promises: "Yo haré que, cual Saulo, / si a la virtud hace guerra, / caiga Don Luis en tierra / y imite después a Paulo" (1: 895b). It is needless to say that Luis, like Dionisio in *La madrina del cielo*, changes his ways and marries the dishonored Inés.

Finally, in Tirso's *El condenado por desconfiado*, the imprisoned Enrico, the worst scoundrel in all of Naples, refuses to repent of his many crimes and to confess his sins. His father Anareto then enters the prison cell to tell him that if he remains disobedient to his father and obstinate about his sins, then he will disavow him as a son. Enrico immediately changes his ways and declares, as have all of Tirso's other converts: "Confieso, padre, que erré; / pero yo confesaré / mis pecados, y después / besaré a todos los pies, / para mostraros mi fe" (2: 496b). He is executed for his crimes, but he is saved because he confessed his sins and took communion before he death, for angels bear his soul to heaven in plain sight of the spectators, testifying thereby to the efficacy of someone humbly repenting, confessing, and begging for God's mercy, which is infinite. The father Anareto thus functions in this play as a human proxy for the divine mediator who appears to Tirso's other Saul-like sinners. As will be explained later in this chapter, those who are not saved, such as Paulo in this play, Don Juan in *El burlador de Sevilla*, and Doroteo in *La madrina del cielo*, are the hard-headed men who disobey their father's wishes and obstinately refuse to recognize the authority of supreme beings over their lives.

Many of the variations of the dramatic pattern of conversion at closure that Tirso utilized in *La ninfa del cielo*, *El condenado por desconfiado*, and the other plays are brought together in *Quien no cae no se levanta*. While Ninfa was an isolated female with repressed desires that erupted suddenly out of control, Margarita is a complicated young woman whose character Tirso analyzes from multiple perspectives by dedicating the first half of Act One to a litany of reasons for her rebellious nature. She is an only child whom her father loves excessively and with whom her deceased mother was too permissive. In fact, Tirso leads the spectator to believe that Margarita's mother is being punished in the afterlife for her leniency, as an angelic voice will later inform the young girl (3: 866b). Margarita also resents her father's attempts to discipline her, calling him a dog in the manger who won't allow her to do what he and her mother did when they were young (3: 849a) and who wants her to live the same sterile, toothless existence he now lives. Finally, Tirso presents Margarita as a genuinely undisciplined girl full of curiosity who is always leaning out of the window ogling the street life, and who follows her inclinations and sees nothing wrong with wanting to try everything once. "En todo quiero picar" (3: 853a), she tells her servant; and one of the things that most interests her is love, because she has read about it in the many fictions – specifically Boccaccio's novels, Ariosto's *Orlando furioso*, and the works of Petrarch (3: 847a) – with which she occupied her time rather than the more appropriate prayer books and spiritual exercises.

These reasons incline Margarita to try to run away with her lover Valerio in Act One, then to attempt to have an affair with Lelio – a married man who beats his wife and injures his father-in-law – in Act Two. But Margarita has a divine friend who, as the angel did with Ninfa, desires to save her from a life of sin. Precisely in the middle of Act Two, as she is preparing to go to meet Lelio, she hears an angelic voice that warns her of her sinful state and offers her another lover, who was killed for her sake, and a rosary of precious mysteries. Margarita ignores this divine counsel, however, and goes to a church to meet her lover. While awaiting his arrival, she hears a sermon by fray Domingo de Guzmán, and his words do convince her to convert to the pious life. Nevertheless, after a year of piety through devotion to the rosary, she again succumbs to her passion for Lelio. When she gets out of the bed in which they have consummated their love, however, she falls. Interpreting it as a "caída en la cuenta" (3: 887b), she determines to stay and maintain her honor; but Lelio calls and she starts to leave with him, only to fall again, and a third time. At this point her guardian angel appears to remind her "que Dios en su gracia no niega / al que hace lo que es en sí" (3: 889b), and offers his help so she won't ever fall again. *Tire una cadena y esté el Ángel acostado en una cama* (3: 889b).

If Tirso described Ninfa's salvation as a divine wedding of two lovers, here he dramatizes the consummation itself and ties the sacred marriage motif directly to the Mary Magdalene type of sin-conversion-grace program. Evoking again passages from The Song of Songs, the angel invites Margarita to share his bed among the jazmines and roses. *Sube desde la cama el Ángel al cielo y lleva consigo a Margarita* (3: 890a). All the other characters now come on stage and are made aware of Margarita's salvation by a final discovery: *Descubren un jardín arriba con muchas rosas y en él, echada, a Margarita, sueltos los cabellos, con un Cristo,* COMO PINTAN A LA MAGDALENA, *los ojos en el cielo* (3: 891a). The moral drawn from her life is clear:

> No desespere el caído
> que, aunque más pecados tenga,
> quien no cae no se levanta,
> Margarita ejemplo sea.
>
> (3: 892a)

The uniformity of all these plays is simply astounding, for they present the same basic pattern of events, dramatizing some form of disobedience, which leads to sin, but which is curtailed by a divine intervention that awakens the sinner to the past life of sin and causes a conversion to godliness consisting of a confession of sins and acts of penance to atone for them. All of the sinners are saved, and the other participants in the plays – as well as the spectators – receive an eye-opening assurance of the sinner's salvation by witnessing some kind of visual apparatus at the closure. Moreover, in the three cases of Paulo in *El condenado por desconfiado*, Juan in *El burlador de Sevilla*, and Dión in *El mayor desengaño*, where the sinner will be condemned to Hell, the spectator will witness the incineration of the body on stage.

In fact, every one of Tirso's religiously oriented plays closes with the elevation or the exposition of a saintly person by means of stage machinery. The purpose of the scene is to assure the viewers that there has been a divine recognition of the saintly person's actions. N. D. Shergold called these moments "discoveries" (202), and they certainly function in that way. Sebastián de Covarrubias used the term *apariencias* in his 1603 dictionary, describing them as "ciertas representaciones mudas, que corrida una cortina, se muestran al pueblo y luego se buelvan a cubrir; del verbo *apparso*" (130). Another popular term was *tramoya*, which Tirso used in his plays to describe moments when people would appear as if by magic on stage (see *Mari-Hernández la gallega* 2: 70a). Both terms were closely associated with saint's plays, as the contemporary author Agustín de Rojas noted in a poetic history of the genre: "Llegó el tiempo que se usaron / las comedias de apariencias, / de santos y de tramoyas" (223). In effect, Tirso's thirteen saint's plays *La joya de las montañas*, the three *Santa Juana* plays, *La ninfa del cielo*, *El condenado por desconfiado*, *Quien no cae no se levanta*, *Santo y sastre*, *La elección por la virtud*, *Los lagos de san Vicente*, *Doña Beatriz de Silva*, *El mayor desengaño*, and *El caballero de Gracia* close with some kind of *tramoya* or *apariencia*.

Also, Tirso's religiously oriented historical plays *La dama del olivar*, *La peña de Francia*, *El árbol de mejor fruto*, and *Las quinas de Portugal*, which Blanca de los Ríos appropriately called "comedias historicorreligiosas" (3: 1319), all dramatize at the close a moment of discovery that provokes the veneration of a miraculous image. These plays form a genre of their own that could be called *comedias de apariencias milagrosas*. They aren't specifically *comedias de santos* because they dramatize the appearance of a holy image rather than the actions of a saint and they have a historical foundation related to a Spanish theme. As will be demonstrated in the next chapter, they are exceptional examples of Counter Reformational closure, because they ingeniously interweave a secular history with a religious component that promotes veneration of holy images. The action of the plays effectively proves thereby the historical validity of the images and the experiential veracity of their efficacy to advance a person's way to salvation.

A good encapsulation of all the conversion motifs used by Tirso de Molina is Antonio Mira de Amescua's *El esclavo del demonio*, which presents a complete exposition of the Magdalene type in Lisarda and the Saul type in don Gil Núñez de Atoquía, with various *tramoyas* and *apariencias* to vivify the miraculous ways God has at His disposal to advertise the outcomes people can expect from lives dedicated to acts of penitence.

The saintly Gil succumbs to the desires of the flesh and seduces Lisarda under the guise of her lover Diego de Meneses. Believing that his actions show him to be predestined to damnation, Gil becomes a bandit and, willing to give anything to seduce Lisarda's sister Leonor, sells his soul to the devil. Rather than receiving the real Leonor, however, he gets a skeleton. At the same moment that he realizes life's pleasures are not just brief but also lies, he hears an angelic voice warning "hombre, ¡ay, hombre pecador! / tu vida me da molestia, / muda la vida" (vv. 2746-48). Gil immediately undergoes a radical change of mind and proclaims: "Líbrame, Señor, de mí; / y seré en buscaros Pablo / si Pedro en negaros fui" (vv. 2753-55). A celestial battle then takes place for Gil's soul (similar to the one between Virtud and Vicio in Tirso's *La madrina del cielo*), in which his guardian angel defeats the devil and advises him:

> Pues la suma omnipotencia
> del cielo te ha rescatado,
> vive, Gil, con advertencia:
> pues asombró tu pecado,
> asombre tu penitencia.
>
> (vv. 2871-75)

So the next time the spectator sees the converted sinner at the end of the play he is *con un saco de penitencia, una soga a la garganta*, announcing his intention to join the Dominican order to serve the Lord.

Lisarda follows the same path as the many Magdalene types in Tirso's plays. In outspoken defiance of her father Marcelo's express wishes, she plans to let Diego de Meneses into her room to consummate their love for each other. Gil enters instead, and tells her Diego let him seduce her as a cruel trick. Swearing vengeance on Diego, Lisarda joins Gil in a life of violence and banditry. She is taken aback, however, when Gil sells his soul to the devil, and begins to consider the weight of her sins (vv. 1549-52). Shortly thereafter, although now deeply examining her conscience about the brevity of life's pleasures, she comes upon Diego and attempts to shoot him with her pistol. It misfires, and Lisarda realizes fully that her life is misdirected. Swearing to do penance for her sins, she releases Diego, aids a distraught girl – "que si esta ha sido Marta / yo puedo ser Magdalena" (vv. 2096-97) – and sells herself as a slave to her own father to help a poor old man with two sons because only thus can she undo the crimes of disobedience against Marcelo: "Perdíme no obedeciendo, / y he de ganarme obediente" (vv. 2134-35).

In the play's last scene, Gil informs everyone of Lisarda's penitence, declaring that she died of her miseries, although pardoned by God and absolved of her pain: "María la pecadora / la llamad; tal nombre tenga" (vv. 3185-88). *Descúbrese Lisarda con música, muerta, de rodillas, con un Cristo y una calavera, en el jardín*.

All these plays visualize the same closing moment quite simply because they all have the same message of salvation through submission – both physical and spiritual – to divine authority. It is the one truly important tenet of the Counter Reformation because it assures loyalty to Catholic Christianity through obedience and service. The obedience is demonstrated through faithful acknowledgement of the Catholic apparatus of divine mediators, who fortunately are ready and eager to work with the sinner for the salvation of the soul. The service is through acts of penitence, by which one shows the completely voluntary resolve necessary for winning divine forgiveness, which will always come from the merciful Lord who magnanimously recognizes even the slightest truly heartfelt act of contrition as sufficient for His pardon.

God's mercy is so easy to attain, in fact, that good Catholics must wonder how anyone ever gets condemned to Hell; yet many do. The Bible records the condemnation of a rich man for not attending properly to the poor (Luke 16: 19-31), and Tirso faithfully presented his damnation in *Tanto es lo de más como lo de menos,* where Nineucio appears *sentado a una mesa, abrasándose, y muchos platos echando de los manjares llamas* (1: 1153a), condemned to participate eternally in a fiery inversion of the divine meal because in life he was a "mísero avariento" (1: 1153b). Dión in *El mayor desengaño* was considered by all to be a saint whose soul would fly directly to heaven; but when he died his soul was placed in judgment by God and found wanting. The spectators learn that before his death Dión had proudly declared that he would not need God's mercy to enter heaven because his own virtue and patience had already merited his salvation; "y quien fía de sí tanto, / que por santo se averigua, / condenarse no es milagro" (2: 1222b). Doroteo in *La madrina del cielo* was condemned forthwith by Christ for being "un hombre remoto, / gran pecador y atrevido" (1: 559b). Doroteo appealed his case to the Virgin as his intercessor, but she gruffly responded: "Cuando tuviste lugar / no gozaste la ocasión" (1: 559b).

These are the same last words directed to don Juan Tenorio in *El burlador de Sevilla* when he pleads for a moment to confess his sins and receive absolution: "No hay lugar; ya acuerdas tarde" (2: 684b). Don Juan, like Doroteo, had his chances. Everyone he encountered during his dramatic life warned him in one way or another that his destructive actions would eventually condemn him. Don Pedro begins a litany of admonitions when he exclaims "¡Castígate el cielo, amén!" (2: 636a) in the first scene. Catalinón warns him later in the Act that death is the payment for those who deceive women as Juan does; but the trickster glibly responds: "¡Qué largo me lo fiáis!" (1: 648b). The essence of this motto is that the young man believes that he has a long time to repent before his death. Don Juan knows that salvation depends on an examination of conscience, a true sense of contrition, confession of sins, and acts of penitence; but he thinks that he can sin as much as he wishes during his youth and change his ways to live a life worthy of divine forgiveness in old age. Theologically, this is the height of blasphemy, because Juan – unlike Dión, who believed that he did not need God's mercy – believes he can manipulate God's mercy.

Another theological component of "¡tan largo me lo fiáis!" is its rejection of the notion of *memento mori* (hence the importance of the statue's comment "ya *acuerdas* tarde"). All traditional Christian theology is based on the doctrine that death comes suddenly because it is part of God's indecipherable plan for each person, so a pious person should be constantly prepared to undergo God's judgment. A good Catholic should therefore always be as thoroughly absolved from sin as is possible through regular confessions of sins and subsequent acts of penitence, and the best way to remain aware of the transitoriness of life on earth is the contemplation of death. Don Juan does precisely the opposite, thinking only in worldly terms.

Another aspect of the rogue's character is that he flatly refuses to consider his dependence on a divine creator, a concept referred to in Catholic dogma as *memoria Dei*. If Juan were to ponder correctly his own creatureliness and subordination to a higher creative authority, he would not attempt to create his own universe of action in the terrestrial sphere.

Both *memento mori* and *memoria Dei*, the doctrines that Juan ignores, have to do with the memory. Don Juan is characterized by a supreme intelligence, one so brilliant that he can seduce and deceive all those with whom he comes in contact. He also has a frightfully powerful will, for he can and does do anything he desires; and it becomes increasingly apparent throughout the play that no mere mortal can stop him. His powerful will and intellect serve him no good for salvation, however, if his memory is blank. Don Juan simply refuses to think about the women he has beguiled or the men he has deceived, moving methodically from one trick to the next without any thought to what he has done or to what the consequences may be. At the drama's close, the stone guest will painfully remind him of all these things, but Juan will not get an opportunity to change his ways precisely because he was given so many opportunities to repent beforehand. Tisbea warned him at the end of Act One that God punishes those who break their word (2: 649b). In

Act Two Don Juan's father stated explicitly his son's blasphemous sins:

> Mira que aunque al parecer
> Dios te consiente y aguarda,
> su castigo ha de haber
> para los que profanáis
> su nombre, que es juez fuerte
> Dios en la muerte.
>
> (2: 658b)

The rogue scoffs at these warnings, as he does also at those of Gonzalo de Ulloa (2: 661b), Catalinón (2: 669a), and Aminta (2: 670b).

The final admonitions come in the form of divine manifestations in the famous two-part format of banquets, which has fascinated artists and critics for centuries. In the initial meeting between the stone statue and the rogue, the Comendador could have easily taken Juan to Hell when he grasped his hand; but Tirso delayed the punishing execution for a second meeting. He could have done so because he was following so faithfully the Spanish versions of the legend (which with but one exception have the double-invitation motif) that it never occurred to him to write the drama otherwise. It may also be that Tirso desired to increase the dramatic effect of the encounter between Juan and the stone guest by bringing them together twice rather than once. The most justifiable explanation for including the double-invitation motif, however, is that, for theological reasons, Tirso wanted to show that his protagonist receives every possible chance to acknowledge the power of God and the supernatural before being condemned to Hell. If God were punishing Juan solely for seducing four women, murdering Gonzalo de Ulloa, and desecrating a graveyard, he would have taken him away at the first meeting, as Doroteo was whisked away without a second chance in *La madrina del cielo*. The utilization of the second encounter illustrates that Tirso wanted his audience here to see that God condemns Juan for the youth's mindless refusal to recognize God's power and authority, which were made astonishingly clear to him by the arrival at his home of an animated stone statue. In this play, in other words, Tirso presents a God who makes sure that Juan receives every possible opportunity to repent of his sins, assuring thereby the conviction by the spectators that Juan is wholly responsible for his own destiny and is in no way destined to Hell by exterior forces.

Paulo in *El condenado por desconfiado* is not condemned for ignoring death's arbitrariness and God's sense of justice, as was Juan; nor is he guilty of depending wholly on his own merits for salvation, as was Dión in *El mayor desengaño*. Paulo's problem, as R. J. Oakley has noted, is simply that he loses confidence in God's infinite capacity to forgive and thereby throws away his many chances for salvation; for, like Juan Tenorio, the hermit-turned-bandit is given every possible opportunity to repent, and foolishly rejects them all. In fact, the very postulate of the play is an opportunity for Paulo to wake up to the presumption of his questioning God about his destiny. The Devil enters to inform the spectator that God is offended by Paulo's lack of faith, pride and mistrust, but has decided to give Paulo a chance to show his true worth by allowing the Devil to test him. "Sepa resistir valiente / los combates que le ofrezco" (2: 457a), comments the Devil before initiating his efforts to trick Paulo into believing he will somehow have the same end as Enrico.

The Devil is not allowed to function without a competitor, however, so in Act Two God sends a Pastorcillo to speak to Paulo about God's infinite love and mercy, which are open to all, regardless of their past sins: "Esta es su misericordia; / que con decirle al Señor: / *pequé, pequé*, muchas veces, / le recibe al pecador / en sus amorosos brazos" (2: 480a). The hermit listens attentively, contemplates what he has been told, and actually understands what he has heard, but then rejects outright that a person as sinful as Enrico could every be pardoned by God. Paulo doesn't even listen to Enrico himself in the next scene when the ruffian informs him that despite his sins he believes that God could forgive him, since "tengo confianza / en su piedad, porque siempre / vence a su justicia sacra" (2: 487a).

Paulo receives a more specific visit by the Pastorillo in Act Three, who again does everything possible to convince the bandit of God's readiness to forgive all those who confess and repent of their past sinful lives, but to no avail. Even the miraculous vision of angels lifting a soul to heaven and Pedrisco's informing him that Enrico won God's pardon by his pious acts of contrition before the execution fail to sway Paulo, who obstinately sticks to his foolish belief that God would never pardon someone as wicked as was Enrico. Like his overconfident counterpart in *El burlador de Sevilla*, who was also given every possible opportunity to see the error of his ways, Paulo's lack of confidence gains him the eternal fires of Hell: *Húndese, y sale fuego de la tierra* (2: 503a).

The aggressively violent nature of these conversions and condemnations in Tirso's theater are characteristic of Counter Reformational closure during the crucial period from 1580 to 1620. Afterwards, as noted in Chapter Two of this study, the sharp edge of physical penitence began to disappear, and by mid-century the conversion model for closure had lost its initial sense of an opportunity to atone for sins to take on more of a social function as a personally-motivated voluntary decision to live outside the typical family-oriented Spanish social structure.

Perhaps the best example of this shift in literary closures is the corpus of courtly novelettes by María de Zayas y Sotomayor (1590-166?). Her first book of ten tales, titled *Novelas amorosas y ejemplares* (1637), has three stories that end with a religious closure by conversion in which a woman who has been mistreated or jilted by a man seeks a better, more comfortable life in the convent: "Aventurarse perdiendo," "El prevenido engañado," and "La fuerza de amor." In all these cases, the women make personal decisions unmotivated by religious fervor to voluntarily enter a convent. Moreover, their move is facilitated by their bringing along maids and lots of money. The result of their voluntary conversions to the religious life therefore is of only social importance, assuring that the three women will have a happier and safer life than the one experienced in their relationships with men.

The same convent closure can also be employed in a callous, misogynous vein. The courtly tale "Quien todo lo quiere, todo lo pierde" by Alonso Castillo Solórzano (1584-1648), incorporated into the novel *La garduña de Sevilla* (1642), presents the Valencian socialite Isabel who tries to maintain two fiancés at the same time, in case one of the gallants should change his mind about marrying her. Unfortunately, the men discover what is going on and leave her for other brides. Isabel, feeling herself dishonored by these events, enters the Royal Monastery of Zaydía, cursing her bad luck, while in the community "atribuyeron todos esto, no a lo que pasó, sino a que Dios tiene muchos caminos por donde llama a los suyos" (88). So the hypocritical young lady who unsuccessfully deceived the two man successfully deceives the entire city of Valencia. They assume she underwent the kind of religious conversion narrated so often in

Spain's early seventeenth-century literature, but the reader knows her decision was exclusively a social one prompted by her failure at maintaining simultaneously two fiancés.

María de Zayas and Alonso Castillo thus utilize the convent in the same way as a social alternative, but Zayas reverses the roles of her protagonists so that the convent becomes a refuge from the cruel persecutions by brutal men rather than a punishment for immoral actions against men. The tales in Zayas's second book, titled *Desengaños amorosos* (1647), are eye-opening love tragedies, as the title indicates. Four end with the murder of the female protagonist, while the other six use religious closure by conversion to separate socially the persecuted female from the world of treacherous men. "La esclava de su amante" is a good example of how María de Zayas manipulates a Counter Reformation motif now empty of its original force, for the tale is a global socialization of literary themes. Isabel participates in a series of adventures that come from earlier fiction models which in their original context often had moral, religious, or cultural significance but now serve only to advance the storyline. She is raped by Manuel, but decides to forgive him because he claims to love her. He abandons her to go to Sicily, and she disguises herself as a slave to follow him. They are captured by Moors, but an Algerian princess falls in love with Manuel and escapes with him and Isabel to Zaragoza. There, Manuel again tries to abandon Isabel to marry the Moorish princess, but Felipe, a poor servant who is also in love with Isabel, kills him. Isabel then decides to enter a convent to become a slave to God, whom she is sure will be a more faithful companion.

There is no indication anywhere in this courtly novelette that Isabel has any inkling of piety, religious fervor, awareness of the state of her soul, contrition, or repentance. Her decision to become a nun is a social one motivated by social circumstances and serving the social end of establishing a proper social closure to her turbulent life in a way socially acceptable and appropriate for a lady of her social status. Her only real concern about her decision is therefore not the acts of penitence she may wish to undergo as a nun but rather the money she needs to get into a socially agreeable convent. She tells her friend Lisis that "en mis joyas me parece tendré para cumplir el dote y los demás gastos" (65), and Lisis assures her that "si las joyas que decís tenéis no bastaren, os podéis servir de las mías, y de cuanto yo valgo y tengo" (65-66).

"La más infame venganza," "La inocencia castigada," "Amar sólo por vencer," "Engaños que causa el vicio," and "La perseguida triunfante" all proffer the same utilization of the convent as a place for social reclusion rather than for pious service and penitence. With the possible exception of Beatriz in "La perseguida triunfante," which is the only truly religious tale of the lot, the characters in these novels are no longer Counter Reformation protagonists, nor is the closure of their histories part of the sincere Counter Reformation mentality. By the 1630s, what had earlier been a serious literary technique to direct the reader towards a specific religious posture has become a mechanical technique for ending courtly tales about women who seek a safe haven from the hazardous masculine world. The earlier aggressive imposition of certain religious structural models – in this case the model for closure on a religious note of humbly obedient contrition that initiates a desire to withdraw from the secular world to a life of devout penitence – was so successful that by the next generation those models can be used as options in a purely social setting. The Church had truly accomplished its goal of appropriating to itself responsibility for all the important functions of a citizen's life.

CHAPTER SIX

CONVERTING HISTORY

One thing about which Counter Reformational fiction writers had no qualms was the manipulation of facts to adjust a historical person's life to the Counter Reformation technique of closure with a conversion. This chapter will examine in some detail three "historical" *comedias* in which the author conscientiously adjusted historical material about one of the peninsula's national heroes to include towards the end of the play a Counter Reformational conversion that – within the context of the dramatized events – appears to be the causal impulse for that character's later heroic feats of conquest against the infidel Moors. Moreover, the historical figure was adjusted in each case to fit the career of the greatest religious hero, the biblical David.

Las mocedades del Cid by Guillén de Castro y Bellvis (1569-1631) is a rigorously historical play in the sense that Castro believed that the source materials in the chronicles he followed so closely were factual. Furthermore, he added a strong sense of historical authority to his play by incorporating many old ballads directly into the dialogue.

The only scene in the play which is entirely of Castro's own invention, in fact, is the first one in which Rodrigo is made a knight. It is a highly visual moment, presenting the spectator with what Hesse and McCrary called a *forma simbológica*, "un modo visual de ser o posición física, una representación plástica muy análoga a la pantomima" (1), that transmits the idea of the action through the visual apparatus. What the spectator sees as the curtain rises on *Las Mocedades del Cid* is the entire cast on stage in various pairs, with King Ferdinand I "el Grande" standing in front of an altar of Santiago but facing Rodrigo, who is kneeling before him. The rest of the cast occupies the sides of the stage: Urraca and Jimena, Sancho and the queen mother, Count Lozano and Peransules, Diego Laínez and Arias Gonzalo. The choreography thus creates three distinct levels. On the first and lowest plane is the kneeling Rodrigo Díaz, member of the Vivar family whose *padre* Diego Laínez stands beside him. On the next plane stands Ferdinand, king of Castilla and *padrino* of the young Rodrigo, flanked by his wife and nobles. On a third, higher plane is the altar of Santiago Matamoros, Spain's great *santo patrón* whose mission is to protect the Christian faithful from the infidel Moors. The three levels thus represent social-geographical planes (Vivar, Castilla, Christendom) and political-military planes (Rodrigo defender of his family, Fernando defender of Castilla, Santiago defender of Christianity).

It is this visual moment of Castro's own construction which encapsulates the three separate plots that alternate on the stage throughout the play: the individual efforts of Rodrigo first to defend his family and then to win the hand of Ximena, the corporate efforts of King Ferdinand to resolve the problem of his succession, and the cosmic role that Santiago plays to assure the Christian reconquest.

In the first Act, Rodrigo's family problems dominate the stage, but by Act Two the second plot begins to encroach on the youth's personal career, to become the only unresolved dilemma by the end of the play. The third "Santiago" plot reaches the dramatic foreground in three specific moments of investiture. The first is the initial nucleus of the entire cast with the altar of the patron saint. The second occurs towards the end of Act Two when Rodrigo enters to present his king with the Moorish kings he has captured. Interestingly, the entire cast is again on stage, with the sole exception of the defunct Conde Lozano. Rodrigo kneels before the king (*Arrodíllase delante el Rey*), but this time Ferdinand comes forward and raises the "famoso Godo" (v. 1687) to his feet. Then the captive Moorish king comes forward and kneels before the warrior, exclaiming "¡Gran Rodrigo! ... / ... ¡el Mió Cide!" (vv. 1693-94), causing the amazed Castilian king to declare: "Llamalle 'el Cid' es razón, / y añadirá, porque asombre, / a su apellido este nombre / y a su fama este blasón" (vv. 1709-12). The young man thus passes from being a member of the Gothic race to being the knight named Rodrigo to being "el Cid," an epithet which by royal decree becomes a part of his name. He has thus moved from an equivalency with his brothers to an equivalency with the king, visualized in the action on stage when Ferdinand raises the youth to his feet and then witnesses another king kneel before the young warrior as if Rodrigo were the king.

The third moment is also a visual event. Halfway through Act Three, Rodrigo enters with his soldiers. They have just made a pilgrimage to Santiago de Compostela and, giving thanks "a nuestro Santo español" (v. 2138), they sit down to eat. A shepherd who is with them mocks Rodrigo for his devoutness, but the hero responds that "el ser Cristiano / no impide el ser Cavallero" (vv. 2165-66) because a well-intentioned soldier can become a "galán divino" (v. 2188).

The following moment in which Rodrigo willingly helps the repulsive leper out of a pit and lets him eat from his own plate is a visual projection of his unusual double role, as the leper affirms: "Todo es menester, Rodrigo: / matar allá al enemigo, / y valer aquí el hermano" (vv. 2218-19). Rodrigo then falls asleep, and the leper proclaims him "¡Oh, gran Cid! ¡Oh, gran Rodrigo! / ¡Oh, gran Capitán Cristiano!" (vv. 2302-03). *El Gafo aliéntale por las espaldas, y desaparécese; y el Cid váyase despertando a espacio, por que tenga tiempo de vestirse el Gafo de San Lázaro.*

It should come as no surprise that Castro substitutes here Religion for Humanism in the famous Renaissance debate concerning the active life of Arms and the contemplative life of Letters. One of the Counter Reformation's initial challenges was precisely to incorporate secular life into the Church's realm of authority, so Castro's conversion of Letters to Religion is not at all remarkable. What is remarkable, however, is that the scene is rigorously historical. The events as they appear in the *Crónica rimada del Cid*, one of the earliest documents that attempts to organize the various legends about the Cid into a coherent biography, are as follows.

After Rodrigo marries Ximena to resolve the conflict between their families, the warrior promises to win five battles before consummating the marriage (which pertains best to Castro's Act Two). He then wins one battle against the Arabs and returns to Burgos to learn that Martín González has challenged Fernando to a duel over the rights to Calahorra and Tudela. Rodrigo promises to defend Castilla for the king, but first asks permission to visit the shrines of Santiago de Compostela and Sta. María de Rocamador. On his return, he meets a *malato*, whom he helps cross a stream and covers with his green raincoat.

> E en siendo dormiendo, a la oreja le fabló el gapho:
> "¿Dormides, Rodrigo de Bivar? tiempo has de ser acordado.
> Mensagero so de Christos, que non soy malato.
> Sant Lasaro so, a ti me ovo Dios enbiado,
> que te dé un resollo en las espaldas, que en calentura seas tornado;
> que quando esta calentura ovieres, que te sea menbrado
> quantas cossas comensares, arrematarlas con tu mano."
> Diól un rresollo en las espaldas que a los pechos le ha passado.
> (vv. 569-77)

Rodrigo awakens and, without comment, proceeds to Calahorra where he defeats and beheads Martín González. Then comes the investiture of Ferdinand as a knight of Santiago in Zamora (reminiscent of Castro's first scene in Act One), and the battle of San Esteban against the five Moorish kings (dramatized in Castro's Act Two).

Castro thus respects dutifully the historical events in Rodrigo's life, but he shifts their order of occurrence to form progressive thematic groups under the three headings of Rodrigo-Ximena-family, Cid-Moors-country, "Capitán Cristiano"-Santiago-Christianity. Whereas the medieval chronicler simply put the events in the order in which they came, our seventeenth-century dramatist organized them ingeniously so that personal events come first, then national ones, then spiritual ones for closure. Furthermore, the duel with Martín González over Calahorra and Tudela is in precisely the same order in the *Crónica rimada* as in *Las mocedades del Cid*; but Castro – who has decided to make it the closing event in his play – charges the duel with biblical significance by equating it with the David and Goliath episode narrated in First Samuel (1 Regum) 17. Frank Casa considers this Rodrigo//David analogy "the major metaphor of the play" (8), and Russell Sebold claims it is the key to Castro's "new" Counter Reformation vision of Spain's national hero: "Decir *David* a secas equivalía en la época de Castro a decir desprecio de lo mundano, angustia ante la muerte, desconfianza de sí, caridad con los afligidos y lucha penosa por arribar a la gloria, así decir en España en esta época que Rodrigo era como otro David, casi bastaba para la revalorización del carácter del guerrero español que Castro quería efectuar" (233).

Guillén de Castro thus follows closely the order of historical events, but by injecting references to David and Goliath he creates the notion that Rodrigo can defeat the Navarran giant and save his people because he has been infused with divine power by God through St. Lazarus precisely the same way that little David defeated Goliath because he had been anointed by God through Samuel (1 Sam. 16) as Israel's savior. In both the *Crónica rimada* and the Bible the consecrations took place towards the beginning of the hero's career; but the Counter Reformational Castro relocates it as a closure, a culmination of ascending events that began on the level of the basic passions and ended in the heavens. The last investiture in which Rodrigo recieves an infusion of the Holy Spirit is thereby the confirmation of the opening scene's tri-partite nucleus exhibited *da sotto in su*, for it lifts the knight Rodrigo who defended his family name in Act One and then his country in Act Two – for which he received the second name of "el Cid" – to the level of Christian Captain, the name given to him on the divine level.

Las mocedades del Cid catholicizes Spain's epic hero by adjusting the historical facts regarding Rodrigo de Vivar's life to a tripartite ascension that culminates in the young man's Davidic sanctification. Lope de Vega's *Las paces de los reyes y judía de Toledo*, on the other hand, will adjust the historical events in the life of Alfonso VIII to a later episode in David's career (2 Sam. 11-12). Alfonso VIII will act out the same disastrous errors with the Jewess Raquel as did his biblical type with Bath-sheba; Alfonso will only see his errancy when a divine messenger shocks him into admitting his error, as David was reprimanded by Nathan; and Alfonso will be punished by the death of his only son, as David was also punished by the loss of Bath-sheba's firstborn.

The play dramatizes two distinct events that occurred in 1168 and 1186 to Alfonso VIII (1155-1214), the famous warrior king who suffered a tremendous defeat against the Moors at Alarcos in 1195, but then achieved the most important victory of the Reconquest in 1212 at Las Navas de Tolosa. The first Act presents the entrance of young Alfonso into Toledo and his taking of the castle of Zurita from Lope de Arenas. All the action is rigorously historical, copied at times word for word from the *Crónica general*, which, according to Marcelino Menéndez Pelayo, served as Lope's source, although the dramatist could have used the material in Chapter X of

Juan de Mariana's *Historia de España* just as well. The only moments in Act One not historical are the investiture of Alfonso before the altar of Santiago in Toledo's Iglesia Mayor, the character of Costanza (wife of Lope de Arenas), and the creation of the Díez coat of arms when Alfonso paints ten bands on the shield of Pero Díez.

The other two Acts of *Las paces de los reyes* present actions that appear totally foreign to those in Act One. In Act Two, Alfonso, now a grown man and married to Leonor of England, returns to Toledo after a ten year absence, falls in love with a Jewess, and retires with her to the gardens of the Tajo for seven years, prisoner of his amorous passions. In Act Three, Leonor finally instigates the nobles to kill Raquel, causing Alfonso to seek vengeance on them. On the road to Madrid, however, an angel of light appears and reprimands him for his past actions. Alfonso repents and makes peace with his wife.

All of the above is also rigorously historical, although it occurred many years after the events in Act One. Mariana, for example, relates Alfonso's relations with the Jewess in Chapter XVIII after a long section on the many civil wars among the Christian kings. Lope, for his part, made no changes to the historical material nor the chronology of Alfonso's life; but he did make two significant adjustments in his dramatization of the events. First, he selected only these two from the many events in the chronicles and put them side by side, giving the impression that the taking of the castle of Zurita had some causal relationship to the affair with the Jewess. Second, he dramatically adjusted both episodes so that they would appear to mirror each other in their structure, giving thereby the impression to the spectator that history is somehow repeating itself in the life of Spain's famous monarch. A close examination of the play's material will clarify these adjustments and show their Counter Reformational purpose.

Las paces de los reyes begins *in medias res* with Esteban Illán and Count Manrique proclaiming that their ward Alfonso is the legitimate king of Castile. An ensuing dialogue between these guardians and two noblemen of Toledo, Fernán Ruiz and Lope de Arenas, explains to the audience the events leading up to the opening of the play. Sancho III, "el Deseado," died in 1158, leaving his three-year-old son Alfonso as successor to the throne. In his will, however, Sancho appointed don Manrique and Esteban Illán as guardians until his son should reach the age of fifteen years. Alfonso's uncle, Fernando de León, seized this opportunity to confiscate several Castilian cities and to declare himself regent for Alfonso. Toledo, one of these cities, was forced to recognize Fernando as regent and to pay taxes to him. In 1166 Esteban Illán and don Manrique, cognizant that the people of Toledo felt oppressed under the harsh rule of Fernando, carried out a daring plan for regaining the city from him. The action of the play begins with the execution of this stratagem. Having stationed himself with don Manrique in the highest part of the city – the tower of the San Román cathedral – Esteban asks Lope de Arenas: "¿No fue concierto que, si entrar pudiese / Alfonso en la ciudad, se obedeciese?" (1: 504a). Lope replies affirmatively, and the guardians present their royal ward to the citizens of Toledo.

For Alfonso, this sudden appearance before his subjects after a decade of exile marks the first public action in which he has participated, and can be considered as a kind of public "birth." Lope has visually enhanced this significant event by revealing the young prince to his people in that spatial position which he symbolically holds in their eyes. Alfonso is seen in the tower as if midway between heaven and earth, and, still a child, he is flanked by the faithful guradians who have been so instrumental in achieving that exalted position for him.

Fernán Ruiz immediately recognizes the legitimacy of Alfonso's claim to the city of Toledo, but Lope de Arenas rejects the promise he had earlier made to Esteban Illán and decides to hold the castle of Zurita until Alfonso reaches the appointed age as prescribed in King Sancho's will. Accordingly, Lope retreats to defend the Zurita fortress and Alfonso preceeds to the Iglesia Mayor to be knighted.

Before the altar of the great cathedral, Alfonso receives the sword essential for uniting the kingdom together with the spurs required for controlling the natural instincts symbolized in the warrior's horse. As seen in *Las mocedades del Cid*, investiture ceremonies were common dramatic techniques for launching a young man's career because the spectator would assume that the ritual somehow legitimized the hero's subsequent actions. The advice given in the investiture ceremony by the guardians – in this play that the young prince should defend "la ley de Dios" (1: 506b), drive the Moors from Christian lands, and protect the fair sex – also serves to establish criteria of conduct against which the spectator can judge those future actions. The dramatization of the ceremony, deployed as it is between the public recognition of Alfonso as heir to the throne and his attempt to gain Zurita, establishes that the youngster has received the moral and doctrinal advice needed to wield properly the instruments of power.

The investiture is solely a bestowal of attributes, however; it does not temper the spiritual nature of the knight, nor does it guarantee success in future ordeals. It follows, then, that the knight must be tested in some way to determine how well he will perform when confronted with a real situation. Rodrigo Díaz faced the *amor//honor* dilemma between his personal desires and tribal loyalty; and he correctly chose the latter. Alfonso will face a subtler test before the walls of Zurita castle, because he will have to choose between expediency and professional rectitude.

As Alfonso and his guardians approach the contested fortress, he exercises his newly conferred responsibility by advancing in front of the others to speak with doña Costanza, the wife of Lope de Arenas, about arranging for a peaceful settlement, thus accomplishing the first public act he has attempted alone. The absence of any aid or advice from Alfonso's elders is emphasized when the traitor Dominguillo offers his plan for gaining the citadel. Alfonso himself listens to the man and agrees "a fe de rey" (1: 511a) to pay Dominguillo for carrying out the treacherous murder of his master.

The climax of the first Act follows when Pero Díez volunteers to allow himself to be wounded by Dominguillo so that Alfonso can take possession of the castle. The monarch, on witnessing the valor and fortitute Pero has exhibited, demonstrates a full awareness of the significance of such a sacrifice by dipping his fingers in the blood shed by Pero and marking the knight's shield with ten bands, thus acknowledging the courageous deed.

Pero Díez has done no less than offer up his life as a sacrifice for the harmony of the kingdom, an example for Alfonso which is recognized and rewarded, but not imitated. In Act Two Alfonso will effectively perform deeds precisely the opposite to those of Pero Díez by refusing to make sacrifices for the peace of his realm. Nevertheless, something of a polemic has formed concerning Alfonso's actions in Act One, with some scholars, Castañeda and de Armas in particular, viewing the king as a "rey ideal" throughout the play, while others, such as McCrary, have seen Alfonso's actions in Act One as an example of lèse majesté that shows the reason for

Alfonso's weaknesses in Act Two and God's reprimand and punishment in Act Three.

One clue to the appropriateness of Alfonso's decisions in the first Act is the character Lope de Arenas. His insistence on obeying the statute of majority and his death at the hands of the traitor Dominguillo come from the chronicles. His relation with his wife Costanza comes from Lope, and it is here that the knight shows himself disobedient to the petitions of his friends and king as well as a person who has forgotten his military mission to defend the castle by delighting in the love of his wife and by leaving his own security in the hands of Dominguillo, "la llave / de cuanto secreto tengo" (1: 508b). When the servant – whom the spectator knows from the beginning to be a traitor – warns Lope of the military danger, the knight responds: "Reírme quiero de ti / y de Alfonso; que los dos / parecéis niños, por Dios; / él en venir contra mí, / y tú en decir que me guarde" (1: 509b). This attitude shows Lope de Arenas to be blinded to the danger around him by his overconfidence in the strength of the castle and the loyalty of his servant; moreover, he is blinded further by his love for Costanza, as de Armas has indicated: "Thus, don Lope de Arenas neglects his duty on two counts. First he pursues love while he should be thinking of war. And secondly, he delegates power on a *mal nacido*. Blind passion and blind trust lead to a third and more definitive blindness, death" (70). The unfortunate Lope de Arenas thus passes through three stages of ignorance in Act One: passionate blindness, treacherous blindness, and deadly blindness. The author "awakens" him before his demise, however, so he can confess his error. "Túvele amor, / que mira el mal desde lejos" (1: 513b), Lope confesses of Dominguillo. He thus ends his life at peace with his wife, to whom he did not listen, with his king, whom he disobeyed, and with his God, from whom he refused to seek aid.

All of this is related to the other action of blinding in Act One, which is faithfully historical. When Dominguillo asks the king for his reward, Alfonso grants it to him, but also gouges out the traitor's eyes, "pues tú los sacaste a quien / te crió y te hizo bien" (1: 514b). So the entire Act is an interlocked progression of treachery, blindness, passion, blindness, treachery, blindness, death, blindness.

The events in Act Two occur historically a full decade after those of the first Act. During this period Alfonso's achievements have been astounding: he has united his kingdoms, has conquered the Syrians in Asia Minor, and, because of his valor in the Crusades, has won the hand of Leonor, the daughter of Henry II of England. *Hombre ya* (1: 515b), he enters as a character totally independent of the men and events in Act One, ingeniously dramatized by Lope in the fact that all the earlier characters have been replaced by an entirely new cast, without exception.

Critics of the play, especially McCrary and de Armas, have viewed this Act as a continuation of the events in the first Act in the sense that the first is a dramatization of Alfonso's "niñeces" and the second of his "mocedades." At the same time, they see a juxtaposition of actions because in the first Alfonso returns from a long absence to conquer Toledo and in the second he returns from a long absence to lose it. Of much more importance is the fact that the action here in Act Two is a *repetition* of the action in the first Act, for Alfonso repeats step by step the errors of his passionate and desobediente predecessor Lope de Arenas. He abandons his vigilence to dally with Raquel in a garden – trusting thereby in a "mal nacida" (1: 520a) analogous to the low-born Dominguillo – who blinds him to the reality of his circumstances and causes his "death" for the nation (Leonor and her son Enrique will come on stage at the beginning of Act Three *de luto los dos* [1: 523b]). Alfonso thus repeats the same pattern of passion, blindness, treachery, blindness, death that was exhibited by Lope de Arenas earlier.

This repetition of a transgression is surely one of the most important connections between the first events and the subsequent ones, and it pinpoints the question of the legitimacy of Alfonso's action in Act One. Why didn't the young king learn from Lope de Arenas's example? How could he have been so blind as to repeat the same steps of passion, overconfidence, treachery, and death as his predecessor? Castañeda (30) and de Armas (68-71, 73) insist that the young Alfonso was an ideal prince who did the right things in Act One when he consented to let Dominguillo kill Lope de Arenas, but then blinded the traitor. This is actually an opinion shared by the *Crónica general* (Menéndez Pelayo 100) and by Juan de Mariana, who commented that "fue ejemplo señalado de castigo contra los traidores" (310). Lope de Vega, however, sees matters differently, for he makes clear in the play that the just punishment of a traitor should not mask the young prince's unjust consent to a traitorous act. In this Alfonso committed a serious crime because he did not keep his word to Costanza, nor to the statue of Santiago, nor to himself. By consenting to Dominguillo's treacherous plan, Alfonso is shown to have fallen into the classical net of utility versus honesty.

The great Roman thinker Cicero faced precisely this dilemma in his moral treatise *On Duties*, a book Lope de Vega would have read many times. The part in question is the famous anecdote about the Greek emperor Pyrrhus and the Roman general Caius Fabricius (which Lope could have also found in Plutarch's *Lives*). Cicero charges the tale with the essence of his fundamental doctrine that only honest actions are valid in politics, regardless of the ends. The Spanish version available to Lope relates the following:

> Por cierto debemos tener que ninguna cosa es útil si no es honesta. Y puesto que muchas veces haya sido esto experimentado en nuestro senado y pueblo romano, fue así juzgado de Cayo Fabricio en aquella guerra que, siendo la segunda vez consul, tuvo con Pirro. Y es así que como el rey Pirro moviese guerra al pueblo romano sin otra causa de malquerencia más solamente fuese la contienda con aquel rey generoso y poderoso sobre el imperio, un cierto hombre se pasó del a los reales de Fabricio y le prometió si le mandase por ello algún premio, que así como vino se volvería secretamente a los reales de Pirro y lo mataría con veneno. Entonces Fabricio lo mandó prender y llevar a Pirro, lo cual fue muy loado del senado.
> Pues si aquí miramos y consideramos la apariencia y opinión de la utilidad, cierto es que aquel hombre pudiera fenecer aquella guerra y quitar delante aquel gran adversario del imperio. Pero fuera grande infamia y gran deshonra y maldad ser aquel rey vencido y sobrepujado no con virtud sino con traición, con el cual era la contienda sobre el señorío y no por otra codicia o enemistad. Pues luego, ¿cuál fue tenido por más provechoso de Fabricio, que en esta ciudad tal cual Arístodes en Atenas o del senado (que nunca apartó la utilidad de la dignidad): contender por fuerza de armas con el enemigo o con ponzoña? Vengo pues a decir que si el imperio se codicia por causa de gloria no se debe por traición, porque donde hay ésta no puede haber gloria. Y si potencias o riquezas se buscan (comoquiera que sea), no pueden ser provechosas siendo con infamia. (176-77)

It is pretty clear that Alfonso VIII is no Caius Fabricius and certainly no "idealized figure of kingship in childhood" (de Armas 73). Alfonso cannot even compare himself to Shakespeare's weak-willed Pompey in *Anthony and Cleopatra*, who is offered precisely the same chance to have his enemies Antony, Lepidus, and Caesar traitorously eliminated and rejects the opportunity with the response: "'Tis not my profit that does lead mine honour; / Mine honour it" (2.vii.82-83).

The Spanish monarch thus makes a terrible mistake in consenting to Dominguillo's treachery because he chooses an expedient tactic based on profit rather than the honest one based on professional integrity. In consequence, he will blindly repeat in Act Two the very actions that he witnessed his enemy commit in Act One by falling subject to his passions, obstinately ignoring warnings from all quarters, and dying from a lance thrust (in his case by Cupid).

The irony of Alfonso's blindness is that he had been given an example of proper actions by Pero Díez, whose humility, obedience and consent to be a sacrifice were opposite postures to Lope de Arenas's refusal to consent, Dominguillo's treachery, and the king's expediency. It is not surprising that Lope presents the valiant soldier as the recipient of so many rewards: a coat of arms commemorative of his deed, the governorship of the castle of Zurita, and – most amazingly – the hand of the widow Costanza with a dowry from the king. All those things Lope de Arenas lost by being obstinate and overconfident Pero Díez won by being humble and obedient.

Lope's answer, then, to the question about the motives for Alfonso's despicable actions with the Jewess is simple. As a child, Alfonso was presented with a crucial Ciceronian dilemma as a test, and he failed the test. He had the opportunity to employ proper moral values in a critical situation, and he did not do it. He had the proper example of Pero Díez, and he did not appreciate it. He saw the destruction that blind love and obstinance can cause, and he ignored it. The play demonstrates in its dramatic structure that these errors are the causes of the errors in Act Two when Alfonso repeats obstinately and blindly the blunders of his enemies. Because he failed the exam, he has to repeat the course; and by doing so he repeats the same vices and crimes. He thus becomes a perfect example of the saying that those who do not learn from the present are condemned to repeat the errors of the past.

The situation in which Alfonso falls into error is intensified histrionically by Lope in a number of ways. First, when Alfonso remarks to Garcerán that he would like to go to the Tajo that afternoon, Garcerán answers:

> Iré a hacerte
> algún reparo primero,
> por ser el calor tan fuerte,
> que los palacios ya son
> más ruinas que palacios,
> (1: 516b)

and explains that the swollen Tajo has flooded the land and "taken possession" of the palace grounds. Secondly, by that strange mystique of time and space, it is at these very *ruinas* that Raquel is preparing to bathe in the Tajo. Thirdly, Raquel, who has earlier seen Alfonso and Leonor enter Toledo, describes the couple to her friend Sibila in richly cloaked terms of heat and cold. She speaks of Leonor as "aquella nieve del norte" "con una hermosura helada," "un ángel tan helado" (1: 516b-517a). The heat of the day, the symbolic effect of the flooded banks of the Tajo, and Raquel's own passionate inclinations all prepare the mood of the scene for Alfonso's discovery of and ensuing infatuation with the infidel – albeit beauteous – Jewess.

The many allusions to the queen's frigidity and to the heat of both Alfonso and Raquel help to explain the immediate attraction between these two young people, especially when understood in conjunction with Garcerán's comment to Alfonso prior to the fateful meeting with Raquel: "¿Qué recelas, / si el amor de tu esposa no te abrasa, / y en la defensa de tu amor te hielas?" (1: 518a). Nevertheless, Lope, through the mouth of his dramatic spokesman Belardo refers to Raquel as "una mujer mal nacida" and draws attention to the forbidden nature of Alfonso's reckless desire: "Y a vos, señor, os defienda / de dar en tan gran error; / porque si cristiana fuera, / ya tuviérades disculpa" (1: 520b).

A warning by Garcerán is much more explicit in so far as it objectively points to the reason for Alfonso's weakness in the face of this new temptation: "Pensar / que es tan infame ley, / y ganar tan gran vitoria / como el vencerse a sí mismo" (1: 520b). During the period of his youthful exploits, the sovereign had overcome every adversary except his own instincts; and now, because of his lack of control over the sensual appetites, he has become a kind of moral

Bellido Dolfos. As Dominguillo in Act One betrayed his master "para tener de comer" (1: 506b), so in Act Two Alfonso's blind subjugation to the appetites makes him a traitor to his crown.

As Alfonso prepares to enter the forbidden garden, where he will remain for seven long years, divine forces come forward to reinforce the previous warnings of Belardo and Garcerán. A mysterious *voz* issues from a thunderstorm to advise him that he is in danger of losing God's grace and protection: "No des lugar desta suerte, / cuando hombre, a tus apetitos. / advierte que por la Cava / a España perdió Rodrigo" (1: 525b). Unswayed, Alfonso then faces a *sombra* dressed in black and armed with sword and daggar, who also attempts to block his path; but the king enters anyway, confessing "que amor me quita el juicio; / y perdida la razón, / conozco el daño, y le sigo" (1: 526a). Lope thus makes it perfectly clear that he, as the author, has done everything possible to warn his own character Alfonso of the serious nature of these actions against God. Alfonso is therefore presented as wholly responsible for what may occur to him.

The chronicles claim that the principal consequence of Alfonso's passion was the loss of the Battle of Alarcos, considered the worst military defeat ever inflicted on the Spaniards by the Moors. Juan de Mariana writes the following:

> Diose la batalla junto a Alarcos, a 19 de julio, que fue miércoles, el año de 1195. Fue grande el coraje y denuedo de entrambas las partes; pero el esfuerzo de los nuestros fue vencido por la muchedumbre de los enemigos, porque mereciéndolo así los pecados del pueblo y por voluntad de Dios amedrentados los nuestros, les faltó el ánimo y corazón en la pelea. ... Túvose por cierto que con aquel desastre tan grande castigó Dios en particular un pecado del Rey, y fue que en Toledo, menospreciada su mujer, se enamoró de cierta judía ... . (330)

Lope de Vega never mentions Alarcos in the play, nor the great victory of Las Navas de Tolosa in 1212. The only punishment directly inflicted on Alfonso in Lope's text – and in the *Crónica general* (Menéndez Pelayo 101) – is the declaration that Alfonso will not have a male heir to the throne, whose biblical analogy with the penalty imposed on King David for his adultery with Bath-sheba allows Lope to make specific comparisons between the two events.

Lope's vision of history thus goes beyond specific occurrences, which his audience would probably already know, to a larger historical-religious analogy between Alfonso and Rodrigo "el último godo" on the one hand and Alfonso and King David on the other, an analogy McCrary called "a diachronic montage which leads our experience from the present back to Rodrigo, David, and eventually to Adam himself" ("Plot" 12). The most immediate analogy, however, is with the transgressors in Act One, for Alfonso repeats the crimes of both Lope de Arenas and Dominguillo. Blinded by passion, he falls into error; warned of his sins, he responds with hardheaded obstinance. Thus doubly blinded, he dies to the world.

As Act Two dramatized the *repetition* of the events in Act One, so Act Three dramatizes the *rectification* of the events in the previous two Acts. The nobles are instigated by Queen Leonor and her son Enrique – who enter *de luto los dos* (1: 526b) to emphasize the moral demise of Alfonso – to assassinate Raquel for the good of the realm; then Alfonso and Raquel drag up the body of a child while fishing (a premonition of the penalty Alfonso will pay for his sins).

After Raquel's death, Alfonso remains obstinate and sets off for Illescas planning to avenge her death. Along the way, however, he undergoes the typical Pauline transformation. *Óyese una música celeste y aparece un Ángel al Rey* (1: 534b). This time Alfonso listens attentively to the repeated admonition "vuelve en ti" and – as have all other dramatic characters who have undergone similar conversions – humbly declares: "Pequé, Señor, ofendí / vuestra majestad; perdón" (1: 534b).

This scene repairs and rectifies the earlier moments of action. The image of the Virgen de la Caridad closes the work with the true ceremony of investiture as opposed to the mechanical one that opened the play, as McCrary has noted: "The real investiture which elevates the ordinary mortal to a plane of superior consciousness is celebrated by the Angel, a stark contrast to the man-made engine which simulated the initiation rites of Act I" ("Plot" 8-9). Likewise, the appearance of an angel of light does what the dark shadow in Act Two could not.

Finally, the peace made with Leonor repairs the rupture of matrimony caused by Raquel and also countermands the relation between Lope de Arenas and Costanza, in which the former ignored the counsels of his wife and died because of it. Costanza lost Lope de Arenas, but gained the exemplary knight Pero Díez. Leonor lost her obstinate husband also, but – thanks to divine intervention – gained a humbly renovated monarch. The man in Act One who refused to be "piadoso ni enamorado" (1: 512b) now is.

As with all the other Pauline conversions, there remains here the question of Alfonso's redemptive state. The king rightly describes himself as a Saint Paul thrown from his horse (535a), for like his predecessor his future actions were considered by the chroniclers to be divinely directed. Juan de Mariana, for example, details precisely the appearance of the angel of light and the king's repentance; then, after narrating the victory at Las Navas de Tolosa, he comments: "Nunca la gloria del nombre cristiano pareció mayor ni las naciones cristianas estuvieron en algún tiempo más gloriosamente aliadas. Los españoles asimismo parecían igualar en valor la gloria de los antiguos; el mismo rey don Alonso comenzó a ser tenido como príncipe venido del cielo y más que hombre mortal" (339).

Neither Lope nor the chroniclers explain why Alfonso VIII was guided by divine powers to become a Pauline defender of the faith; but what Lope does that the chroniclers don't do is present the spectator a patterned life of error, repetition, rectification, and salvation. In Lope's Counter Reformation view of history, the Davidic Alfonso participates in a series of events without the necessary honest attitude, repeats the same events in his own life, is awakened by a divine admonition to rectify his life, recognizes his error, repents, and is forgiven. Remarkably, none of this was "invented" by Lope. All he did was arrange history in such a way that it would conform to the typical Counter Reformation pattern of conversion that closes so many other literary works of the early seventeenth century.

Tirso de Molina's *Las quinas de Portugal* is a late play that dates from about 1630, and it is also the one which divinizes most the historical material it dramatizes. The drama presents a hagiographic biography of Alfonso Enríquez (1094-1185), the first king of Portugal. Its principal source is Manuel de Faria e Sousa's *Epítome de las historias portuguesas* (1628), itself a Counter Reformation view of Portuguese history that highlights every miraculous occurrence associated with the wars of reconquest against the Moors, and which apparently used the figure of Fernán González as its direct model for the sequence and content of the events in King Alfonso's life (Zamora Vicente).

Tirso's dramatic version begins with the already mature Alfonso lost in the forest during a hunting trip. He comes upon a strange grotto and meets Giraldo (the historical Archbishop of Braga), who reprimands him for having neglected his duties to live a life of idle pleasure with his mistress Elvira Gualtar. Alfonso immediately sees the errors of his past life and calls his nobles together to have them swear with him that none of them will remove their armor until they have ousted the infidel Moors from Portugal. This play thus begins with a moment analogous to the last scene in *Las paces de los reyes* and then dramatizes the miraculous victories that follow the conversion from a life subject to the passions to one dedicated to the reconquest.

Tirso attempts to create dramatic interest in his play by introducing an Islamic foil for the Christian Alfonso in the character of Ismael (a historical king, also known as Ismar, defeated by Alfonso at the battle of Santarém in 1239), who functions in the play as a mocked parody of the Christian. Whereas the Portuguese king throws off his domination by the passions to dedicate his life to the reconquest, Ismael falls in love with the noble Leonor, imprisons her, and holds her as his captive in the Castle of Palmela (the historical castle of Palmira, which Alfonso besieged and won from the Moors). Tirso highlights the parodic contrast between the parodied sentimental Moor and Alfonso Enríquez in the middle of his play by having the Christian enter dressed in full battle gear, but with a surplice over his armor – *trae puesto sobre las armas un roquete* (3: 1334b) – while Ismael enters with Leonor's glove as his standard – *con adarga y lanza, y en el extremo de ella, en lugar de banderola, el guante de Doña Leonor* (3: 1335a). The glove also parodies the very purpose of the play, which is to establish the legitimacy of the miraculous donation of Portugal's coat of arms to Alfonso by Christ Himself (Roig).

The figure of Ismael degenerates further at the end of Act Two when Egas Muñiz (Leonor's lover in the play and also an important historical figure during Alfonso's reign) and the *gracioso* Brito pretend to be magicians and dupe the superstitious Ismael so Leonor can escape. By Act Three, Ismael's personality has completely deteriorated into that of a pompous fool, very similar to the vain Martín González in *Las mocedades del Cid*; so when Alfonso kills the Moor in combat everyone rejoices. The other Moors in the play fare no better. Brito constantly uses all the common insults when referring to them, makes fun of their dress, and mocks Islamic dietary laws. In the last scene of the play, he brags that he has chained up a pack of rabid dogs: *Descubre un montón de moros muertos unos sobre otros en diferentes posturas* (3: 1355b).

There are actually only two historical events dramatized in the play, and those two are switched by Tirso. Act One dramatizes the taking of Santarém by Ismael in 1147, and Act Two has various references to the events that followed, such as the interest shown by St. Bernard of Clairvaux (1090-1153) in Portugal, the continuation of the reconquest in the southeastern part of the country, and the siege of Palmira. Act Three then dramatizes the famous battle of Ourique, which took place almost a decade earlier on 25 July 1139. Faria e Sousa narrates the same visit by a hermit, the miraculous vision of Christ crucified, the signal with the bells to start the battle, and the donation by Christ Himself of the Portuguese coat of arms, consisting of five shields with coins in the shape of a cross, that Tirso uses in his play; so – as in *Las mocedades del Cid* – the miraculous events are "historical." Moreover, Tirso has opted for a Counter Reformational closure – as did Guillén de Castro – by putting these miraculous events as the last great moments in Alfonso's life rather than the first ones. In other words, Faria e Sousa has 1. early years, 2. Ismael, 3. battle of Ourique with its miracles, 4. defeat of Ismael, 5. taking of Santarém, 6. St. Bernard and further conquest, 7. Palmira, 8. summary of accomplishments (marriage to Mafalda of Savoy, establishment of the military orders of Avís and Ala). Tirso alters the order of events to 1. early years, 2. Ismael, 5. taking of Santarém, 6. St. Bernard and further conquest, 7. Palmira, 3. battle of Ourique with its miracles, 4. defeat of Ismael, 8. summary of accomplishments (marriage to Matilde of Savoy, establishment of the military order of Avís).

Tirso also creates the same aura of "galán divino" for Alfonso Enríquez that Castro did for Rodrigo. Act Two opens on a discussion of the warrior's devoutness in virtually the same terms that Castro used, for one of the king's nobles comments that "no es inconveniente / ser religioso y valiente" (3: 1333a), since true warriors combine the sword and the scourge, the breastplate and the surplice: "Lo uno y otro al cielo agrada / alentando el corazón, / con Moisés en la oración / y Josué con la espada" (3: 1334b).

The biblical references here only serve to reinforce a plethora of analogies created by Tirso to assure that his audience views Alfonso as a reincarnation of divinely guided Hebrew warriors such as Abraham, Moses, Samson, Joshua, and Gideon. The primary type, however, continues to be King David, as it was in both *Las paces de los reyes* and *Las mocedades del Cid*.

Tirso is explicit about his Portuguese hero's model. One of the characters calls Alfonso "David portugués" (3: 1334a) in Act Two, and associates Alfonso's wearing a surplice and singing in the army's choir to David's wearing an ephod and singing psalms. Tirso even has a scene in Act Three in which Alfonso plays the *tolle, lege* game and opens the Bible to Psalm 19 (20 in the King James Version) to gain inspiration before the battle of Ourique. Immediately following this moment, Giraldo foretells that Alfonso will be the first in a long line of kings, as was David. Further, the final defeat of Ismael is parallel to David's defeat of Goliath.

The entire play thus becomes a recapitulation of diverse events in the Old Testament: the calling of the chosen people from a life of sinful idleness, the creation by Hagar and Ishmael of the Arab race of renegades to the true faith, the struggles of Moses and the pre-Davidic warriors against their enemies, the rise of the savior figure David as a miraculous giant killer and warrior, the eventual coming of Christ to save the faithful, and even the final confirmation of Christianity at the battle of Mulvian Bridge, where Constantine had his vision of the IHS banner and heard the same words as Alfonso does: "Vencerás en nombre mío" (3: 1348a). The battle of Ourique thus recapitulates all earlier divinely guided struggles against those who would seek to harm God's chosen people and establishes for Portugal a covenant with its God equal to the earlier one Israel had, but which was lost because of that nation's infidelity. It is for this reason that Tirso can make every effort to assure that his audience sees the Portuguese nation under Alfonso as a recapitulation of Israel under David, yet at the same time have *Cristo* refer in the play to Jews as "el pueblo fementido" (3: 1348b). Tirso wanted his audience to see that Portugal's destiny was more than a mere imitative copy of Israel's; it was a divinely sanctioned and guided renewal of the covenant relationship, an Israel *redivivus*, born again to war against the Ishmaelites precisely as David warred against the Philistines. The events thus pass beyond being a recapitulation of the Old Testament relationships between God and His people to become a restoration of them in Christian times.

History in all of these dramatists' hands has become a malleable property which on the physical level is restructured to present climatic closures to the lives of its protagonists and on the spiritual level is made to recapitulate the biblical descriptions of divine intervention in the lives of God's chosen vessels (the term used for Paul in Acts 9:15). As historically defined warriors who fight against ages-old enemies of Christianity, these Iberian heroes show no mercy for their defeated opponents, nor do they give the infidels the opportunity to convert to Christianity. All three dramatists, in fact, identify implicitly or explicitly Spain and Portugal as the new Israel, the nations chosen by God to defend the faith and to smite His enemies. Each of their heroes becomes a divinely sanctioned man endowed with miraculous powers to win great victories against the infidels. In each case the material the dramatists used was rigorously historical, but in each case they manipulated its presentation to assure that their audience would note the crucial importance of the divine guidance in the heroes' lives that caused them to be so miraculously successful in their reconquest of the Iberian peninsula.

CHAPTER SEVEN

CONVERTING LANDSCAPES

A pilgrimage doesn't necessarily have to be a Catholic enterprise. The first Protestant groups to seek refuge in North American were pilgrims. The universal Christianity of the Middle Ages was charted on pilgrimage routes that led to the ends of the known world. The theme of *Peregrinatio Vitae* is long and consistent in Western literature, from Odysseus's voyage home and Aeneas's pious travails, through the myriad of allegorical journeys that culminate in works like the Humanist *Peregrinación de la vida del hombre*, written by Pedro Hernández de Villaumbrales in the mid-sixteenth century; and the Protestant countries all have a pilgrim's progress of one form or another in their literary repertiore. The picaresque novels are also kinds of pilgrimage narratives, although in a parodic fashion, since the journeys of pícaros like Guzmán de Alfarache are undertaken away from the moral center and encompass a wasted life of directionless wandering (Hahn 160).

Counter Reformation Spain has three masterpieces of the canonical pilgrimage narrative. Lope de Vega's *El peregrino en su patria* (1604) is a strange, semi-autobiographical novel with intercalated tales by Montserrat monks, journeys to most of Spain's famous shrines (Zaragoza, Toledo, Guadalupe), and four full-length *autos sacramentales*. Avalle-Arce is therefore correct when he concludes that "el *Peregrino* es un panegírico religioso, con fuertes dosis de propaganda catequística, todo muy propio de las directivas del Concilio de Trento acerca de los usos de la literatura" (26).

Avalle-Arce adds that "todo ello se reflejará también en el *Persiles* de Cervantes," referring to the second great contribution, *Los trabajos de Persiles y Sigismunda* (1617). It too is peppered with declarations of the Catholic faith and framed by a regular series of "temple experiences" (Forcione 45) ranging from the first lines of the poem that describe the exit from a dark pit located on the extreme northern confines of the world through visions on the top of a mountain (Antonio and Ricla's hideaway), the frozen hermitage of Renato and Eusebia, the temples of Lisbon, the monastery of Guadalupe, the forest cave of the prophet Soldino, Toledo, Valencia, Barcelona, and – the goal of every pilgrim's journey – the hills of Rome.

Furthermore, *Persiles y Sigismunda* has various underlayers of allegorical material. The most obvious is the biblical pattern in the plot, which recapitulates the story of Israel (Wilson 136-41). Another is the incessant warfare between *Caritas* and *Cupiditas* in the novel, which is most visible in Periandro's long narrative in Book Two, but which can be found in every episode. Those who die in the novel are the ones who put their desires on a created object rather than on the creator, on an object as the end of their love rather than as a means to divine approbation. As occurs in Periandro's narrative (2.15), the good life awaits those who conquer greed and lust in favor of a life ordered by continence and modesty. A third related allegory is the Augustinian doctrine expressed explicitly two times in the novel that "están nuestras almas siempre en continuo movimiento, y no pueden parar ni sosegar sino en su centro, que es Dios, para quien fueron criadas" (275), which is for Julio Baena the "center-center" of the novel (112), and that "nuestras almas ... siempre están en continuo movimiento y no pueden parar sino en Dios, como en su centro" (458), which prefaces the last moments in the narrative. Life itself is like the travails of Persiles and Sigismunda, who wander the earth seeking repose from the turmoils that beset them and which they find only at the Roman center when they become passively receptive to whatever providential outcome God may wish for them.

The third Spanish contribution, Baltasar Gracián's *El Criticón* (1651, 1653, 1657) also begins on a distant island (St. Helena) and moves through all of Catholic Europe to end in Rome. Its characters are for the most part allegorical, and there are therefore very few references to religion or religious shrines. The two pilgrims Andrenio and Critilo journey in search of Felisinda (their mother and wife, respectively), directing their steps first to Madrid (Part One) and then to Aragón (Part Two), stopping in Huesca at the palace of

Gracián's benefactor don Vincencio Juan de Lastanosa. They next cross into France, where they hope to encounter Virtelia, who will in turn lead them to Felisinda. They discover Virtelia, with her four ministers (the cardinal virtues), and she directs them to the court of Ferdinand Augustus III (1608-1657) in Germany, because Felisinda is reportedly in the house of the Spanish ambassador at the Imperial capital. Entering Germany through Picardy, they discover that the ambassador no longer resides at the German court, but has moved to Rome; so they change direction and cross the alps into Italy (Part Three), reaching the Ambassador's residence in Rome and discovering that Felisinda has died to this world and now resides in heaven. This final disillusionment opens their eyes to the mortality of all things in this life due to the destructive nature of time, and causes them to leave Rome for the Isle of Immortality, where they find, not Felisinda, but Fama.

This program is clearly Humanist rather than Religious, and *El Criticón* was actually denounced in a contemporary *Crítica de reflección* (1658) for its neglect of religion and the Catholic spirit (*Obras* xciv, clxxxiii); but, as Arturo del Hoyo emphasizes, *El Criticón* is nevertheless characteristic of late Counter Reformation thought because of its constant tone of deception with this world, expressed as "la prudencia como desengaño" (clxxxiv), as will be demonstrated at length shortly.

The most obvious Counter Reformation characteristic in all three of Spain's pilgrimage novels is their slavish adaptation of the Byzantine structure and its divinization for Catholic purposes, which has been adequately deciphered by Alban K. Forcione and Diana de Armas Wilson. What is of more interest here is the closure of pilgrimage novels, for they all end happily for the pilgrims involved; actually, they end in the typical marriage format of comedies rather than the conversion format of the serious literature examined in the earlier chapters. This alone would disqualify them as candidates for Counter Reformational closure were it not for the fact that the endings created for the protagonists all appear quite arbitrary; the closures therefore do not fit into the traditional ones for *comedias de enredo*, for example, where the marriages at the denouement are justified by the characters' compatibility with each other (in terms of age, class, humor, profession, etc.) within the social structures of Spanish Golden Age society. Everyone deserving a peaceful married life, in other words, gets it in these pilgrimage novels, but through no special effort on their part, nor through any particular consummation of a vow nor through any stipulated passage of time nor through any particular intellectual discovery of some information or spiritual insight necessary for them to participate in a peaceful future of marital bliss. In sum, the old secular programs for literature do not work for these pilgrimage novels.

The problem, then, is not that the protagonists do not deserve the closure in which they all participate; it is that they do not exercise any particular individual effort to bring it about. On the contrary, they are all just as passive at the end of their novels as were Ozmín and Daraja – two outsiders striving as best as they could to find a way to live together in a hostile world which they found themselves forced to adopt and imitate in their own lives – at the end of their story. The closure is thus imposed on these worthy people rather than earned, and it is imposed when it is simply because that is when it occurs, not because any particular event or action by other characters causes it to occur when it does. Time and human actions in time thus become irrelevant in these pilgrimage tales.

In other Spanish literature, time and human actions are vitally important. Calderón's *La vida es sueño*, as explained in Chapter Three, presents Segismundo as gaining control over his own passions, memory, and rational faculties to thus be able to control his destiny and the destinies of all the other characters in the play by directing properly his free will to the eternal. His actions thus fit Anthony J. Cascardi's notion that "control" is the key word in Counter Reformational Spain:

> Phrased in other terms, Calderón's Segismundo not simply as the subject of an ideal moral itinerary but as *subject to* the "passions of the soul" mirrors a crisis of subjectivity that leads to a vision of the self as *requiring* (political) control. Indeed, it could be said that a work like *La vida es sueño* provides one of the best examples of the ways in which an encounter between the inherited principles of psychology and the problem of the legitimacy of authority leads to manifestly conservative ends, for what is ultimately at stake in Calderón's play can best be described in terms of the relationship between Segismundo's subjective self-consciousness and the need to restore authority in his father's State. Counter-Reformation ideology served in this context as the means by which the State could reassert, reassure, or legitimize

its rule, not so much by dominating subjects as by producing subjects who would not wish to escape its control. ("Subject" 243-44)

In *El burlador de Sevilla*, also used by Cascardi as a model for Counter Reformational control, time is the fundamental factor in don Juan Tenorio's demise. As explained in Chapter Five, the youth is warned repeatedly by don Pedro, Catalinón, Tisbea, his father, don Gonzalo, Aminta, and the Stone Guest at the first invitation that time will catch up with him and destroy him if he does not amend his ways. In this case, "the 'resolution' is itself the source of a 'higher' authority (whether of society or of God) and its principles of control" ("Subject" 246). As will be seen at the end of this Chapter, Cascardi's notion of control also applies to the timeless, haphazard world of the pilgrimage novels where the protagonists are constantly buffeted by unexpected events and surprised by deviations from their projected pathways, but in a very different way, because the control will function through a comedic romance closure rather than one of disillusionment or chastisement.

Baltasar Gracián's *El Criticón* is the last pilgrimage novel, and because of its political nature falls outside the format of conversion at closure which characterizes the literature previously studied here. Nevertheless, it expresses most adamantly the Catholic vision of a world so out of control that its inhabitants must resign themselves to – at best – becoming undeceived (the ubiquitous Baroque idea of *desengaño*) about understanding its nature or achieving the ability to control it in any kind of mechanical way. Gracián presents this anti-scientific, anti-modern – although very Humanist – philosophy through three interconnected themes that occur repeatedly in the book.

The most easily discernable theme in Gracián's novel is the presentation of a universe in which all is out of joint. Indeed, the vision of an inverted world permeates almost every Crisi (the term he uses for his chapters) in the three Parts. At the very "Entrada del mundo" (1.5), Critilio warns Andrenio: "De estas cosas toparás muchas en el mundo, que no son lo que parecen, sino muy al contrario" (554b). The theme is then given form in the narrative when the unwary youth witnesses his first topsy-turvy situation, for the beautiful woman who appears to be guiding children along the right path in life suddenly hands them over to the lions, tigers, bears, wolves, serpents, and dragons who tear apart their tender bodies.

In the next Crisi, entitled "El estado del siglo," the guide Quirón leads Critilo and Andrenio to the Plaza Mayor to show them that people live by their passions rather than by reason, and, consequently, people always accomplish exactly the opposite goals from what they intended to achieve. Critilo and Andrenio see persons who "caminaban hacia atrás, y a este modo todas sus acciones las hacían al revés" (567a); and they watch "uno que yendo a caballo en una vulpeja caminaba hacia atrás, nunca seguido, sino torciendo y revolviendo a todas partes" (568a). The spectacle culminates at the end of the Crisi when they notice "que no solo anda el mundo al revés en orden al lugar, sino al tiempo" (574a); "todo va al revés, en consecuencia de aquel desorden capital" (575a).

This vision of the condition of the civilized world remains constant throughout *El Criticón*. In Crisi Eight, when the prudent old man frees Andrenio from the Palace of Falimundo, he tells the youth how to see "alguna realidad" among the false coverings: "No ha de ser de ese modo – dijo el viejo –, sino al contrario, volviendo las espaldas, que las cosas del mundo todas se han de mirar al revés para verlas al derecho" (595b). In "El golfo cortesano" (1.11), the youth is guided by Fortune's pageboy, who "comenzó al mismo instante a revolverlo todo, sin dejar cosa en su lugar, ni aun tiempo. Guiaba siempre al revés" (626a). Gracián presents the same theme in many of the sections without using the typical terminology. In Crisi Six, for example, the narrator describes personages "que caminaban de tan graves, con las cabezas hacia bajo por el suelo, poniéndose del lodo, y los pies para arriba, muy empinados, echando piernas al aire, sin acertar a dar un paso; antes, a cada uno caían, y aunque se maltrataban harto, porfiaban en querer ir de aquel modo tan ridículo como peligroso" (566a).

The second Part of *El Criticón* offers the same picture of society. Critilo, when asked in what age he considers his century to pertain, replies: "Yo diría que en el de hierro; con tantos, todo anda errado en el mundo y todo al revés" (692a). In the last Crisi of the second Part, where Andrenio observes "La jaula de todos," "todo cuanto miraba le parecía andar al revés, todo al trocado, lo de arriba abajo, y como en realidad de verdad así va el mundo y todas sus cosas, al revés, nunca más acertado iba él ni mejor le conocía que cuando le miraba al revés, pues entonces le veía al derecho y como se había de mirar" (824a).

Part Three tenders a world view even more upside down than that of the earlier sections, because old men are by nature Janus figures, growing old but pretending to be young (1.1). It comes as no surprise, therefore, that an Acertador comments: "Digo que todo anda al revés y todo trocado de alto abajo" (845a). And in the opening statement to Crisi Five, Gracián notes: "Ahora me confirmo en que todo el mundo anda al revés, y todo cuanto hay en él es a la trocada" (894b).

These disparate examples demonstrate how consistent Gracián is in presenting his topsy-turvy world. They are well substantianted by a simple enumeration of the appearances of "al contrario" and "al revés" in the work. Gracián employs the term "al revés" some fifty-one times: twenty-one in Part One, fifteen in Part Two, and fifteen in Part Three. "Al contrario" appears no less than 124 times: thirty-seven in Part One, thirty-four in Part Two, and an astonishing fifty-three times in Part Three.

It is patent that such a view of civilization, while prevalent in the Counter Reformation period, was not the world as it should be viewed. Gracián wants the reader to be well aware that something or someone must have made the world topsy-turvy, and throughout *El Criticón* he continually reminds the reader that the culprit is none other than the reader. In the opening Crisi, the narrator comments that "todo cuanto inventó la industria humana ha sido perniciosamente fatal y en daño de sí misma" (522b). In the third Crisi, Gracián remarks that people are constantly at war with themselves (the topos *vita hominis militia est* runs throughout the work); and in the sixth Crisi Quirón finally places the blame for the upturned world where it belongs. Andrenio asks: "¿Quién le trastornó de alto a bajo, como hoy le vemos?" Quirón replies that some say it was Dame Fortune, others that the world became thus when Satan landed on it, and others that women are to blame.

> Mas yo digo que donde hay hombres no hay que buscar otro achaque; uno solo basta a desconcertar mil mundos y el no poderlo era lo que lloraba el otro grande inquietador. Mas digo que si no previniera la divina Sabiduría que no pudieran llegar los hombres al primer móvil, ya estuviera todo barajado y anduviera el mismo cielo al revés: un día saliera el sol por el poniente

> y caminara al oriente, y entonces fuera España cabeza del mundo, sin contradicción alguna, que no hubiera quien viviera con ella. Y es cosa de notar que, siendo el hombre persona de razón, lo primero que ejecuta es hacerla a ella esclava del apetito bestial. Deste principio se originan todas las demás monstruosidades: todo va al revés, en consecuencia de aquel desorden capital. (574b-75a)

This explanation for the upside-down social order does not change in *El Criticón*. It is repeated in more or less the same terms throughout the work and it reaches a climax in Crisi Five of Part Three. Critilo laments the sad state of the universe, and The Seer of All explains to him that he should not ask who made the world, but rather who unmade it, "porque habéis de saber que el Artífice Supremo, muy al contrario lo trazó de como hoy está" (895a). Who is to blame, then, asks Critilo. "¿Quién? Los mismos hombres, que no han dejado cosa en su lugar; todo lo han revuelto de alto abajo, con el desconcierto que hoy le vemos y lamentamos" (895a-b).

Gracián knows all too well there is little that the individual can do to change the lamentable condition of things, since the entire civilized world (which for him includes Spain, France, Germany, and Italy) is completely inverted from the way it should be, and since every stage of human development from childhood through youth and manhood to senectude exhibits the same foibles. One certainly cannot leave the world. Andrenio wanted to do precisely that in Crisi Six of Part One, but Critilo responded: "Eso es lo que ya no se puede. ¡Oh, cuántos volvieran atrás, si pudieran! No quedaran personas en el mundo. Advierte que vamos subiendo por la escalera de la vida, y las gradas de los días, que dejamos atrás, al mismo punto que movemos el pie, desaparecen. No hay por donde volver a bajar, ni otro remedio que pasar adelante" (575a). Andrenio then wishes to know what one can do to live peaceably in such a topsy-turvy world, and the response is: "Ver, oír y callar" (575b). Only if Andrenio does this will be become a "persona."

This pessimistic doctrine is the third constant theme in this late Counter Reformation novel, for the author continually warns his heroes – and his readers – to be on the alert and to command their lives with the mind rather than with the passions. At the beginning of Crisi Two in Part One, Gracián has God declare that man must rule the world "con la mente, no con el vientre; como persona, no como bestia" (528a). At the entrance into society, Critilo warns his friend: "Ya estamos entre enemigos: ya es tiempo de abrir los ojos, ya es menester vivir alerta. Procura de ir con cautela en el ver, en el oír y mucho más en el hablar" (544a). In the following Crisi Critilo tells him that "no son lo que parecen, sino muy al contrario. Ahora comienzas a vivir; irás viviendo y viendo" (554a); and a little later he advises "que abras los ojos y vivas siempre alerta entre enemigos" (556b). In Crisi Seven Critilo gives Andrenio a "regla de vivir" that repeats the same advice: "Nota dónde y cómo entras, considera a cada paso que dieres dónde pones el pie y procura asentarlo. ... Nada creas de cuanto te dijeran, nada concedas de cuanto te pidieren, nada hagas de cuanto te mandaren. Y en fe de esta lición, echemos por esta calle, que es la del callar y ver para vivir" (583a). Critilo then frees himself from the clutches of Falimundo because he "rompió con todo, que es el único medio, y saltó por el portillo de dar en la cuenta, aquel que todos cuantos abren los ojos le hallan" (590b-91a); and Andrenio escapes from the palace because "en el ver y conocer consistía su total remedio" (595b).

The warnings continue in the same vein throughout the novel. In Crisi Four of Part Three the reader is told: "Advertid que va grande diferencia del ver al mirar, que quien no entiende no atiende: poco importa ver mucho con los ojos, si con el entendimiento nada, ni vale el ver sin el notar" (879a). Two Crisis later, when the Zahorí has to escape from the doorless palace, "apretó lo pies, digo las alas, y huyóse al sagrado de mirar y callar" (909a). And in the tenth Crisi, which is the last one before Death and Immortality, the Cortesano tells Andrenio: "Buen remedio, ser prudente, abrir el ojo y dar ya en la cuenta" (974b). Only by opening his eyes to reality, by looking instead of merely seeing, can Andrenio consider himself a "persona."

In summary, Gracián converts the landscape of southern Europe with an allegorical message that is repeated throughout *El Criticón*, for the objective world does not change as people grow old, only the individuals and their subjective perception of it do. The landscape first confronts the reader with the view of things "al revés" and "al contrario" to the way they should be. It next shows that mankind is at fault for the topsy-turvy social order because people for one reason or another have chosen the physical realm of *engaño* as their residence rather than the mental realm of *desengaño*. The principal cause is that people make decisions based on information supplied by the senses rather than by the intellect. Yet Gracián also gives the reader the key to deciphering the deceitful illusions of life: "ver, oír y callar." If people do this, they will realize the true appearance of things.

Lope and Cervantes will present no such philosophy, and they will close their novels with joyful comedic marriages rather than flight from the world; nevertheless, their protagonists are just as unable to control their environment and their destiny as are Andrenio and Critilo. Furthermore, Lope and Cervantes will present a clear early Counter Reformational philosophy of religious dependence, while Gracián endows his characters with a Stoic political doctrine that allows them to attempt to seek a trajectory through the pilgrimage of live that will enhance the possibility of their finding felicity.

The final thematic constant that appears in all three Parts of *El Criticón* is the allegorical map the pilgrims follow to reach the Isle of Immortality. When Andrenio and Critilo approach the Entrada del mundo (Crisi Five), they discover the roadway of life. To their surprise, the path does not bifurcate into virtues and vices, but proceeds in three different directions: "Siendo la tradición común ser dos los caminos – el plausible, de la mano izquierda, por lo fácil, entretenido y cuesta abajo, y al contrario el de la mano derecha, áspero, desapacible y cuesta arriba – halló con no poca admiración que eran tres los caminos" (557b). Critilo nears a column and reads a sign on which is written the slogan "There is a middle way to all things. Never go to the extremes":

> Estaban de relieve todas las virtudes con plausibles empresas en tarjetas y roleos. Comenzaban por orden, puesta cada una en medio de sus dos viciosos extremos y en lo bajo la Fortaleza, asegurando el apoyo a las demás, recostada sobre el cojín de una columna, media entre la Temeridad y la Cobardía. Procediendo así todas las otras, remataba la Prudencia, como reina, y en sus manos tenía una preciosa corona con este lema: "Para el que ama la mediocridad de oro." (559b)

The long journey that the two heroes undertake will be an attempt to tread this middle path, although more times than not they will take by mistake or follow out of curiosity the extreme paths of vice and/or excess. The counsel, however, is always to follow the mean.

After noting that most people take the extreme highways at the trifurcated way, Critilo remarks to Andrenio: "Todos, al fin, verás que van por extremos, errando el camino de la vida de medio a medio. Echemos nosotros por el más seguro, aunque no tan plausible, que es el de una prudente y feliz medianía, no tan dificultoso como el de los extremos, por contenerse siempre en un buen medio" (561a). The two travelers always have in mind this mean. In the sixth Crisi, for example, when Andrenio wishes to know how to avoid the extremes of "el rico, más rico" and "el pobre, más pobre," Quirón recommends: "Echemos por el medio y pasaremos con menos embarazo y más seguridad" (566a). When they reach the "Golfo cortesano," the Sabio tells them that "el que se contenta con una medianía, ese vive" (628b); and in the final Crisi of Part One they find "Pitaco, aquel otro sabio de la Grecia, andaba poniendo precios a todo, y muy moderados, igualando las balanzas, y en todas partes encargaba su *ne quid nimis*" (655b).

Part Two teaches the same philosophy. In the opening Crisi, Argos tells them of middle age: "Aquí ya están en su punto, ni tan pasados como en la vejez, ni tan crudos como en la mocedad, sino en un buen medio" (674a). The same counsel is repeated in Crisi Eight: "La varonil edad está en su sazón, y del valor tomó el renombre de varonil. Es en ella valor lo que en la mocedad audacia y en la vejez recelo: aquí está en un medio muy proporcionado" (768b). The pilgrims also find that in Fortune's palace (Crisi Six) the wise man "ni tomó la corona, ni la tiara, ni el capelo, ni la mitra, sino una medianía, teniéndola por única felicidad" (751b). Likewise, the error is to miss the mean and to stray into the extremes: "Siempre van los mortales por extremos, nunca hallan el medio de la razón" (782a).

In the first Crisi of the third Part presentations of the extremes dominate the scene, mainly because people who enter into old age tend to be two-faced Janus figures; but Gracián does not allow the reader to forget the proper path. In Crisi Six he comments: "Casi todos los mortales andan por extremos, y el saber vivir consiste en topar el medio" (913b). Later, when Andrenio and Critilo become separated, "fue cosa notable que ambos a la par, aunque tan distantes, parece que se orejearon, pues convinieron en dejar cada uno el extremo por donde había echado, el uno de la astucia, el otro de la sencillez. Y poniendo la mira en el medio, descubrieron la Corte del Saber prudente y se encaminaron allá" (915b). The same remedy is employed when Vil Ocio tries to drag Andrenio into "La cueva de la nada" and a Fantástico forces Critilo into "El palacio de la vanidad," "fatales ambos escollos de la vejez, tan por extremos opuestos que en el uno suele peligrar de ociosa y en el otro de vana. Pero fue único remedio darse ambos las manos, con que pudieron templarse y hacer un buen medio entre tan peligrosos extremos" (955a).

Lope and Cervantes present no such philosophy as this either, for they close their novels with events that occur irrespective of the pathways trod by their pilgrims; nevertheless, their protagonists encounter the same Felicity as did Gracián's two travelers. The problem in *El peregrino en su patria* and *Persiles y Sigismunda* is that only the main protagonists survive life's journey to Felicity and that the journey is through a continuum of time in which contingency has replaced controlled conditions.

Lope's novel has few extraneous characters or episodes because it dedicates most of its pages to the eerie psychodrama that Pánfilo undergoes in his search for Nise, which takes him literally from one imprisonment to another: Doricleo's bandits, Barcelona's jail with Evarardo, Valencia's madhouse, an Arab captivity (narrated), Barcelona's jail again, Valencia's madhouse again, Godofre's parents' house, Nise's home. "Mirad cuán medrado llevamos nuestro Peregrino," Lope comments to his reader, "después del largo proceso de sus trabajos, pues de cortesano vino a soldado, de soldado a cautivo, de cautivo a peregrino, de peregrino a preso, de preso a loco, de loco a pastor y de pastor a mísero lacayo de la misma casa que fue la causa original de su desventura" (472-73). Along the way, the reader learns of a terrible shipwreak, the disastrous events in Doricleo's life which led the man to a career of banditry, the tragic murders of Lucrecia and Telémaco that led to Evarardo's imprisonment, tales by the Montserrat hermits of diabolical possession, Celio's murder in France of a suitor for Finea's affections, dangerous adventures in north Africa, another terrible shipwreck, the wounding of Jacinto, the wounding of Nise, Godofre's murder, and Pánfilo's demonic adventures outside Zaragoza.

It would not be an exaggeration to say that Lope does everything possible to make sure that the reader rejects any notion of a human being's capacity to organize and plan a life free from contingency. Indeed, at the precise center of Lope's book is a discourse on

Fate and Providence, which would be strangely out of place if it were not the intellectual core of the Counter Reformation message. Quoting from St. Augustine's *City of God* (Book Five), Lope informs the reader through Celio (who is speaking to Pánfilo, Lope's alter ego), "que este nombre hado sólo se puede atribuir a la voluntad de aquel sumo y verdadero Dios, que verdaderamente ve y conoce todas las cosas antes que sean, cuya alta providencia es la que las gobierna y rige con el medio de las segundas causas, la orden de las cuales pende del mismo Dios, y de algunos es llamado hado" (244). Life on earth is experienced as contingent and chaotic, and there is little that humans can do to assuage its haphazard nature other than accept it as it is. As Lope remarks at the end of the novel: "Ovidio, reprendiendo a Icaro, dijo: 'dentro de su fortuna viva el hombre'" (473), because if we know our limits we can restrict fate's influence. Yet, Lope continues, to live a life secure from fortune's vicissitudes is hardly to live at all, since it eliminates possibilities of completing actions that may be part of one's assigned role in life as a noble creature. "Mas también es flaqueza indigna de un noble el no atreverse," continues Lope, "pues si los que acabaron grandes cosas no las comenzaran, era imposible haberlas conseguido. Comenzar es generoso ánimo de un hombre; el suceso da el cielo, que dispone los fines" (473).

This is a solid philosophy of life that simultaneously explains the haphazard, contingent world in which we live and the value of striving to acheive those ends we desire. It is at once anti-pessimistic and voluntary, and it emphasizes the necessity for human endeavor while maintaining the notion that we are all dependent on divine guidance, since the ultimate ends in life are provided by God, not achieved by our own efforts. More specifically, it is anti-Stoic. Lope follows the statement about human endeavor with a rejection of Seneca's philosophy of the tranquil spirit. "Quien no ha peregrinado, ¿qué ha visto?" Lope asks his reader. "Quien no ha alcanzado, ¿qué ha sabido? ¿Y qué puede llamar descanso quien no ha tenido fortunas o por la mar o por la tierra?" (474). Life may be topsy-turvy, the human race may well be a species of passionate beasts, and we are all assuredly blind to the reality of things; but the noble heart still must strive to achieve what the will desires. Fifty years later, Gracián can recommend a moderate middle way derived from disillusionment with the extremes as the path to one's goals; but the early Baroque Lope sees striving as an open-ended enterprise undertaken with maximum effort. In Gracián's journey – a political odyssey – the dangers are mental and the remedy is simply to open one's eyes, to undeceive oneself about the reality of things; in Lope's world the journey is a physical exercise of dangers and imprisonments that – regardless of how long one continues to strive – has no remedy at all, because life is itself the very reality of things. For Gracián, the pilgrimage is life itself, an enterprise all human beings undertake by the mere fact that they live; for Lope, the pilgrimage is a voluntary, individual endeavor initiated by those of noble spirit who refuse to let their lives pass without attempting to fulfill completely the role their divinely guided free will tells them is theirs to realize. "¿Qué fama puede dejar de sí el que murió dentro de la cáscara de su nacimiento," Lope again questions his reader, "y desde los pañales a la mortaza apenas ha salido de la línea?" (474).

Life is not a pilgrimage, in other words, unless you make it one; and if you do, the outcome will invariably be happy. All pilgrimages, if undertaken in the appropriate spirit, necessarily bring salvation. At Lope's closure, all the major protagonists intermarry in a quintuple ceremony: Pánfilo with Celio's and Lisardo's sister Nise, Celio with Pánfilo's sister Finea, Leandro with Pánfilo's sister Elisa, Lisardo with Jacinto's sister Tiberia, plus Jacinto with Lucinda. Unlike the typical comedy, however, there were no actions undertaken by any of the characters that could have guaranteed these felicitous closures. The relationship between intent and outcome is based solely on Lope's philosophy of meritorious effort. As the last lines in the important discourse examined here declare, Pánfilo's constant subjection to fortune's blows are what win him a happy ending: "Haber merecido por medio de tan inumerables trabajos el fin del descanso de la patria" (474).

In reality, then, the Counter Reformation logic of Lope's world is only accidentally expressed in the series of sanctuaries visited (Montserrat, Valencia, Zaragoza, Guadalupe) and in the cumulative doctrinal material in the four intercalated *autos sacramentales*. The substantial logic is in the Catholic philosophy of active, willing participation in a world that is really (not merely illusionally) contingent, hazardous, and unpredictable, yet equally really (no merely illusionally) organized providentially by an active divinity who rewards with existential merits those who strive optimistically to achieve the goals they believe to be part of their appropriate role in life. It is at once a positive philosophy which permits freedom of the will and an authoritative philosophy that leaves all the ultimate decisions and outcomes to a sovereign power.

Cervantes' world is in many ways little more than a Baroque expansion of the one created by Lope de Vega. If *El peregrino en su patria* narrates six acts of violence, *Persiles y Sigismunda* narrates two dozen. In the first part, consisting of Books One and Two, whose events transpire in the northern areas of Europe farthest from Rome and therefore the least influenced by Catholic charity, everyone who is not incorporated into the core group of pilgrims that journeys to the south is either defeated or put to death.

In Book One, the demises begin with that of the barbarian Corsicurbo, the first voice heard and the first named character. His drowning at sea is followed by the violent death of Bradamiro, who is pierced through the mouth by an arrow, which initiates a pell-mell conflict among numerous barbarians who murder each other and then consume themselves in a universal conflagration.

Cloelia is the next to die, confessing her faith, then – skipping over the unnamed witch killed years before by Rutilio – Manuel de Sosa Coitiño perishes, confessing his love. After a ten-chapter respite on the island of Golandia (1.11-20), the reader absorbs the shock of two men who fight to the death over possession of the ill Taurisa, who also dies, followed immediately by the mysterious death of Rosamunda, apparently caused by her disgust at failing to seduce the young Antonio. With the exception of Clodio (who is accidentally murdered by young Antonio early in Book Two), everyone who has appeared so far and has a name and dies in the novel does so in this first Book; or, to put it another way, none of the other people who participate in the action of Book One and who have names die in the novel. They constitute the remnant who escapes to the south (which, as Julio Baena has intuited, is their "north" [134]) and whose names Cervantes repeats in summary form at key moments in the novel: the women Auristela (Sigismunda), Transila, Constanza, and Ricla, and the men Periandro (Persiles), Ladislao, Mauricio, old Antonio and young Antonio, Rutilio (who will stay behind but reappear in Rome at closure), and the itinerant Arnaldo.

Book Two takes another course and presents no significant violence or deaths (only Clodio's and the witch Zenotia's). It serves as a profound study of godless civilized peoples, in contrast to the presentation of godless uncivilized peoples in Book One.

Book Three brings the core remnant (Ricla, Constanza, the two Antonios, Periandro, and Auristela) to southern Europe and broaches a whole new packet of Christian themes based on charity. Nevertheless, the violence and death of uncivilized barbarians in Book One returns as a hallmark of uncivilized Christians in Book Three. In Chapter Four the group stumbles upon the murdered Diego de Parraces, whose assassin, Sebastián de Soranso, is never caught. In Chapter Nine they encounter the murdered Count, also assassinated from behind. In Chapter Fourteen Domicio kills himself and almost kills Periandro when the two fall from a tower. In the next chapter Rupertino is killed by the young Antonio while trying to abduct Feliz Flora. In Sixteen and Seventeen the group hears the story of Rubicón's murder of Lamberto de Escocia, and in Twenty-One they witness the voluntary death of Alejandro Castrucho, who simply quits living when he discovers how his niece Isabela tricked him so she could marry Andrea Marulo.

Book Four, the reconciliatory finale, also has sporadic violence and a number of deaths. The Duke of Nemurs and Arnaldo wound each other over a portrait of Auristela, Luisa kills Ortel Banedre when he tries to beat her up for running off with Bartolomé el Manchego, the reader learns that Policarpa has died, Sinforosa is refusing to marry anyone, and the barbarians have repopulated their island and instituted their savage rituals again. Pirro el Calabrés tries to murder Periandro, and the older brother Maximino succumbs to the Neapolitan disease.

All these deaths are sudden, violent, and totally unexpected. Many are vicious attacks from behind, and quite a few are unresolved. Poetic justice clearly is not a part of this barbaric European society through which the core remnant of pilgrims is traveling, nor does life become any easier or safer or provident as one nears the holy city of Rome. As in Lope's novel, life is unpredictable for everyone, everywhere, regardless of the nationality, gender, rank, lifestyle, age, or religion of the participants.

The south, then, is a dangerous, contingent society of people just as motivated to action by their baser passions as were the barbarians in Book One. The difference is in the series of counterweighted episodes which creates within the pilgrimage text a battery of characters with lives of their own, who come to project an exemplary moral focus onto the main event. Diana de Armas Wilson has done a magnificent job of isolating the thirteen most important episodes and analyzing their contribution to the narrative, for "the common denominator of all the 'templates' or exemplary novels interpolated into the *Persiles* is erotic love – fables of 'delicious love' for their readers or listeners, if not always for their protagonists" (160). Further, the "as-is" novelistic nature of the eroticism in the episodes coexists as a contrast to the "as-if" romance love of the main narrative. Indeed, every one of the episodes involves a dangerous, often illegal liaison, such as those concerning 1. Antonio-Ricla, 2. Rutilio, 3. Manuel de Sosa, and 4. Transila in Book One; 5. Leopoldo, 6. Sulpicia, and 7. Renato-Eusebia in Book Two; and 8. Feliciana de la Voz, 9. Ortel Banedre, 10. Ambrosia Agustina, 11. Claricia, 12. Ruperta-Croriano, and 13. Isabela Castrucho in Book Three. Book Four is the revelatory final part that unites the disparate characters and brings them together for closure.

While only Rutilio actually participates in the special couple's Roman denouement, almost all the other episode protagonists are mentioned in Book Four, often in closure terminology. For example, the young Antonio marries Feliz Flora on the last page, and Croriano and Ruperta are also mentioned as returning contentedly to France. The reader learns in Chapter Eight that Transila, Ladislao and Mauricio left Ireland and settled in England, where they are living happily, that Leopoldo pardoned the errant lovers and has remarried to assure a successor to the crown, and that Ortel Banedre's death has allowed Luisa and Bartolomé to marry. So – with the exceptions of the widowed Sulpicia and Claricia – the unresolved episodes eventually reach closure directly or indirectly in the last Book, ending happily in marriages.

The only exemplary tale that breaks the mold is the one concerning Manuel de Sosa Coitiño's death; but, as Alban Forcione observed, this tale is the only one that truly looks forward to the final scenes of the work because it is the only narrative that shows the victory of holy charity over secular desire in the bride's selection of Christ for her groom rather than Coitiño (64-65).

The multiplication of episodes in the first three Books, where they are evenly distributed, followed by no new characters in Book Four but rather the direct or indirect resolution of many of the tales, gives the end of *Persiles y Sigismunda* an eerie sense of completeness and universal harmony at closure quite different from those found in contemporary plays and novels. The person who has perceived this subtle technique best is Anthony J. Cascardi. In a perceptive study of Cervantes' romance, he observed:

> Whereas the order of signs established by the old symbolic regime could best meet the demands of a moral law through the sacrificial logic of violent revenge we see in the work of dramatists like Guillén de Castro, Lope, and Calderón, the *Persiles* seeks to establish what is essentially a new law, together with new conditions for moral discourse. These do not depend, as in the *comedias*, on a sublimation of those sacrificial demands through an idealist reshaping of the past, nor do they depend, as in the novel, on the generic institutionalization of an ironic point of view, but require instead the projection of a reconciled community of mankind. ... Any attempt to read the persuasive power of the romance in light of a demand for novelistic verisimilitude, and to stake its projections of community, identity, happiness, and belief on the plausibility of events would be to resist the more powerful thrust beyond the ethical toward the moral that it makes. ("Reason" 289-90)

It is this projection of an accomodating world in which human happiness is achieved through mutual reconciliation and cooperation by capitulating one's personal desires that marks both Cervantes' and Lope's romances as Counter Reformational. The religious aspects of the two novels, especially the "temple experiences" at the many religious shrines along the way, are not the important key here, nor is it true that "las peripecias del *Peregrino* y del *Persiles* son, en su esencia, experiencias religiosas," as Avalle-Arce once claimed (Lope, *Peregrino*, 30). Pánfilo and Periandro never consider religion as an appropriate closure for their lives. They are more like Ruy Díaz and Alonso Enríquez, who believed that being a knight did not preclude in any way being also a pious person. In effect, the lowest psychological moment in *Persiles y Sigismunda* is when Auristela, recovering from Hipólita's hex on her, adopts the Augustinian philosophy of the *ordo amoris* and decides to become a nun: "En sólo conocer a Dios está la suma gloria, y todos los medios que para este fin se encaminan, son los buenos, son los santos, son los agradables, como son los de la caridad, de la honestidad y el de la virginidad" (459).

This moment is certainly the emotional climax of the novel, and it does contain the ultimate meaning of the work, as Alban Forcione has observed, but not for the reasons he proffers. "The ultimate meaning of the *Persiles*," he writes, "is the acceptance of man's duty to participate in the life cycle, to make his way through the dark labyrinths of human history, and with the aid of faith and revelation discover the light that is ever partially obscured" (76-77). Faith and revelation have no specific role in the closure of this novel, nor even in Auristela's immediate decision to not enter the nunnery but rather to seek Periandro and marry him. What dissuades the heroine (now confessing publicly that she is Sigismunda) is the realization that the moral value of the reciprocal love she and Persiles have for each other, regardless of the dangerous vicissitudes of an active life to which that love exposes her, is worth more than the safe life of a cloistered virgin: "Hijo de rey es; hija y heredera de un reino soy; por la sangre, somos iguales; por el estado, alguna ventaja le hago; por la voluntad ninguna; y con todo, nuestras intenciones se responden, y nuestros deseos, con honestísimo efecto se están mirando; sola la ventura es la que turba y confunde nuestras intenciones, y la que por fuerza hace que esperemos en ella" (462).

Sigismunda's recognition of the appropriateness of human marriage as a controlling force in the violent, unstable, secular world is, according to Cascardi, the whole point of the novel: "Indeed, the very structure of the *Persiles* as a romance seems designed to illustrate the principle that despite the contingencies of time and chance and the fluctuations of fortune, there exists a transcendent plane on which our individual differences can be reconciled and the vagaries of our fortunes justified" ("Reason" 288).

There is thus an acute difference between Lope's and Cervantes' romances and the *comedia de enredo*, which – as will be noted in the Conclusion – also invariably ends in marriage. The dramatic project is a realistic enterprise to establish a stable social fabric in which the desires of the young are satisfied by incorporating their energies into the established order. The romance project is an idealistic enterprise to establish visionary closure to all human endeavor in which the individual willingly submits to divine providential direction, hence the extreme passivity of all the recipients of the connubial rewards at the end of these tales. Unlike the young dynamic men and women in the *comedia de enredo* who actively forge the destiny most appropriate for them in urban society, these Counter Reformation characters are coerced by the haphazard structure of the secular world in which they live to adopt a God's-eye view of time and its development, wherein they cannot presume to control events. They therefore eventually find it best to become as passive as possible before life's bewildering circumstances and to await a bountiful outcome based on God's providence.

It is this posture that makes the closures moral transactions, explains Cascardi with specific reference to *Persiles y Sigismunda*, rather than merely ethical ones: "In contrast to the ethical, the moment of the moral is produced when the freely-acting (novelistic) subject is brought willingly to submit to some more powerful agent of social and cultural control" ("Reason" 289). That this is accomplished through closures of transcendentally significant marriages intertwined with equally emblematic deaths should come as no surprise, because, as the following concluding pages will attempt to explain, these were the only non-religious avenues of passage available for those whose journeys through life became the subject matter of Counter Reformation literature.

CHAPTER EIGHT

CONVERTING AFFECTIVE EXPECTATIONS

If I were asked to choose three words to describe the entire apparatus of Counter Reformational closure by conversion that this study has examined, the first word I would choose would not be Cascardi's "control," but rather it would be the one José Antonio Maravall made so famous in his *La cultura del Barroco*: "directed." "Todo lo propio del Barroco surge de las necesidades de la manipulación de opiniones y sentimientos sobre amplios públicos," writes Maravall; "por eso destacamos precedentemente el carácter de 'dirigida' que la cultura del Barroco posee, su condición – por debajo de otras muchas cosas admirables – de técnica manipuladora" (198). A directed culture must be one in which four major areas are tightly manipulated from above:

> Una economía fuertemente dirigida, al servicio de un imperialismo que aspira a la gloria; una literatura comprometida a fondo en las vías del orden y de la autoridad, aunque a veces no esté conforme con ambos; una ciencia, tal vez peligrosa, pero contenida en manos de unos sabios prudentes; una religión rica en tipos heterogéneos de creyentes, reunidos en una misma orquesta por la Iglesia, que ha vuelto a dominar sobre el tropel de sus muchedumbres, seducidas y nutridas con novedades y alimentos de gustos raros y provocantes. (133)

The second and fourth of these areas are of interest here, and in particular how the fourth manipulated the second, because everything about all the literary materials examined here has the sense that it was "directed" by unseen powers to reach a religious closure;

from hence comes perhaps the sense of superficial, repetitive artificiality that haunts this kind of literature.

The ultimate reason for the sense of directedness is that the authors – while doing everything possible to assure that the reader understands all the protagonists' actions to be outcomes of the exercise of their own free will – must guarantee the reader that the lives of Christians are providentially directed by God to the end most appropriate for each one. As Cervantes noted at the closure of *Persiles y Sigismunda*, "aquella que comúnmente es llamada Fortuna, que no es otra cosa sino un firme disponer del cielo" (474). Lope de Vega's final philosophical discourse in *El peregrino en su patria* was on the same theme that "todo consiste en la disposición del cielo, cuya influencia armónica guía los pasos de nuestra vida donde quiere, porque aunque sobre todo tenga imperio el albedrío, pocos resisten a su sentido. ... Comenzar es generoso ánimo de un hombre, el suceso da el cielo, que dispone los fines" (473).

Very conservative authors like Francisco de Quevedo were always aware of the social implications of this message, and used it to protect their seigneurial status. The knowledge that "nunca mejora su estado quien muda solamente de lugar, y no de vida y costumbres" (1: 350) is what Quevedo presents Pablos de Segovia as learning only at the end of a disastrous career as a *buscón* aspiring to be the gentleman whom he can never be. Lope, Cervantes, and the other writers examined here preferred to express the idea in ethical terms of obedient resignation to God's designs which, being supremely provident, are the ones that direct people's lives to the happiest outcomes. As the proverb says, "*El hombre propone y Dios dispone.* 'Ref. que enseña que el logro de nuestras determinaciones pende precisamente y únicamente de la voluntad de Dios'" (Campos 239); or, in the words of Cervantes' *gitanilla* Preciosa, "uno piensa el bayo y otro el que le ensilla; el hombre pone y Dios dispone; quizá pensará que va a Oñez, y dará en Gamboa."

For those living in early seventeenth-century Spain, moreover, the variety of happy outcomes disposed by God was fixed at only two. Allowing for certain strange exceptions noted where appropriate, the literary characters whose careers end happily either get married or take religious orders. There are really no other options available for a felicitous closure in Counter Reformation Spain.

No piece of literature brings together better the themes of divine guidance in a seemingly unpredictable world and the necessary closures in marriage or the religious life than Mira de Amescua's *El esclavo del demonio*. In the opening scene, the aged Marcelo determines to dispose of his daughters in the standard two-part way, marrying Lisarda to don Sancho de Portugal and placing Leonor in a convent. Marcelo makes both of these decisions with the best of intentions for the good of the two girls. Furthermore, as their father he has the right to determine their futures. The girl's reactions to their father's plans are immediate: Leonor – "Tu esclava he de ser" (v. 74); Lisarda – "Y yo / una hija inobediente" (vv. 74-75). Marcelo then responds by angrily "destining" his two children with a curse on Lisarda and a blessing on Leonor.

> [to Lisarda] Plega a dios, inobediente,
> que casada no te veas,
> que vivas infamemente,
> que mueras pobre y que seas
> aborrecible a la gente.
>   Plega a dios que, destruida
> como una mujer perdida,
> te llamen facinerosa,
> y en el mundo no hay cosa
> tan mala como tu vida.
>   (vv. 121-30)
>
> [to Leonor] Plega a Dios que desigual
> tu vida a tu hermana sea,
> y este viejo ya mortal
> tan venturoso te vea
> que reines en Portugal.
>   (vv. 181-85)

Marcelo clearly exaggerates. As Mira portrays him, this old man certainly does not expect Lisarda to become "infame," "aborrecible," "perdida," and "facinerosa." He will in fact later agree to her own stated plan to marry Diego de Meneses, the family's mortal enemy (vv. 888-94). It is equally improbable that Leonor, whom Marcelo has destined for the convent, should somehow become the sovereign of her country. Yet curses and blessings of this type always come true in Golden Age drama, where they function as an ironic device to insinuate forthcoming dramatic events.

Many of the works examined here – especially those with a heroic adventure structure like *Las mocedades del Cid*, "El bandolero," *Las quinas de Portugal*, the pilgrimage novels, but also *El condenado por desconfiado*, *La ninfa del cielo*, and *El burlador de Sevilla* – have various types of premonitions and forewarnings which all come to pass, regardless of the expectations of the protagonists. The curses and blessings in *El esclavo del demonio* are somewhat different because Marcelo has no expectation at all that they will ever come to fruition. Mira de Amescua's *La rueda de la fortuna* and *El animal profeta* are also constructed around such blind predictions. Another classic example of empty threats that come true is the admonition that Sancho Ortiz de la Roela hurls against King Sancho in Act One, scene ten, of the anonymous (although often attributed to Mira de Amescua) *La estrella de Sevilla*. Diatribes like Roela's are often given in fits of rage, and the speaker does not normally intend for them to be taken literally. In this sense they are "rhetorical truths," empty threats that ironically come true by the end of the play.

Marcelo comes to understand the irony of his rhetorical curses and blessings at the resolution of the events in his life when he exclaims in an apostrophe to his deceased daughter: "Mi maldición te alcanzó; / mas si Dios en sí te trueca, / maldición dichosa ha sido" (vv. 3284-86). Equally ironic is the veracity of Marcelo's unwitting benediction to Lisarda when she was disguised as a male bandit in Act Two:

> Ya que con sano consejo
> pides bendición a un viejo,
> Dios desta vida te saque.
> Él te perdone y te aplaque,
> que perdonado te dejo.
> (vv. 1378-82)

Indeed, the outcome of the play is precisely the opposite from Marcelo's initial designs. In a secular/religious vein parallel to the political reversals of fortune in Mira de Amescua's *La rueda de la fortuna* and *No hay dicha ni desdicha hasta la muerte*, Leonor and Lisarda achieve final destinies totally contrary to their father's designs, endings so unexpected that the spectators would have to marvel at how far from their original planned outcomes the daughters have gone. Who would have ever expected that Leonor, destined for the convent, would marry, but not Sancho de Portugal (a second destiny), but rather Sancho the king of Portugal? Who would have ever expected that Lisarda, destined for marriage to Sancho de Portugal, would not even marry Diego de Meneses, but would be seduced by the holiest man in the kingdom, become a bandit, repent, become a slave to her father, and finally be purified by God to die a saint? Both young women go through analogous four-fold cycles of 1) other-proposed lives, 2) self-destined intentions, 3) actual events, and 4) final unexpected outcomes. Lisarda 1) is proposed by Marcelo to marry Sancho de Portugal, 2) plans to escape with Diego, 3) flees with Gil to become a bandit, but 4) finishes her career a Magdalene "esclava de Dios." Leonor 1) is proposed by Marcelo to enter a convent, 2) plans to obey him, 3) then falls in love with Sancho de Portugal, but 4) finishes her career as queen of her country.

The same kinds of plans frustrated by events leading to unexpected outcomes characterize the two male protagonists in the play, whose lives parallel those of the two women. Gil 1) is supposed to win souls from sin (that is what he sees as his planned career), and 2) he intends to save Lisarda and Diego from a sinful act; but 3) he instead seduces Lisarda and becomes an "esclavo del demonio," to then 4) finish his career as a saint of the Church. Diego 1) is supposed to be the family's mortal enemy, but 2) he intends to steal Lisarda from her father, only 3) to repent and decide to make peace with Marcelo. At this point, still only in Act One, Diego loses control of his destiny to become a bewildered onlooker to events. He first thinks Lisarda's father has murdered her, then is arrested and sentenced to die for her death, only to be absolved through the last-minute intervention of Gil – "No es bien que Don Diego muera" (v. 3227) – the very person who "saved" him at the beginning of the play.

Diego's continual confusion about the reality of events places him in the unique role of participant/spectator, much like the *spitzel* in old paintings who points to the significant event in a picture, who is in the action but not necessarily part of it. Repeatedly accused of sins he never committed, hunted down by everyone, castigated undeservedly by Lisarda, Gil, Marcelo, and King Sancho, Diego never has control of his own destiny nor a voice concerning his circumstances. He is present at the play's resolution, but has nothing resolved; he simply stands there, pointing at the others' completed lives. Diego becomes an onstage spectator, just as amazed about the outcome of events, just as dumbfounded at the unimagined destinies of the other personages, just as convinced of some guiding hand that disposes people's lives in the way most appropriate for each individual, as are the spectators in the audience. His comment to close the play is thus the same as ours: "Merecen estos sucesos / una admiración eterna" (vv. 3290-91).

The eternal admiration comes from the simple yet ingenious technique that Mira de Amescua uses to generate the play's action: expectations never match outcomes, regardless of the plans and intentions of the participants. *El hombre propone y Dios dispone.* The events in the lives of Lisarda, Gil, Leonor, Sancho, Prince Sancho, Diego, Marcelo, and even the gracioso Domingo show that personal desires and plans are never guaranteed. One must therefore adopt the Counter Reformation posture of creaturely dependence exhibited by Gil at the play's end and expressed in his declaration "confío / en Dios y en mi penitencia" (vv. 3234-35). This is the simple message about the appropriate roles in regard to authority and obedience in Catholic society that all readily understand because they hear it every week from the pulpit. It is a theology meant to inculcate humility about earthly expectations, but it also inspires eternal admiration about God's providence in disposing our lives to their most appropriate end.

The closures thus leave no gaps and no ambiguities. Everyone's life which ends happily necessarily ends in marriage or religion, and conversely everyone's life which ends sadly necessarily ends in death or extirpation from the society. You're either out or in. If you're out, nobody cares about you. If you're in, you have taken up the religious life or gotten married. It's as simple as that to the Counter Reformation mind.

The ubiquity of these two choices and their universal acceptance by the populace are what make novels like *Guzmán de Alfarache* and *El buscón* so shocking and "picaresque." In those tales the protagonists, led astray by their "mala inclinación" to be gentlemen without acquiring the concomitant virtue necessary to live as one, abuse, mock, and parody the religious life and marriage. Pablos ends his narration describing how he and his band took refuge from the law in a church (the "Iglesia Mayor" no less) and perverted its purpose by letting in prostitutes (for whom he uses the "pagan" term *ninfas*) and learning new ways to continue their corrupt life: "Estudié la jacarandina, y a pocos días era rabí [note the non-Christian reference] de los otros rufianes" (1: 350a). The closure mocks both religious conversion and marriage, because Pablos declares that while in the church he met the prostitute Grajales, with whom "propuse de navegar en ansias con la Grajales hasta morir" (1: 350b), words which invert the happily-ever-after endings of all comedies and the author's own courtly love poetry, such as his sonnets to Lisi (2: 116 ff.).

Guzmán de Alfarache specifically enters into both sacraments, only to pervert them to ends opposed to their Catholic intentions. After a series of frustrated affairs with women in Part One and the first two books of Part Two, Guzmán dedicates almost all of the third book to destroying marriage and religion. The theme of the female dominates. It starts in Zaragoza (II.3.1), where he decides to court an apparently rich widow. His problems begin before he even meets her, because two other lively girls flirt with him in the street and steal all his money, leaving him stranded. Then, on his way back to his lodgings, he is again solicited by a lady; but that episode ends worse, because he eats dung and vomits in front of her house. He again pursues the widow (II.3.2), but desists when he realizes she is a respectable person who will never pay any attention to an unknown out-of-towner.

Guzmán subsequently goes to Madrid and begins a relationship with the mistress of the inn where he is staying and then with the daughter of a friend of hers. The women conspire to get him to spend money on them, then accuse him of deflowering the daughter to extort two hundred ducats from him. Guzmán's response is a long discourse on rape, which he considers a fiction used by women to trick men into paying them money or marrying them. Nevertheless, he immediately marries a woman who is so insignificant to him that he never tells us her name. She spends all his money and, when he is impoverished, comes to hate him (II.3.3). This leads to a long discourse against all women and the torments he suffered during his six years of marriage, which ends with his liberation from the wife: "De una enfermedad aguda murió, sin mostrar arrepentimiento ni recebir sacramento" (348b).

Having thus made a travesty of the sacred event that serves as the ultimate happy ending for all comedies and courtly novels and summarily dispatching his wife to Hell, the narrator turns to religion as a proper vocation, as indeed it is. In Guzmán's case, however, the priesthood is no more than an easy way to get free room and board: "Tendré cierta la comida y, a todo faltar, meteréme fraile, donde la hallaré cierta. Con esta no solo repararé mi vida, empero la libraré de cualquier peligro, en que alguna vez me podría ver por casos pasados" (351a). So he moves to Alcalá de Henares and studies theology for seven years (II.3.4). During the interval he denounces house mothers and women who board students, which seems strange, until we learn that in his last year of studies he is swept off his feet by Gracia, the oldest daughter of his house mother: "Volví de nuevo como Sísifo a subir la piedra" (363b).

The situation worsens. After a long discourse on sexual passion (II.3.5), he describes how he and his new family lose their inn and have to work in it for the new owners to subsist. His mother-in-law then prostitutes her daughter (with Guzmán's consent), and they all move to Madrid to make more money from Gracia's services. They are soon caught, and he and Gracia are exiled to Sevilla, where his mother is already a madame for another girl and takes over the chores of prostituting her daughter-in-law (II.3.6). Gracia eventually runs away with a Neapolitan ship captain, and his mother leaves Guzmán to fend for himself. Befriended by a good priest, he is given a job as an administrator for a kindly woman, whom he cheats and robs (II.3.7). This is rock bottom, because both his benefactors are charitable people who truly wish to help him; and it is for these specific deeds of ill-will that he is put into jail and sentenced to public flogging and six years in the galleys.

The last two chapters of *Guzmán de Alfarache* describe Guzmán's tortuous conversion (whether real or feigned), described earlier in Chapter Five; but even in closure the narrator cannot leave the subject of marriage aside. In the very last pages, Guzmán inserts a section in which the knight he serves asks him how he should respond to an unmarried man who insists that he get married. Guzmán replies with two tales that warn the knight against it, because only one in a thousand couples finds happiness. Honestly, there was no reason at all for Mateo Alemán to have inserted this intrusive moment in his finale unless he specifically wanted to satirize the happy marriage closure that populated all the other literature in 1600.

The ubiquity of the marriage and conversion closures is also what makes books like *Don Quijote de la Mancha* so humanistic and refreshing, for the novel stands out as a positive alternate vision to the mass of Counter Reformation materials that limit life's options to two careers. It is not unusual for the greatest literature of an age to go against the grain of the epoch it most patently represents; *El poema de mió Cid* is a democratic anti-noble, anti-courtly tale about an older man and his family seeking an honorable life on their own land, *El libro de buen amor* extols physical love as an end in itself rather than an instinct to be used in marriage but never enjoyed; *La Celestina* views life as a selfish existence of alienated individuals seeking instant gratification for personal desires; and *Don Quijote de la Mancha* is replete with people who take the notion of Free Will literally and choose the destiny they themselves consider to be the most beneficial. Tell Marcela, the "galeotes," Ricote, Ginés de Pasamonte – to say nothing of Don Quijote and Sancho – or any of the other characters who populate the tale that there is an *Autor* like the one in Calderón's *El gran teatro del mundo* who has distributed the appropriate roles to all creatures because "así mi ciencia previene / que represente el que viva. / Justicia distributiva / soy, y sé lo que os conviene" (3: 208a). They would respond with the traditional Humanist philosophy that God may know, but no one else does; so people must depend on their own natural inclinations – what Cervantes refers to over and over as the "ventajas naturales" – to reach the destiny God has deemed most appropriate for them. Cervantes' independent characters would add that, even though the achievement of personal desires may depend ultimately on the will of God, there are many things people can do to sway the divine will to their benefit or their detriment, such as work in a cooperative way with divine intermediaries to win God's mercy or, contrarily, obstinately ignore the advise and warnings the divine mediators bring to them about their destiny.

All seventeenth-century readers would capture immediately this notion of cooperative Free Will, because it is a part of their Counter Reformation culture and the major bulwark to the Protestant notion of divine election. Predestination was the core of the first religious crisis between Erasmus and Luther in the 1520s, as we have seen, and the Council of Trent had confirmed the traditional teachings of the Church that all human beings have sufficient control over their own lives to establish by their own actions their own salvation or condemnation. God may know what we are going to do, but that does not mean that he has elected for us to do it nor even desires for us to do it; therefore, we all create our own outcomes. In the words of Alejo Venegas, "a Dios no hay cosa pasada, porque todas le son presentes; y por consiguiente el conocimiento eterno de Dios constriñe ni fuerza al libre albedrío:"

> De manera que hace muy mala cuenta el que dice 'ya sabe Dios lo que ha de ser de mí. No puedo escaparme del fin que Dios sabe que tengo que haber,' porque con la libertad del libre albedrío puede aparejarse a la divina gracia para obrar bien. ... Así diremos que el conocimiento que Dios tiene del fin de los hombres no fuerza a los hombres para obrar de una o de otra manera, mas los deja libres para obrar lo que ellos quisieren. (xxiv)

In effect, Free Will is the one thing someone like Francisco de Quevedo most defends in books with appropriate titles such as *Providencia de Dios* against the false arguments about predestination held by Martin Luther, who rejected Free Will (1: 1428). The Protestant theology of election – understood as a God-driven process in which the human's part in salvation is limited to faith alone, regardless of any special voluntary acts of penitence – is simply a demonic deceit, a diabolical ruse to persuade simple believers to lose their faith in their ability to win God's infinite mercy by actively cooperating with divine intermediaries through established religious rituals and works.

The same ideas of an open eschatological system are also expressed well in the popular lore of the time, such as in proverbs and folk sayings. The surprising and unexpected turns of events for Gil and the many other characters in *El esclavo del demonio*, and for the countless sinners in the other works examined here, are fully subsumed under ageless sayings such as *Quien yerra y se enmienda, a Dios se encomienda* or *Quien se muda, Dios le ayuda* or *No hizo Dios a quien desamparase*: "Manifiesta que Dios no se olvida de nadie, y que no debe perderse la esperanza en ningún caso, por desesperado que parezca" (Campos 180-81).

Lamentably, this traditional Catholic philosophy of self-direction loses much of its force in the Counter Reformation times of authority and obedience, to hardly appear at all after 1615, as is seen in *Persiles y Sigismunda*, which falls back into the pattern of marriage or religion for appropriate options to happiness. All other participants in the novel either die or, like Bartolomé "el Manchego" and his Talaveran mistress, parody the pilgrimage motif by wandering off into a wasted life of directionless perdition. Lope's pilgrimage novel with its closure of quintuple marriages is the most blatant acquiescence to the mode, followed by virtually the entire corpus of early seventeenth-century comedies.

Moreover, the novelists and playwrights do everything possible to make it appear that the final pairings are precisely what the individuals and society most want to occur, otherwise the closures would not be completely happy. They therefore create characters who, as Matthew Stroud astutely observed, joyously adopt their new matrimonial roles: "These characters *want* to believe that they are marrying as a logical extension of their imaginary love. They *want* to get married, to trade their individual fantasies for the collective security of the society" (90-91).

There is not better proof of the latter genre's conformity to the Counter Reformation pattern than the eighty plays attributed to Tirso de Molina. Of those, forty-seven can be classified as pure *comedias de enredo*, with no religious or historical reference. In fact, when religion does become a factor, it is always in the form of satire or parody, as in *Marta la piadosa*. When history appears to support the plot, as in the lone example of *El vergonzoso en palacio*, the author himself presents an auto-criticism of its presence, claiming that the sole intention is "fabricar, sobre cimientos de personas verdaderas, arquitecturas del ingenio fingidas" (*Cigarrales* 159).

All forty-seven *comedias de enredo* end with weddings, and – concomitantly – all forty-seven shun violence in the closure, with the only deaths at all being catalytic murders in the initial moments of five of the comedies (*Como han de ser los amigos, Ventura con el nombre, La villana de la Sagra, Habladme en entrando, El honroso atrevimiento*). In effect, matrimony is so important in the outcome of the *comedia de enredo* that when a character decides not to marry, as in *La firmeza en la hermosura*, it is a shocking surprise to everyone. When Juan and Elena win the necessary permission to wed, Josefa, who had vied for Juan's love, declares that she has decided to remain unmarried so that her relatives can inherit her estate. This unusual decision prompts the gracioso Buñol to comment parodically: "Y habremos comedia visto / que no acaba en casamientos / ... / porque pueda rematarse, / sin cura y sin padrinos, / una comedia soltera" (3: 1443b).

It is worth repeating that for Tirso and the other playwrights entrance into a convent is not an option in the *comedia de enredo*. In

Tirso's thirty-three historical and religious plays, on the other hand, which have serious plots consistently involving the death of a principal character and often ending in disillusionment with political and social life, many women and men choose the religious life as a proper closure to their careers.

Such overwhelming evidence of strict conformity to only a pair of possible outcomes leads me to the second word that best describes the entire apparatus of Counter Reformational closure: "agenda." José Antonio Maravall discusses this motivation also, referring to the fact that Baroque culture does everything necessary to assure that there be a previously established goal, "un resultado programado" (172) to which the people can be directed; and, as Maravell stresses, to do this the directors must know how the directed ones think and adjust their agenda to match those thoughts, assuring thereby a successful reception for the program: "Ni se dirige a los hombres de cualquier manera, sino como técnicamente sea adecuado (según estiman el moralista o el político del XVII), ni mucho menos se les dirige hacia donde se quiere, si no es contando con las respuestas que cabe esperar de la opinión constituida previamente entre los mismos dirigidos" (*Cultura* 153-54).

Once the authorities discover what works, they only need to limit production to those models, what Maravall calls the "patrones de la literatura y del arte barrocos" (*Cultura* 161). This is why, I believe, the Baroque literary genres – like the purportedly revolutionarily innovative *comedia* structure – are so stable decade after decade. The agenda established for the medium was integrally connected with the medium's structural mechanisms, which depended on the established expectations of the recipient. It would never occur to Tirso de Molina, for example, to end one of his *comedias de enredo* with the demise of a principal character; yet every one of his religious or historical plays has a demise or disappearance of some kind. More strictly, there are certain theatrical techniques and literary stereotypes that Tirso never used in a *comedia de enredo* but always used without exception in his serious religious or historical plays.

The most obvious theatrical technique is the use of stage machinery, which has already been discussed briefly in Chapter Five. There were three basic ways to create a vertical action on stage to counter the typical horizontal action of coming and going. The most impressive was the *tramoya*, where personages or objects would be lifted over the stage or fly through the air or witness divine beings descend from above the stage. It should come as no surprise that every one of Tirso's religious plays calls for the use of a *tramoya* somewhere in the drama, because it is the *tramoya* that puts the protagonist into contact with the divine realm, proving visibly to the spectators the validity of the heavenly visit which sanctifies the protagonist.

The second theatrical technique was the previously discussed *apariencia*, which N. D. Shergold called "discovery" (202) and which was defined so succinctly by Covarrubias (130). Again, every play by Tirso de Molina that has a religious context has some kind of "discovery" where a vision from the divine realm is revealed through the personages on stage to the audience, precisely as in the church a curtain or panel is pulled aside to reveal the host or a relic or a divine image.

The third theatrical technique is a horizontal one that permits the sudden dramatic exhibition of a corpse. It could also be termed a "discovery" because Tirso usually introduces the exhibition of the corpse with the phrase "*Descúbrese*." These moments invariably occur at closure, and they can be found in Tirso's biblical plays (with the exception of *La mejor espigadera*, which has a true *apariencia*) and in the plays he called tragedies. Their use is clearly programmed, because each exhibition of a corpse is the same. *La adversa fortuna de don Álvaro de Luna: Descúbrese un teatro de luto, y Moralicos, de luto, con un plato pidiendo; el cuerpo aparte y la cabeza aparte* (1: 2038b). *La mujer que manda en casa: Descúbrese tendido en el suelo Nabot, muerto, en camisa y calzones de lienzo; él y el vestido manchado de sangre, entre un montón de piedras, también ensangrentadas* (1: 617a). *Los amantes de Teruel: Córrase un tafetán, y aparezca Marsilla armado sobre un túmulo negro con una celada en las manos y hachas a los lados* (1: 1396b). *Escarmientos para el cuerdo: Descubre a Doña Leonor ya difunta, y a Diaguito, ensangrentado* (3: 259b). And so on.

Tirso does not use repeatedly these basic theatrical devices because he has a limited repertoire of techniques. On the contrary, he uses them because he knows precisely the response that they will elicit from his spectators; he uses them as part of his agenda for controlling their emotional dispositions towards his material and bringing them into his illusion.

Tirso de Molina also has some strictly formal techniques related to the theme of divine providence that he uses to elicit programmed responses from his audience, and they too depend on the generic nature of the dramatic material. Patently Counter Reformational is Tirso's repeated use of an act of desperation by a main character. In the religiously oriented plays *La ninfa del cielo*, *Santa Juana II*, *No le arriendo la ganancia* (*auto*), and *Los hermanos parecidos* (*auto*) a character attempts to commit suicide in a moment of desperation about God's saving mercy, only to be detained by a divine being (an angel, Santa Juana, "Acuerdo," Cristo, respectively). In every instance the motive for suicide is deep remorse for past sins, and after being deterred the character decides to lead a pious and saintly life. Mari Pascuala in *Santa Juana II* tries to take her life by hanging herself, while "Honor," Ninfa and Hombre in their respective works seek to throw themselves off a precipice. These kinds of desperate acts can be counted on to elicit programmed responses from spectators, so they form an agenda of techniques, actions, remarks, scenic sets, stage postures, pertinent clothing, and symbolic props that convey the appropriate message – here one of divine succor for those in need – to the spectator.

One more example of a programmed item that is relevant here is the depiction by Tirso of the scorned woman. In at least six plays of serious subject matter Tirso creates interchangeable actions, tones, and language to portray a woman seduced and abandoned by her lover. His utilization of this formula is unrelated to the particular histrionic mode of the play, because the scene – while not appropriate for *comedias de enredo* – appears in an *auto sacramental*, hagiographic dramas, a tragedy, and a biblical play. The presentation of the scorned woman forms part of *La madrina del cielo* (*auto*), *Santa Juana II*, *La ninfa del cielo*, *La dama del olivar*, *El burlador de Sevilla*, *Escarmientos para el cuerdo*, and *La venganza de Tamar*. In every situation the female – Marcela, Mari Pascuala, Ninfa, Laurencia, Tisbea, María, and Tamar, respectively – is either seduced or raped by the male – Dionisio, Jorge, Carlos, Guillén, Juan, Manuel, and Amón, respectively – and then cast off and abandoned by him.

Scorned women appear in countless other works of literature, so it is not surprising to find seven examples in Tirso's dramatic corpus of eighty plays. It is unusual, however, to find seven examples so similar in their physical actions, their language, and their outcome. In the religious plays, which constitute the first four, the men are eventually forgiven for their seduction and abandonment because in one way or another they go through the requisite cycle of examination of conscience, confession, and desire for forgiveness. In the last three plays the men are punished by death because they refuse to enter into the requisite cycle of conversion.

The final and perhaps most appropriate word to describe the Counter Reformational culture in Spain is "propaganda," a term now part of every Westerner's vocabulary, but which was coined only in 1622 by the Roman curia. It means the systematic manipulation of public opinion, generally by the use of symbols such as flags, monuments, oratory, and publications. It derives from the *Congregatio de Propaganda Fide*, the office of the Vatican that was established by Gregory XV to assure uniform propagation of Catholic doctrine.

Propaganda makes the message of prime importance and nullifies the integrity of the medium; and in effect the mode of transmission becomes irrelevant, as we have seen in this study. Every literary or artistic genre or medium becomes a legitimate vehicle for the Catholic Church to appropriate from its secular origen and to reinstitute as a vessel for a religious message, regardless of the vehicle's prior purpose. Emblems, popular songs, public festivals, comedies, tragedies, farces, novels of every type, erudite poetic rhyme schemes, Classical models, jokes, games, proverbs, nothing is exempt from the Church's appropriation of media for its message.

It goes without saying that the message being transmitted 1) must reach its destined ears in a convincing, affirmative way, and 2) must retain for the recipient the same meaning that it had for the sender. If the propaganda isn't accepted by the receiver or isn't interpreted as the sender wished, then it has failed as propaganda. Today most propaganda practices the technique of inverting the relationship between difficulty and didacticism; in other words, the more the sender wishes to have the import of the message received intact and properly interpreted, the clearer the message will be. The accompanying attractants – the entertainment factors – will therefore be non-verbal so as not to cloud the message. Music, dance, costumes, theatrical devices (*tramoyas, apariencias*, exhibitions), fancy rhythms and rhymes, and other implements will be utilized to capture the receiver's attention while the message is being sent. These non-verbal techniques certainly proliferate as well in the Spanish Golden Age, as has been seen in the examples presented here.

Clarity of language to assure a precise, direct, understandable, unambiguous message is another hallmark of today's propaganda. It is not necessarily the typical character of Counter Reformation propaganda, however, because of an innovative technique that all modern scholars have recognized as a definitive characteristic of Baroque culture: *admiratio*. If you can startle the recipients of your message to suspend their train of thought, then you can impose more readily your message on their mind. The technique is so universally recognized that it really needs no elaboration here. It is the one that prompts the typical list of Baroque characteristics, such as those by Fernando Checa Cremades y José Miguel Morán Turina in *El Barroco*: "Un sentido dramático, emotivo, retórico, teatral y anticientífico de la imagen" (27).

Unfortunately, the technique has been viewed by most scholars as an end in itself and not as a means to a much more significant closure, whose proper usage I believe José Antonio Maravall was one of the first to emphasize. In *La cultura del Barroco* he mentions the technique of *admiratio*, but correctly brushes it aside in favor of its purpose for winning over the will of the recipients:

> Mover al hombre, no convenciéndole demostrativamente, sino afectándole, de manera que se dispare su voluntad: ésta es la cuestión. Sólo así se consigue arrastrar al individuo, suscitando su adhesión a una actitud determinada, y sólo por esa vía se logra mantenerlo solidario de la misma. Para la mente barroca es la única manera de conseguir atraerse una masa cuya opinión cuenta e imponerse a ella, canalizando su fuerza en la dirección querida. (171)

The appropriate word is therefore not *admiratio* but rather *adfectio*. You don't want to just startle your recipients; you want to move them to love you, to respond with the "affection" that you show for them.

No one saw the difference between these two techniques better than Baltasar Gracián. Primor XII of *El héroe* states the following: "Poco es conquistar el entendimiento, si no se gana la voluntad; y mucho, rendir con la admiración la afición juntamente" (23-24). *Oráculo manual y arte de prudencia* presents the same aphorism in a different form: "Mucho es conseguir la admiración común, pero más la afición" (164).

There is no question that the Counter Reformation writer does indeed use every technique available to impose a sense of *admiratio*, including the exaltation of the passionate emotions of fear, love, desire, hate, joy and sadness. Regrettably, these bodily sensations are also referred to in the nomenclature of the art historians as "afetti," which refer specifically to the expression of passionate emotions, not the turning of the will towards an affectionate object. The Counter Reformation *adfectio* that Gracián defines so well is closer to "benevolencia" (24), a movement of the will to the good, a reciprocal, warm feeling of loving communion and sense of belonging.

Although usually appreciated for its clear declarations about roles in life, Calderón's *auto sacramental El gran teatro del mundo* also expresses this notion of *adfectio*. The play which the Autor (God) has decided to present is titled *Obrar bien, que Dios es Dios*, and this idea of good works forms the core of the anti-Protestant theology in the play. To assure that all the actors (humanity) have precisely the same opportunity to perform good works during their time on stage, God distributes their attributes to them based on His prescience of their abilities. All thus receive the role that is most appropriate for them to play, so all thus have exactly the same chance to perform their roles well. Whether they be kings, peasants, nuns, beautiful women, or rich men, all have the same opportunity to "obrar bien." People should therefore not worry about what their role or anyone else's role is in this life, because their role neither favores nor prejudices their salvation. The only important factor is how well they perform. As the Autor explains to the Pobre: "Haz tú bien el tuyo y piensa / que para la recompensa / yo te igualaré con él [el rey]" (3: 208a).

There is certainly nothing affectionately benevolent about this equalizing system of thought, since it deemphasizes the work ethic and the culture of success in favor of a static system of appropriate roles. Yet there is more to *El gran teatro del mundo* than the role one plays in life. Along with one's attributes comes the dramatic part, which entails the lines one must speak in the play.

After all have received their roles, represented by the clothes they will wear, Ley de Gracia enters and announces that although every actor will have a different role, all will have precisely the same lines in the play: "Ama al otro como a ti / y obra bien, que Dios es Dios" (3: 211b). The second line informs them *what* they have to do to gain salvation, but the first line tells them *how* to do it. At the end of the theater play, then, only Discreción is recognized as having accumulated truly good works capable of being transferred to the afterlife in her favor, and those are her "sacrificios, afectos y oraciones" (3: 220a).

Interestingly, we all know what sacrifices and prayers are, but the precise meaning of the "afectos" has been lost within the Counter Reformation culture that fostered it. The closest meaning to "afecto" in this Calderonian context is probably "devotions" in the archaic sense of "religious observance or worship; a form of prayer or worship for special use" (*Random House Dictionary of the English Language: College Edition*). Francisco de Quevedo used the term in this sense when he titled one of his religious sonnets *A la limosna y su afecto y su poder con dios* (2: 88), and when he delivered an apostrophe to a very poor church with a single clay lamp that ended "se verá en tu afecto cuánto vales" (2: 88); but Quevedo also used the word repeatedly to describe the ardent emotions he experienced from being in love, both of the "sensitive" and the "intellectual" type (2: 114). One of his most famous love sonnets is titled *Afectos varios de su corazón, fluctuando en las ondas de los cabellos de Lisi* (2: 118), and many other sonnets have the word in singular and plural forms as an equivalent for "passionate desire" (2: 126).

In all these cases, one gets the sense of a total capitulation to *adfectio*, a willing surrender of the sensitive and intellectual faculties to reach a cooperative relationship with another entity. For a paradigmatic case for this submissive Cooperative Love we only need to go back to the *Introduction to the Devout Life* by Saint Francis of Sales, which Quevedo translated into Spanish in 1634. After going through all the different stages that a normal lay person can utilize for leading a devout life, including traditional prayer and the sacraments, the practice of virtue and the avoidance of temptations, Saint Francis of Sales discusses the exercises of self-examination necessary to renew the soul and confirm it in the devout life. Chapter Eight, a brief "aviso" towards the end of the book, is titled *Aficiones que debemos tener después del examen* and states the following:

> Después de haber con blandura considerado cada punto del examen y visto el estado en que estás, darás lugar a las aficiones siguientes:

> Darás gracias a Dios por la enmienda que hubieres hallado en tu vida después de tu resolución; y reconoce que ha sido su misericordia sola que ha obrado en ti y por ti.
> Humíllate cuanto puedas delante de Dios, reconociendo que si no te has adelantado más, ha sido por tu falta, y por no haber con fidelidad, animosa y constantemente correspondido a las inspiraciones, claridades y movimientos que te ha dado en la oración. Y entonces
> Prométele alabar para siempre por las gracias recibidas; y así te retirarás de tus inclinaciones, y llegarás a la enmienda.
> Pídele perdón por la infidelidad y deslealtad con que has correspondido.
> Ofrécele tu corazón para que se haga de todo punto señor dél.
> Súplicale te haga fiel de todo punto.
> Invoca a los santos, la Virgen, tu ángel, tu patrón, San Josef, y otros. (Quevedo 1: 1710b-11a)

The entire section – virtually a summary of Counter Reformation doctrine – is replete with gentle advice that the pious readers stop what they are doing, accept a passive role in life, and cooperate with the host of invisible intermediaries who will lead them to the fulfillment that comes with surrender to the Church; thank God for their decision to cease living a sinful life, and recognize that He alone has done this; humble themselves and recognize their faults and weaknesses; retire from their past inclinations; seek pardon for past infidelities; turn their very hearts over to the Lord to do with it as He wishes; pray to all the invisible Catholic intermediaries who populate this world.

This is the end of the line, because it entails a culture of emotional passive cooperation rather than rational assertive responsibility. Willing abnegation of one's self-worth to the Church brings a sense of affectionate belonging to something of much greater worth, while resistence only brings melancholy and self-deprecation.

Happiness, then, comes from cooperative submission to the divine plan, whose platform allows cooperation either through marriage or through relinquishment of the secular life. In Golden Age Spain there thus is a specific closure for everyone. Those who oppose the system – the Moors, the doubters of their faith, the don Juans, the willful, the social climbers – die or leave it, while those who participate can either submit to the loving reciprocal affection of a companion by marrying and living happily ever after or can yield to the spiritual friendship of the Church's many divine intermediaries by taking religious vows. Either choice evokes an inclusive *adfectio* in the participants which leads to a joyous passivity of being. As Maravall noted, this is the only logical closure for a directed culture's agenda: "Así pues, el Barroco pretende dirigir a los hombres, agrupados masivamente, actuando sobre su voluntad, moviendo a ésta con resortes psicológicos manejados conforme a una técnica de captación que, en cuanto tal, presenta efectivamente caracteres masivos" (*Culture* 172-73).

The composite term "Directed Propagandistic Agenda" describes well the Counter Reformation program that I have attempted to describe in this study. At their best, the Church's doctrines, once they became part of mainstream Spanish culture and lost their sharp converting edge, fostered family values, a sense of belonging, benevolence, political homogeneity, and a general sense of confident satisfaction with the religious and secular authorities who affectionately looked after the society's well-being. At their worst, the new doctrines eradicated the outsider and nonconformist, crushed dissent, and restricted career goals to a severely limited number of avenues (which in secular literature come to only two).

Both sides of the Counter Reformation mentality are most clearly seen in the techniques for closure by conversion used by the literary writers examined here. All have to do with some form of conversion quite simply because the purpose of this literature is to show people turning their wills to the Church, freely adhering thereby to the Counter Reformation program of thought and action. Some convert gladly, some sadly; some convert after long periods of transformation, others instantaneously. All convert of their own free will and choice. By presenting their literary characters in this way, the authors who wrote this kind of literature demonstrated their own established convictions about conversion, a program to which they either subscribed or – at the very least – utilized because they knew it to be an efficacious and acceptable technique for closing their fictions. Either way, the closures by conversion are there, and they serve as the cultural artefacts by which readers today evaluate and judge the Counter Reformation mentality of the Spanish Golden Age.

BIBLIOGRAPHY

Abellán, José Luis. *Historia crítica del pensamiento español.* 5 vols. Madrid: Espasa-Calpe, 1979-86.
El Abencerraje. Sendas literarias: España. Ed. David H. Darst. New York: Random House, 1988. 45-69.
Alcalá Yáñez y Rivera, Jerónimo de. *El donado hablador Alonso, mozo de muchos amos. La novela picaresca española.* Ed. Ángel Valbuena y Prat. Madrid: Aguilar, 1966. 1197-1339.
Alemán, Mateo. *Guzmán de Alfarache.* Ed. Amancio Bolaño e Isla. México: Porrúa, 1976.
Alonso, Dámaso. *Poesía española.* 5th ed. Madrid: Gredos, 1971.
Arce, Joaquín. "Boccaccio nella letteratura castigliana: Panorama generale e rassegna bibliografico-critica." *Il Boccaccio nelle culture e letterature nazionali.* Ed. Francesco Mazzoni. Firenze: Leo S. Olschki, 1978. 63-105.
Arias, Joan. *Guzmán de Alfarache: The Unrepentant Narrator.* London: Tamesis, 1977.
Baena, Julio. *El círculo y la flecha: Principio y fin, triunfo y fracaso del 'Persiles.'* Chapel Hill: North Carolina Studies in the Romance Languages and Literatures, 1996.
Bainton, Roland H. *Here I stand.* New York: New American Library, 1950.
Bireley, Robert. *The Counter-Reformation Prince: Anti-Machiavellianism or Catholic Statecraft in Early Modern Europe.* Chapel Hill: The University of North Carolina Press, 1990.
Blanco Suárez, P., ed. *Poetas de los siglos XVI y XVII.* Madrid: Instituto-Escuela, 1923.
Boccaccio, Giovanni. *Il Filocolo.* Trans. Donald Cheney. New York: Garland, 1985.
Bouza Álvarez, José Luis. *Religiosidad contrarreformista y cultura simbólica del Barroco.* Madrid: CSIC, 1990.
Campa, Pedro F. *Emblemata Hispanica: An Annotated Bibliography of Spanish Emblem Literature to the Year 1700.* Durham: Duke University Press, 1990.
Campos, Juana G., and Ana Barella. *Diccionario de refranes.* Madrid: Anejos del Boletín de la Real Academa Española, 1975.
The Canons and Decrees of the Council of Trent. London: Booksellers of London and Westminster, 1687.
Cantimori, Delio. *Humanismo y religiones en el Renacimiento.* Barcelona: Península, 1984.
Caro, Miguel Antonio. *La canción a las ruinas de Itálica del licenciado Rodrigo Caro.* Bogotá: Voluntad, 1947.

Caro Baroja, Julio. *Las formas complejas de la vida religiosa: Religión, sociedad y carácter en la España de los siglos XVI y XVII.* Madrid: Akal, 1978.
Casa, Frank P. "The Self-Realization of the Cid." *Folio* 12 (1980): 1-11.
Cascardi, Anthony J. "Reason and Romance: An Essay on Cervantes's *Persiles*." *MLN* 106.2 (1991): 279-93.
———. "The Subject of Control." *Culture and Control in Counter-Reformational Spain.* Eds. Anne J. Cruz and Mary Elizabeth Perry. Minneapolis: University of Minnesota Press, 1992. 231-54.
Case, Thomas E. "Lope and the Moriscos." *Bulletin of the Comediantes* 44.2 (1992): 195-216.
Castañeda, James A., ed. *Las paces de los reyes y judía de Toledo.* Salamanca: Anaya, 1971.
Castillo Solórzano, Alonso de. *La garduña de Sevilla y anzuelo de las bolsas.* Buenos Aires: Espasa-Calpe, 1955.
Castrillo, Hernando. *Historia y magia natural.* Madrid: Juan García Infanzón, 1692.
Castro y Bellvis, Guillén de. *Las mocedades del Cid.* Ed. Victor Said Armesto. Madrid: Espasa-Calpe, 1913.
Cayillac, Michel. "Les trois conversions de Guzmán de Alfarache: Regard sur la critique recente." *Bulletin Hispanique* 95.1 (1993): 149-201.
Cervantes, Miguel de. *Los trabajos de Persiles y Sigismunda.* Ed. Juan Bautista Avalle-Arce. Madrid: Castalia, 1969.
Checa Cremades, Fernando, and José Miguel Morán Turina. *El Barroco.* Madrid: ISTMO, 1982.
Cicero, Marcus Tullius. *Libros de Marco Tulio Cicerón.* Trans. Juan Jarava. Antwerp: Juan Steelsio, 1549.
Covarrubias Horozco, Sebastián de. *Tesoro de la lengua castellana o española.* Madrid: Turner, 1979.
Crónica rimada del Cid. Romancero general. Vol. 2. Ed. Augustín Durán. *Biblioteca de Autores españoles.* Vol. 16. Madrid: Atlas, 1945. 651-64.
Crosbie, John. *A lo divino Lyric Poetry: An Alternative View.* Durham: University of Durham, 1989.
Cruz, Juan de la. *Obras. Escritores del Siglo XVI.* Vol. 1. *Biblioteca de Autores Españoles.* Vol. 27. Madrid: Atlas, 1948. 1-273.
Darst, David H. "Las palabras y las cosas en la iniciación del cultismo español." *Studies in Honor of William C. McCrary.* Eds. Robert Fiore, Everett W. Hesse, John E. Keller and José A. Madrigal. Lincoln: Society of Spanish and Spanish-American Studies, 1986. 91-113.
———. "Techniques of Evasion in Montemayor's *Diana*." *Symposium* 43.3 (1989): 184-93.
de Armas, Frederick A. "Passion, Treason and Blindness in Lope's *Las paces de los reyes*." *Studies in the Spanish Golden Age: Cervantes and Lope de Vega.* Eds. Dana B. Drake and José A. Madrigal. Miami: Universal, 1978. 65-75.
Dickens, A. G. *The Counter Reformation.* Harcourt, Brace & World, 1969.
Domínguez Ortiz, Antonio, and Bernard Vincent. *Historia de los moriscos: Vida y tragedia de una minoría.* Madrid: Revista del Occidente, 1978.
Erasmus. *Paraclesis. Christian Humanism and the Reformation: Selected Writings of Erasmus.* Ed. John C. Olin. New York: Fordham University Press, 1987.
Evenett, H. Outram. *The Spirit of the Counter Reformation.* Cambridge: Cambridge University Press, 1968.
Faria e Sousa, Manuel de. *Epítome de las historias portuguesas.* Madrid: Colección Cisneros, 1943.
Fischer, Susan L. "The Art of Role-Change in Calderonian Drama." *Bulletin of the Comediantes* 27.1 (1975): 73-79.

Forcione, Alban K. *Cervantes' Christian Romance: A Study of 'Persiles y Sigismunda.'* Princeton: Princeton University Press, 1972.
Fox, Dian. *Kings in Calderón.* London: Tamesis, 1986.
Gállego, Julián. *Visión y símbolos en la pintura española del Siglo de Oro.* Madrid: Aguilar, 1972.
García, Carlos. *La desordenada codicia de los bienes ajenos. La novela picaresca española.* Ed. Ángel Valbuena Prat. Madrid: Aguilar, 1966. 1155-95.
Gerli, E. Michael. *Refiguring Authority: Reading, Writing, and Rewriting in Cervantes.* Lexington: The University Press of Kentucky, 1995.
Gracián, Baltasar. *Obras completas.* Ed. Arturo del Hoyo. Madrid: Aguilar, 1967.
Greene, Thomas M. *The Light in Troy: Imitation and Discovery in Renaissance Poetry.* New Haven: Yale University Press, 1982.
Hahn, Juergen. *The Origins of the Baroque Concept of 'Peregrinatio.'* Chapel Hill: North Carolina Studies in the Romance Languages and Literatures, 1973.
Hartt, Frederick. *Love in Baroque Art.* Locust Valley NY: J. J. Austin, 1964.
Heiple, Daniel L. "Life as a Dream and the Philosophy of Disillusionment." *The Prince in the Tower.* Ed. Frederick A. de Armas. Lewisburg: Bucknell University Press, 1993. 117-131.
Hesse, Everett W., and William C. McCrary. "La balanza sujetiva-objetiva en el teatro de Tirso: Ensayo sobre contenido y forma barrocos." *Hispanófila* 3 (1958): 1-11.
Horozco, Sebastián de. *El libro de los proverbios glosados.* Ed. Jack Weiner. 2 vols. Kassel: Reichenberger, 1994.
Jesús, Teresa de. *Obras completas.* Eds. Efren de la Madre de Dios and Otger Steggink. Madrid: BAC, 1974.
Kermode, Frank. *The Sense of an Ending: Studies in the Theory of Fiction.* New York: Oxford University Press, 1967.
Ledesma, Alonso de. *Conceptos espirituales y morales.* Ed. Eduardo Juliá Martínez. 3 vols. Madrid: CSIC, 1969.
León, Luis de. *De los nombres de Cristo.* Ed. José Onrubia de Mendoza. Barcelona: Bruguera, 1975.
López Bueno, Begoña. "Tópica literaria y realización textual: Unas notas sobre la poesía de ruinas en los Siglos de Oro." *Ideologies & Literature* 3.1 (1988): 129-48.
Loyola, Ignacio de. *Obras completas.* Eds. Ignacio Iparraguirre and Cándido de Dalmases. Madrid: BAC, 1982.
Lumsden-Kouvel, Audrey. "*El príncipe constante*: Drama de la contrarreforma." *Calderón: Actas del Congreso Internacional sobre Calderón y el Teatro Español del Siglo de Oro.* Ed. Luciano García Lorenzo. Madrid: CSIC, 1983. 495-501.
Luther, Martin. *Christian Liberty.* Trans. W. A. Lambert. Philadelphia: Fortress Press, 1957.
Mal Lara, Juan. *Filosofía vulgar.* Ed. Antonio Vilanova. 4 vols. Barcelona: Selecciones Bibliográficas, 1958.
Malón de Chaide, Pedro. *La conversión de la Madalena. Escritores del Siglo XVI.* Vol. 1. *Biblioteca de Autores Españoles.* Vol. 27. Madrid: Atlas, 1948. 275-417.
Maravall, José Antonio. *Antiguos y modernos.* Madrid: Sociedad de Estudios y Publicaciones, 1966.
———. *La cultura del Barroco: Análisis de una estructura histórica.* Barcelona: Ariel, 1975.
———. *Teoría española del Estado en el siglo XVII.* Madrid: Instituto de Estudios Políticos, 1944.
Mariana, Juan de. *Obras.* Vol. 1. *Biblioteca de Autores Españoles.* Vol. 30. Madrid: Hernando, 1931.

Mariscal, George. *Contradictory Subjects*. Ithaca: Cornell University Press, 1991.
McCrary, William C. "Guillén de Castro and the *Moçedades* of Rodrigo: A Study of Tradition and Innovation." *Romance Studies in Memory of Edward Billings Ham*. Ed. Urban T. Holmes. Hayward: California State College, 1967. 89-102.
———. "Plot, Action and Imitation: The Art of Lope's *Las paces de los reyes*." *Hispanófila* 48 (1973): 1-17.
Menéndez Pelayo, Marcelino. "Observaciones preliminares: *Las paces de los reyes y judía de Toledo*." *Obras de Lope de Vega*. Vol. 18. *Biblioteca de Autores españoles*. Vol. 197. Madrid: Atlas, 1966. 96-114.
Mira de Amescua, Antonio. *El esclavo del demonio*. Ed. James Agustín Castañeda. Madrid: Cátedra, 1980.
Monçón, Francisco de. *Norte de ydiotas*. Lisbon: Joannes Blavio de Colonia, 1563.
More, Thomas. *Utopia*. Trans. H. V. S. Ogden. Arlington Heights IL: Harlan Davidson, 1949.
Oakley, R. J. *Tirso de Molina: 'El condenado por desconfiado'*. London: Grant & Cutler, 1994.
Parker, Alexander A. "Religion and War: *El príncipe constante*." *The Mind and Art of Calderón*. Cambridge: Cambridge University Press, 1988. 288-311.
Pérez de Hita, Ginés. *Guerras civiles de Granada: Primera Parte*. Ed. Paula Blanchard-Demouge. Madrid: Bailly-Bailliére, 1913.
Pfandl, Ludwig. *Historia de la literatura nacional española en la Edad de Oro*. Trans. Jorge Rubió Balaguer. Barcelona: Juan Gili, 1933.
Pigman III, G. W. "Versions of Imitation in the Renaissance." *Renaissance Quarterly* 33.1 (1980): 1-32.
A Postmodern Reader. Eds. Joseph Natoli and Linda Hutcheon. Albany: State University of New York, 1993.
Quevedo Villegas, Francisco de. *Obras completas*. Ed. Felicidad Buendía. 2 vols. Madrid: Aguilar, 1966-68.
Ribadeneyra, Pedro de. *Vida de Ignacio de Loyola*. Madrid: Espasa-Calpe, 1946.
———. *Tratado de la religión. Obras escogidas del padre Pedro de Rivadeneira. Biblioteca de Autores Españoles*. Vol. 60. Madrid: Hernando, 1927. 449-587.
Roig, Adrien. "*Las quinas de Portugal* de Tirso de Molina: Comedia de blasones." *Nueva Revista de Filología Hispánica* 32.2 (1983): 424-47.
Rojas, Agustín de. "Loa de la comedia." *Preceptiva dramática española del Renacimiento y el Barroco*. Eds. Federico Sánchez Escribano and Alberto Porqueras Mayo. Madrid: Gredos, 1965. 94-103.
Salas, Pedro de. *Afectos divinos con emblemas sagradas*. Valladolid: Gregorio de Bedoya, 1658.
Sales, Francisco de. *Introducción a la vida devota*. Trans. Francisco de Quevedo. *Francisco de Quevedo Villegas: Obras completas*. Ed. Felicidad Buendía. 2 vols. Madrid: Aguilar, 1966-68. 1: 1567-1716.
Sánchez Lora, José L. *Mujeres, conventos y formas de la religiosidad barroca*. Madrid: Fundación Universitaria Española, 1988.
Sebold, Russell P. "Un David español, o 'galán divino:' El Cid contrarreformista de Guillén de Castro." *Homage to John M. Hill*. Ed. Walter Poesse. Bloomington: Indiana University Press, 1968. 217-42.
Shakespeare, William. *Antony and Cleopatra*. Ed. Charles Jasper Sisson. New York: Dell, 1961.
Shergold, N. D. *A History of the Spanish Stage from Medieval Times until the End of the Seventeenth Century*. Oxford: Clarendon, 1967.
Simerka, Barbara. "Early Modern Skepticism and Unbelief and the Demystification of Providential Ideology in *El burlador de Sevilla*." *Gestos* 12.23 (1997): 39-66.
Sloane, Robert. "Action and Role in *El príncipe constante*." *MLN* 85.2 (1970): 167-83.

Stern, Charlotte. "Lope de Vega, Propagandist?" *Bulletin of the Comediantes* 34.1 (1982): 1-36.
Stroud, Matthew D. *The Play in the Mirror: Lacanian Perspectives in Spanish Baroque Theater*. Lewisburg: Bucknell University Press, 1996.
Téllez, Gabriel (Tirso de Molina). *El bandolero*. Madrid: Espasa-Calpe, 1972.
———. *Los cigarrales de Toledo*. Ed. F. S. R. Madrid: Aguilar, 1962.
———. *Deleytar aprovechando*. Madrid: Domingo Gonçález, 1635.
———. *Obras dramáticas completas*. Ed. Blanca de los Ríos. 3 vols. Madrid: Aguilar, 1946-58.
Valdivielso, José de. *Romancero espiritual*. Ed. J. M. Aguirre. Madrid: Espasa-Calpe, 1984.
Vega Carpio, Lope Félix de. *Obras escogidas*. Ed. Federico Carlos Sainz de Robles. 3 vols. Madrid: Aguilar, 1958-61.
———. *Obras poéticas*. Barcelona: Planeta, 1983.
———. *El peregrino en su patria*. Ed. Juan Bautista Avalle-Arce. Madrid: Castalia, 1973.
Villava, Juan Francisco de. *Empresas espirituales y morales*. Baeza: Fernández Díaz, 1613.
Vives, Juan Luis. *Tratado del Alma*. Madrid: Espasa-Calpe, 1942.
Vranich, Stanko B., ed. *Los cantores de las ruinas en el Siglo de Oro: Antología*. Ferrol: Esquio, 1981.
Wardropper, Bruce W. *Historia de la poesía lírica a lo divino en la cristiandad occidental*. Madrid: 1958.
Weisbach, Werner. *El Barroco: Arte de la Contrarreforma*. Trans. Enrique Lafuente Ferrari. Madrid: Espasa-Calpe, 1942.
Whitenack, Judith A. "The *alma diferente* of Mateo Alemán's 'Ozmín y Daraja.'" *Romance Quarterly* 38.1 (1991): 59-73.
———. *The Impenitent Confession of Guzmán de Alfarache*. Madison: Hispanic Seminary of Medieval Studies, 1985.
Wilson, Diana de Armas. *Allegories of Love: Cervantes's Persiles y Sigismunda*. Princeton: Princeton University Press, 1991.
Wilson, E. M. "Sobre la *Canción a las ruinas de Itálica* de Rodrigo Caro." *Revista de Filología Española* 23 (1936): 379-96.
Zamora, Laurencio de. *Monarquía mística de la iglesia hecha de hieroglíficos sacados de humanas y divinas letras*. Madrid: Luis Sánchez, 1604.
Zamora Vicente, Alonso. "Una mirada a *Las quinas de Portugal*." *Tirsiana*. Copenhague: Instituto de Lenguas Románicas, 1990. 263-76.
Zayas y Sotomayor, María de. *Desengaños amorosos*. Ed. Agustín G. de Amezúa. Madrid: Aldus, 1950.

NORTH CAROLINA STUDIES IN THE ROMANCE LANGUAGES AND LITERATURES
I.S.B.N. Prefix 0-8078-

Recent Titles

"EL ÁNGEL DEL HOGAR". GALDÓS AND THE IDEOLOGY OF DOMESTICITY IN SPAIN, by Bridget A. Aldaraca. 1991. (No. 239). *-9243-2.*
IN THE PRESENCE OF MYSTERY: MODERNIST FICTION AND THE OCCULT, by Howard M. Fraser. 1992. (No. 240). *-9244-0.*
THE NOBLE MERCHANT: PROBLEMS OF GENRE AND LINEAGE IN "HERVIS DE MES", by Catherine M. Jones. 1993. (No. 241). *-9245-9.*
JORGE LUIS BORGES AND HIS PREDECESSORS OR NOTES TOWARDS A MATERIALIST HISTORY OF LINGUISTIC IDEALISM, by Malcolm K. Read. 1993. (No. 242). *-9246-7.*
DISCOVERING THE COMIC IN "DON QUIXOTE", by Laura J. Gorfkle. 1993. (No. 243). *-9247-5.*
THE ARCHITECTURE OF IMAGERY IN ALBERTO MORAVIA'S FICTION, by Janice M. Kozma. 1993. (No. 244). *-9248-3.*
THE "LIBRO DE ALEXANDRE". MEDIEVAL EPIC AND SILVER LATIN, by Charles F. Fraker. 1993. (No. 245). *-9249-1.*
THE ROMANTIC IMAGINATION IN THE WORKS OF GUSTAVO ADOLFO BÉCQUER, by B. Brant Bynum. 1993. (No. 246). *-9250-5.*
MYSTIFICATION ET CRÉATIVITÉ DANS L'OEUVRE ROMANESQUE DE MARGUERITE YOURCENAR, par Beatrice Ness. 1994. (No. 247). *-9251-3.*
TEXT AS TOPOS IN RELIGIOUS LITERATURE OF THE SPANISH GOLDEN AGE, by M. Louise Salstad. 1995. (No. 248). *-9252-1.*
CALISTO'S DREAM AND THE CELESTINESQUE TRADITION: A REREADING OF *CELESTINA*, by Ricardo Castells. 1995. (No. 249). *-9253-X.*
THE ALLEGORICAL IMPULSE IN THE WORKS OF JULIEN GRACQ: HISTORY AS RHETORICAL ENACTMENT IN *LE RIVAGE DES SYRTES* AND *UN BALCON EN FORÊT*, by Carol J. Murphy. 1995. (No. 250). *-9254-8.*
VOID AND VOICE: QUESTIONING NARRATIVE CONVENTIONS IN ANDRÉ GIDE'S MAJOR FIRST-PERSON NARRATIVES, by Charles O'Keefe. 1996. (No. 251). *-9255-6.*
EL CÍRCULO Y LA FLECHA: PRINCIPIO Y FIN, TRIUNFO Y FRACASO DEL *PERSILES*, por Julio Baena. 1996. (No. 252). *-9256-4.*
EL TIEMPO Y LOS MÁRGENES. EUROPA COMO UTOPÍA Y COMO AMENAZA EN LA LITERATURA ESPAÑOLA, por Jesús Torrecilla. 1996. (No. 253). *-9257-2.*
THE AESTHETICS OF ARTIFICE: VILLIERS'S *L'EVE FUTURE*, by Marie Lathers. 1996. (No. 254). *-9254-8.*
DISLOCATIONS OF DESIRE: GENDER, IDENTITY, AND STRATEGY IN *LA REGENTA*, by Alison Sinclair. 1998. (No. 255). *-9259-9.*
THE POETICS OF INCONSTANCY, ETIENNE DURAND AND THE END OF RENAISSANCE VERSE, by Hoyt Rogers. 1998. (No. 256). *-9260-2.*
RONSARD'S CONTENTIOUS SISTERS: THE PARAGONE BETWEEN POETRY AND PAINTING IN THE WORKS OF PIERRE DE RONSARD, by Roberto E. Campo. 1998. (No. 257). *-9261-0.*
THE RAVISHMENT OF PERSEPHONE: EPISTOLARY LYRIC IN THE *SIÈCLE DES LUMIÈRES*, by Julia K. De Pree. 1998. (No. 258). *-9262-9.*
CONVERTING FICTION: COUNTER REFORMATIONAL CLOSURE IN THE SECULAR LITERATURE OF GOLDEN AGE SPAIN, by David H. Darst. 1998. (No. 259). *-9263-7.*
GALDÓS'S *SEGUNDA MANERA*: RHETORICAL STRATEGIES AND AFFECTIVE RESPONSE, by Linda M. Willem. 1998. (No. 260) *-9264-5.*
A MEDIEVAL PILGRIM'S COMPANION. REASSESSING *EL LIBRO DE LOS HUÉSPEDES* (ESCORIAL MS. h.I.13), by Thomas D. Spaccarelli. 1998. (No. 261) *-9265-3.*

When ordering please cite the *ISBN Prefix* plus the last four digits for each title.

Send orders to: University of North Carolina Press
P.O. Box 2288
CB# 6215
Chapel Hill, NC 27515-2288
U.S.A.

www.ingramcontent.com/pod-product-compliance
Lightning Source LLC
Chambersburg PA
CBHW020739230426
43665CB00009B/493